BOOKIES

AND

BETTORS

ALSO BY RICHARD SASULY

I.G. Farben
The Search for the Winning Horse

BOOKIES

AND

BETTORS

TWO HUNDRED YEARS OF GAMBLING

RICHARD SASULY

HOLT, RINEHART AND WINSTON • NEW YORK

Copyright © 1982 by Richard Sasuly
Published by Holt, Rinehart and Winston,
383 Madison Avenue, New York, New York 10017.
Published simultaneously in Canada by Holt, Rinehart and
Winston of Canada, Limited.

Library of Congress Cataloging in Publication Data

Sasuly, Richard, 1913–
Bookies and bettors.
Includes index.
1. Gambling—History. 2. Book-making (Betting)—
History. 3. Gambling—United States. 4. Book-making
(Betting)—United States. 5. Gambling—Law and
legislation—United States. I. Title.
HV 6710.S24   306'.4   81–7139
AACR2

ISBN: 0–03–053756–8

First Edition

Designer: Helene Berinsky
Printed in the United States of America
1 3 5 7 9 10 8 6 4 2

ISBN 0-03-053756-8

ACKNOWLEDGMENTS

SOME OF THE INFORMATION I NEEDED MOST WHILE WORK-ing on this book I received from people I cannot name. I thank them nevertheless.

I can and do thank Bob Martin, Joshua Shelley, Stan Isaacs, Herb Phipps, Stephen Jarrell, John Luckman, and Myles Cooper.

Several scholars took time from their own work to help me with mine. I am grateful for what I gained in conversations with professors David Goldberg of the University of Manchester, Eric J. Hobsbawm of the University of London, Harold G. Vatter of Portland State University, and Peter Stansky of Stanford University.

I received truly excellent assistance from Irene Heller, Lorraine Brown, and Gwen Olmsted, and I thank them for it.

I benefited greatly from the services of a number of libraries, including in particular four in California: The Burlingame Public Library, the William P. Kyne Library at Bay Meadows in San Mateo, the California Thoroughbred Breeders' Association Library in Arcadia, and the San Francisco Room, directed by Gladys Hansen, of the San Francisco Public Library.

As a visitor in Britain I was kindly received and helped by Peter Blackwell of the William Hill Organization, David Brimacombe of Joe Corals, and officials of the Tote, the Bookmakers Protective Association and the Horse Race Betting Levy Board.

Lucille Daneri Sasuly contributed so much, from ideas to execution, that I am tempted to forego the usual absolution. But I do absolve her, and of course all others named and unnamed, from any responsibility for this work.

CONTENTS

Prologue: *The Bookmaker's Genie*   1

1. *In the Beginning*   3
2. *Tattersall's, Bentinck, and John Gully*   13
3. *Interlude: On the Nature of Gambling*   32
4. *Gambling Comes of Age: The First Repression*   44
5. *Saratoga, Morrissey, and the Redcoats' Second Coming*   55
6. *Before the Fall: The First Crop of American Bookmakers*   65
7. *Interlude: An Essay on Reform*   83
8. *Outside the Law*   91
9. *The Racing Wire and the Rise of Moe Annenberg*   106
10. *Layoff Betting: Erickson and Company*   123
11. *Interlude: The Mafia—An Essay on Fact and Fiction*   138

12. *Harry Gross Enterprises—and the Law*   152
13. *The Kefauver Committee: A Numbers Game*   166
14. *A New Style in Bookmaking*   181
15. *Practitioners of the Art*   196
16. *Back to Britain*   219
Epilogue: *Nevada and the Future of Legal Gambling*   233
A SELECTIVE BIBLIOGRAPHY   247
INDEX   255

BOOKIES

AND

BETTORS

PROLOGUE:
THE BOOKMAKER'S
GENIE

THE BOOKMAKER IS A GAMBLER'S GAMBLER. THE BOOKIE and the ordinary gambler are as closely joined as the two sides of a coin, and as different.

The gambler follows the rules of his game, to the limits of his ability. Then luck can make him a winner, or break him.

The bookmaker, if he does his work well, also applies the rules of his game, meticulously. But then luck, with no if's or maybe's, guarantees that he will win.

The ultimate difference lies in numbers, large enough numbers to turn the normal bell-shaped curve of basic statistics into the bookmaker's genie—while holding the plain gambler forever at risk. Because he does depend on numbers, including increasing amounts of money in circulation, the bookmaker emerges full grown quite late in the ages-old history of gambling.

The story of bookmaking as told here begins, properly, in England. Further developments in British bookmaking will be treated in later parts of the book. The rest of the story concerns bookies, and their customers, in America.

For the most part, this book deals with people not generally reckoned among society's leaders. It is in some respects private, or even more or less secret, history. It deals often

1

with covert transactions undertaken by unknowns. Bookmakers, or gamblers in general, have not as a rule recorded their views in *Hansard* or the *Congressional Globe* or *Record*. Few, if any, among them have been known for their diaries or memoirs. It is authentic history for all that. And history of this kind casts light into byways and thereby does its bit to help illuminate the shape of society and its changes.

1

IN THE BEGINNING

SAMUEL PEPYS'S DIARY ENTRY FOR NOVEMBER 23, 1663 begins: "Up and to Alderman Backwell's, where Sir W. Rider, by appointment, met us to consult about the insuring of our hempe ship from Archangel . . ."

Pepys went on to a coffee house. From there he went "to the 'Change, where Sir W. Rider and I did bid 15 percent, and nobody will take it under 20 percent . . .' "

Without consummating any business, therefore, the diarist continued his rounds and, later, again "called at the Coffee House, and there by great accident hear that a letter is come that our ship is safe come to Newcastle. With this news I went like an asse presently to Alderman Backewell [sic] and told him of it. . . . Now what an opportunity, had I to have concealed this and seemed to have made an insurance and got one hundred pounds with the least trouble and danger in the whole world. This troubles me to think I should be so oversoon."

To the student of bookmaking, Pepys's story has a familiar ring. Any bookmaker would recognize at once that Pepys was chiding himself for having missed a clear chance for "past-posting," a kind of coup that bookies fear as much as they worry about insolvent clients. A pet fantasy of gamblers

3

always has been to swindle a bookmaker (or broker, or commissioner) into accepting a bet on an event whose outcome the gambler already knows.

In Pepys's time, bookmakers did not yet exist. Gambling, though, assuredly did, and had existed down through the millennia. Archaeologic digs repeatedly have turned up knucklebones presumably used as auguries and for games of chance. By Roman times the knucklebones had clearly resolved into the modern shape of dice. The Roman dice box—*fritillus*—has handed on its name to a lovely spring flower of mottled hue, and to butterflies.

The professional gambler practiced his trade in Renaissance Italy. Cardano (G. Cardan), in an autobiographical sketch, devotes far more space to his career as a gambler than to the discoveries in probability mathematics that have preserved his name.

For several centuries the English lagged behind their continental neighbors in the development of games of chance. The word *gambling* itself did not appear in the language until the eighteenth century. The earlier term, and the subject of the statutes first addressed to the subject, was *gaming*.

From the late 1600s on, England gradually moved ahead of the rest of Europe in trade, naval strength, imperial reach, industrial production—and gambling. It will be argued here that the connections among these accomplishments were not accidental.

Much will be said in pages to follow about the nature, and character, and the effects of gambling. Here let it be noted only that the ways of assuming risk, in search of possible reward, divide readily into two sorts—the businesslike and the recreational. At the border separating them, the two in fact are virtually interchangeable. The riskier sorts of business have seemed the most pleasant of games to some traders. Conversely, what appears to be recreational gaming has rather often been practiced as a business. Perhaps the clearest difference between the business and recreational forms of gambling lies neither in pleasure nor in profit, but in the amount of social stigma attached to the practice.

In any case, Samuel Pepys's undertaking in marine insurance was only a minor example of a kind of business gamble for which precedent could be found among the Greeks of Demosthenes' time. Less than twenty years after Pepys's death something genuinely new occurred. An outbreak of speculative fever, on a scale never seen before, seized much of Western Europe.

Financial chicanery reached its highest peaks with the South Sea Bubble in Britain and the nearly parallel Mississippi scheme in France. (Holland, as a pioneer of the commercial revolution, had indulged in its own tulipomania in the seventeenth century.) The South Sea and Mississippi ventures on either side of the English Channel in the second decade of the eighteenth century unleashed frenzies of speculation which touched every business center in Western Europe. A few new fortunes were made, but in England, at least, most people with disposable money were badly singed.

The South Sea Bubble did not involve outright swindle. At its peak, bribes passed as freely as gossip at court, but in its mechanics it violated no laws, because no laws regulated public finance or speculation in stocks.

The South Sea Company itself was chartered in 1711. From the start, like its two great (and more durable) rivals, the East India Company and the Bank of England, it used royal—or national—authority to derive profit from an exercise of monopoly power in money changing and foreign trade. The company proposed to conduct trade with South America under an arrangement (the Asiento), which, as part of the complex Peace of Utrecht, ended the Wars of the Spanish Succession in 1713. First and last the company failed in trade. Even the most sinister and presumably most profitable of its ventures—the hauling and sale of African slaves—failed. Where other slavers grew rich, at the cost of a social blight that extended through the centuries like radioactive waste, the South Sea Company lacked even the measures of luck, brutality, and management needed for the slave trade. Its ships (curiously misnamed *Hope* and *Liberty*) found Spanish colonial authorities who essentially ignored the Asiento. The company dumped its human cargo, at a loss, in Jamaica. The company's directors concentrated then on what John Carswell, historian of the Bubble, called its principal undertakings: creation of credit and management of government finances.

To use the term *public finance* is to impose a twentieth-century term on an era in which it did not yet exist. At the beginning of the eighteenth century, Parliament had abolished the old feudal tenures and dues, with rights of purveyance and preemption (in the wake of a previous generation's revolutions and restoration). But then as now warfare was not merely the bloodiest but also the most expensive act of nationhood. The debt owed by the crown, £16 million in 1702, had more than tripled to £53 million by the Peace of Utrecht in 1713. Throughout the eighteenth century the wars continued, and so too did the expansion of the debt, nearly tripling again by the end of the Seven Years War (1763) and nearly doubling again by the time of American Independence in the 1780s.

Lacking the feudal resources, Parliament had recourse to excises and import duties, licenses, and house taxes. It thereby made heroes of smugglers without immediately meeting the country's financial needs.

The South Sea Company, with its powerful political connections and liberal use of bribes at court, acquired the right to handle the public debt. Company stock was given as an exchange to holders of some £9 million worth of government bonds. By 1720 the company proposed to take over the entire national debt. On the promise of gain from this transaction, the price of company shares vaulted during the first half of the year. The boom in South Sea shares touched off a frenzy of stockjobbing and the creation of dozens of companies with the sole purpose of speculative gain by shareholders. The boom collapsed in September 1720 after the price of South Sea shares had passed £1,000, from a price of £128 nine months before.

According to Carswell, foreign investors helped precipitate the collapse, selling South Sea shares to raise bullion for shipment abroad. In England, loans issued on the inflated stock could not be collected. The expansion of credit throughout the country, based on a wild assortment of paper instruments, contracted as if in an economic seizure.

One account holds that every pocket in England was affected by the bursting of the bubble. This may in fact have been true of every pocket that contained a fair amount of money. Among the millions of Englishmen, only between two and three thousand had bought South Sea shares by 1715, perhaps a few thousand more by the crisis of speculative fever in 1720. Certainly most of the names of prominence were connected with the debacle. Isaac Newton, then the head of the mint, had bought early and sold early, at a profit. He too succumbed to the contagion of the final stages of the boom, bought again, and this time lost. Another loser was George I, who at the time of the crash was visiting his native Hanover (where, as was not the case in London, he had at least the comfort of understanding the language spoken around him).

The corresponding collapse of the Mississippi scheme in France took place a month later. The Scottish architect of the French boom, John Law, fled France and eventually died in Venice. According to gossip passed along by the French ambassador to Venice, Law supported himself, appropriately enough, at the gaming tables.

The gambling fever in business fell back into a normal temperature range after the first quarter of the eighteenth century. Gaming as such continued to grow, and by mid-century the word *gambling*, in its modern sense, had entered the language. According to later accounts, fortunes changed hands at the card tables in London clubs. Certainly a number of players thus ruined themselves. But perhaps the most significant form of more or less recreational (as opposed to entirely business) gambling, was betting on races among Thoroughbred horses.

In the spring of 1680, the household of the King of England, Charles II, accompanied by a coterie of gentry, made its way by carriage and saddle horse to the Newmarket Downs, some sixty-odd miles northeast of London. The royal household records, as set down in the *Domestick Intelligence*, take notice of "knights of the road" (highwaymen), who were said to have been "having a good time of it during this meeting." [The quotations are from J. P. Hore, *The History of Newmarket and the Annals of the Turf*, Vol. II, A. H. Bailey & Co., London 1886]. The *Domestick Intelligence* then proceeded to the chief business of the assembly, which was the racing of horses, precursors of Thoroughbreds, across the Downs: "This present Tuesday, being the 6 of April [1680], is a great Horserace run at Newmarket, between Major Astan's Horse and another Gentleman's, the six mile course, for £500 each, carrying ten stone apiece, where a great number of Gentlemen stay, who have laid very considerable sums of money on both sides; but 'tis supposed the odds will lie on the Major's side."

A number of points in this report will strike a twentieth-century reader familiar with racing. The horses carried a staggering burden (140 pounds) over a distance eight times longer than a modern sprint, four times as long as a typical present-day cup race. Only two horses ran—as if two farmers were settling an argument as to which owned the speedier mount. And finally, the total of the stakes, £1,000, was surprisingly large (even leaving aside the considerable but unspecified amount of side betting). The amount at stake could have established a trading business. Carswell, describing the nearly 1,800 merchants listed in a 1677 business directory for the City of London and Westminster, referred to "modest men trading on a capital of £1,000 or so." Some 250 years later, in the 1920s, after substantial inflation of all prices, horses ran at major American tracks for far smaller purses. Thus, on a day taken at random, September 8, 1925, at Belmont Park, the featured race, the Whitestone Handicap, offered a purse of only $1,500, or about £300, and out of this sum the second- and third-place finishers took their earnings too.

Nor should it be thought that all bettors in England in the seventeenth and eighteenth centuries staked vast sums on every issue. Of the eighteenth-century London clubs, White's led in gambling (and was the gathering place for leading politicians and men of fashion). White's betting book has been preserved in Algernon Bourke's *History of White's (With the Betting Book from 1743 to 1878)*.

Gambling, according to Bourke, caused the transformation of a public gathering place, White's Chocolate House, into a private club. Leaders of political affairs already frequented the Chocolate House. But as gambling increased there, adventurers, sharpers, and even highwaymen swarmed in. "It was inconvenient, to say the least, that one of these gentlemen should rub shoulders with the judge who might afterwards have to sentence him for highway robbery," according to Bourke. The elite among the patrons, therefore, first set aside rooms for themselves and then established their own club, known simply as White's, where they could carry on conversation and wagering in private.

What stands out in White's betting book is not the size of the wagers but the variety of subjects on which differences of opinion could be settled. The first item in the betting book (dated "Octr ye 5, 1743," earlier entries having been lost by fire) concerns a wager between two lords: "Ld. Lincoln bets Ld. Winchester one hundred guineas to fifty guineas that the Dutchess Dowager of Marlborough does not survive the Dutchess Dowager of Cleveland."

The question of who survives is one of the most common in the betting book. Usually the two bettors had no apparent relationship to those whose lives were at risk. And the sums bet were not large enough to encourage a bettor to hasten one of the subjects toward his or her end. In some instances the bettors did not survive the subjects. Thus, in the entry of November 4, 1754: "Lord Montfort wagers Sir Jno. Bland one hundred guineas that Mr. Nash outlives Mr. Cibber." Below the entry, in another hand, is the note: "Both Lord M. and Sir Jno. Bland put an end to their own lives before the bet was decided." According to Bourke, Montfort lost heavily at gaming. Bland also went through a fortune, with a £32,000 loss at one sitting. The suicides, nine months apart, followed the wager by less than a year.

The gamblers at White's also wagered on the *start of life*, that is to say, on which of two women would first bear a child, as well as on the outcome of elections and battles. By the end of the eighteenth century and the first decade of the nineteenth, Napoleon Bonaparte and his longevity and successes or failures appeared repeatedly in the betting book.

Club members owned and raced Thoroughbreds, and bets on their horses were entered in the book, though the bets appear to have been smaller than those they made at Newmarket and the other racecourses. In one strange entry, racing and a prospective marriage were entangled in a way presumably clear to the bettors: "Mr. Broderick bets fifty guineas with Gen'l. Mackenzie on Sir John Shelley winning the Derby, against Lord Steward being married to Lady F. V. Tempest in six months from this day. May 22nd, 1818. W. Broderick, A. Mackenzie."

One wager concerned a chess match, and another, for £5, between Lord Ossulton and Sir. F. Cadogan, was laid on whatever form of tennis might have been played in 1844.

Two great names in racing, Glasgow and Bentinck, appear in the betting book. Curiously, their bets at White's had to do with such matters as the length of Sir Robert Peel's ministry, the price of wheat, and the effect of a "protectional government" on the bond market. And they, too, solemnly set down bets for as little as £5, as if to punctuate a conversation.

At the racecourse, Lord George Bentinck made huge bets, and with little conversation.

By the middle of the eighteenth century, Thoroughbred racing had set itself apart as a mix of caste ritual, sport, animal husbandry, and gambling on a very large scale. The horse as a symbol of feudal institutions is clear enough. The roots of the word itself are imbedded in *chivalry* and *cavalier*. But more practical aspects of horse breeding, horse racing, and horse gambling also suggest themselves.

The rise of Thoroughbred racing over the course of the eighteenth century coincided with severe dislocation in British agriculture. The rapid increase in enclosures (some 3,500 enclosure bills during the reign of George III affecting more than five million acres, where previously the whole number was only in the hundreds) was "merely the most dramatic, and, as it were, official and political aspect of a general process by which farms grew larger, farmers relatively fewer, and the villagers more landless," according to E. J. Hobsbawm.

Christopher Hill noted another aspect of the extreme pressures on marginal landowners, even quite large holders: ". . . the victory of the gentry in 1688 led to increasing disgruntlement of the Tory squires as the land tax which paid for the French wars eliminated the economically unfit," and in the same context he referred to the "desperate poverty of the northern Catholic gentry."

It was scarcely an accident that a disproportionate number of the new racecourses were established in the northern counties of England. And it seems highly probable that some of the genuinely great sums staked on Thoroughbred races represented a last hope of paying off debts and preserving a landhold. A direct parallel was seen in backwoods Tennessee early in the nineteenth century. And, at a farther reach in time, place, and social class, something rather similar was seen at the Detroit Race Course in 1980 when recently unemployed automobile workers went to the races in larger numbers than ever before.

Even the emergence of the distinctive line of Thoroughbred runners and intensive breeding to the most successful of these (Flying Childers, Eclipse, Highflier, Matchen, King Herod, among others) fit into the broader picture of British animal husbandry. At the least, some of the eighteenth-century squires who bred to the get of Arab sires must surely have known of the experiments then in progress with new strains of sheep and cattle.

But racing also retained its qualities as sport. Spectators came very close to being participants. When a pair of horses matched speed at Newmarket in the first half of the eighteenth century, a crowd of mounted gentry was likely to dash off behind them in pursuit. Some of the followers nearly equaled the racers in speed. And thus, more and more often, the two horses matched in a race might be joined by a third racer, and then a fourth, and sometimes even greater numbers. The original pair of bettors, in turn, gave way to a crowd eager to back a bewildering variety of opinions with money.

A bet between two gamblers could readily be set down in a betting book. And all the bets among a group of cardplayers could be heaped in plain sight before them on a table. But possible bettors in a crowd of mounted gentry on the downs at Newmarket spread out, literally, over acres might disappear as rapidly after a race as picnickers running from a sudden rainstorm. The massive and increasing growth of horse racing by the mid-eighteenth century thus created a need for a mechanism to regulate wagering on the outcome of races.

The needed machinery, the onset of what a generation later became bookmaking, took shape gradually. The crucial year, if one can be chosen, was 1766.

A number of happenings of greatest importance can be traced to that year, though as Hobsbawm notes, no one at the time could have been expected to know that the sum of events might later be called an industrial revolution. The process of private enclosure of English land was nearing completion after gradually increasing through five centuries; and, as people were pushed off the land, the population of London approached a million. In 1766, James Watt was within three years of obtaining his patent for a practical steam engine. Just twenty years had passed since the English fought their last battle with the Scots, at Culloden Moor. Only nine years before, Clive had defeated the Nawab of Bengal. And just three years earlier, the Seven Years War had ended, leaving England the world's dominant colonial power. In 1766, too, the Scottish essayist on questions of morality, Adam Smith, returned from a visit to the continent with the Duke of Buccleugh and went to live with his mother at Kirkcaldy to begin ten years of work on his *Inquiry into the Nature and Causes of the Wealth of Nations.*

And 1766 was notable, too, in the development of bookmaking. In that year a young man from rural England, Richard Tattersall, having earlier come to London to seek work in the stables of a nobleman, branched out on his own and opened an auctioneering yard for the sale of horses at Hyde Park Corner.

2

TATTERSALL'S, BENTINCK, AND JOHN GULLY

AT BRITISH RACECOURSES TODAY, BOOKMAKERS SET UP their stands in what is called the Tattersall's Enclosure. Thus the Tattersall name is embedded in bookmaking. Curiously, the firm itself took no direct part in betting in any form.

Richard Tattersall, the founding father, was a quick-witted and eloquent man, with a prodigious memory (particularly for the bloodlines of Thoroughbred horses). He used his abilities, and an acquaintance among the horse-buying gentry he had met in the stables of the Duke of Cumberland, to become the leading horse auctioneer of his time. From then on, the firm he thus founded devoted itself exclusively to the buying and selling of horses. His establishment at Hyde Park Corner was an auction yard. For the comfort of his patrons he established a suitable kitchen and dining room at the Corner and at Newmarket as well.

Around 1750 (the exact year is not known, but it was somewhat before Richard Tattersall opened shop at Hyde Park Corner) the gentry who bet heavily and were most concerned with Thoroughbred racing had organized the Jockey Club. As a matter of course, Jockey Club members, then as now leading aristocrats, attended and dominated the sales at Tattersall's.

From the outset the Jockey Club set down rules to govern racing. To ease the pains of settling disputes, racecourses in all parts of England, and eventually in all parts of the world, followed the Jockey Club's lead and, with minor variations, adopted their rules. Above all, the rules were aimed at preventing sharp practices, and at enforcing payment of debts.

For the convenience of his patrons, Richard Tattersall set aside space, eventually known as the Subscription Rooms, in which once weekly, on Mondays, bets were to be settled. Anyone failing to pay up could be ruled off the course. The defaulter therefore could have no hope of making good his losses by future bets. And thus the Tattersall firm, as a convenience to its patrons, gave its name to racecourse betting.

The institution of settling day, backed by the authority of the Jockey Club, served well enough to regulate head-to-head bets. But by the latter part of the eighteenth century, as racing continued steadily to expand, simple betting techniques no longer served. By 1786 racing of two-year-olds was approved. The numbers of horses competing thus further increased. Within a few years most of the historic stakes races had seen their first running. The Jockey Club experimented with the assignment of different weights to try to equalize chances among the increasing numbers of horses competing.

Still lacking was a way to allow any bettor to place a wager, of any size, on the single horse of his choice, without picking his way through a crowd to find the individual bettor with an opposed opinion who might give him satisfaction.

Sometime around 1800, with perhaps ninety racecourses in use in England, and increasing crowds at all of them, the bookmaker finally emerged in an early form. A gambler himself, he was dedicated to the proposition that a majority of other gamblers more likely than not will lose. No exact record remains, but most accounts give the name of the first known bookmaker as Ogden and 1795 as the year in which he stepped forward and offered to book bets on any horse in any race. Other accounts credit "Leviathan" Davis. Still others, Messrs. Greville and Drummond. No matter. The time is clear. The practice arose, promptly, when it was needed.

A now familiar confrontation took place. On one side stood the backer, the person who liked the chances of a horse well enough to register his opinion with a bet. Facing him was the bookmaker (or blackleg, or simply leg), clearly not a gentleman, who laid his money against the horse's chances. The backer, who wagered that a horse would win, stood in the ancient tradition, backing his opinion about the speed of the horse. The bookmaker acted on a new concept: he made his own judgment, not merely about the horse but also about the worth of the bettor's opinion. In addition, he offered different odds on the chances of different horses. He thus tempted a backer to wager on a lightly regarded horse, and, at the same time, the varying odds made it possible for the bookmaker to make a profit (given enough bettors or, as would be said today, enough action) no matter which horse won.

Representative of the bettor at his best and most successful, by all contemporary accounts, was Lord George Bentinck, a son of the Duke of Portland.

Among the bookmakers who faced Lord George in the betting rings, none stood out more boldly than John Gully, butcher's apprentice and son of an innkeeper near Bristol.

"Thormanby," a nineteenth-century racing writer, said of Lord George Bentinck that he was "the idol of the sportsmen of his own day. The commanding personality of the man threw a spell over all with whom he was brought in contact: they were half fascinated, half awed; judgment and criticism surrendered to admiration." Lord George stood out, as Thormanby put it, as "a very Napoleon among betting men." And yet, though most of Bentinck's adult life was devoted to racing, his biography was written by Benjamin Disraeli.

Surely no more than a handful of others in England could have enjoyed as great advantages of birth as Lord William George Frederick Cavendish Bentinck (1802–48), known as Lord George. He was the second son of the fourth Duke of Portland, and the family was closely related by marriage to two other ducal families. Lord George was the grandson of one prime minister, the nephew of another. At the age of seventeen, he served as a junior officer with the 10th Hussars.

Still in his teens, he evidently carried himself with, at the least, assurance and hauteur. His superior, a Captain Kerr, reproved him, on parade. According to Thormanby, Lord George was heard to say, "Captain Kerr ventured to say *on* parade that which he dared not repeat *off.*" The captain sent a challenge which Lord George refused on the grounds that he had vowed never to fight a duel. The captain posted his subaltern, an inquiry followed, and it was the captain who was cashiered. In Thormanby's words, "Captain Kerr was most unjustly cashiered, for, as he pertinently put it, if he had refused to demand satisfaction by duel after Lord George's insulting words he would have been 'sent to Coventry' by his brother officers."

Bentinck's army career lasted only three years. In the course of his service he won a majority simply because his commander-in-chief, the Duke of York, enjoyed his conversation about horses during a ride on Newmarket Heath. His uncle, George Canning, then appointed him his private secretary, and Bentinck resigned his commission. In 1828, Lord George succeeded to the King's Lynn seat in Parliament, which was formerly held by another of his uncles. As nearly as possible, the seat could have been described as excess family property, since Lord George for some years paid little attention to it.

Disraeli observed about Lord George's early parliamentary career: "He was not a very frequent attendant of the house. He might be counted on for a party division, and when, towards the termination of the Melbourne ministry, the forces were very nearly balanced and the struggle became very close, he might have been observed on more than one occasion entering the house at a late hour, clad in a white great coat which softened, but did not conceal, the scarlet hunting-coat."

Lord George nevertheless maintained his popularity among many members of Parliament. Disraeli said: "Although he took no part in debate, and attended the house rather as a club than a senate, he possessed a great and peculiar influence in it. He was viewed with interest and often with extraordinary regard by every sporting man in the house. With almost all of these he was acquainted; some of them, on either side, were his intimate companions and confederates."

The fact is that Lord George had actually made the turf his career. The Duke of Portland, his father, had owned the 1819 Derby winner, Tiresias. In his twenties, Lord George started betting (at first unsuccessfully) and then began buying horses, against his father's wishes. At first he ran them under the names of others, but within a few years there could no longer be a question of concealment. Lord George maintained three breeding farms, owned more than a hundred racers, and kept as many as sixty at a time in training.

But Bentinck's preeminence among his fellows on the turf resulted from more than the size of his stud and racing stables. He seems to have been admired extravagantly (and envied as well) not only for his wealth and unassailable social position, but also for his force of character and even for his appearance.

As Disraeli put it: "He had become the lord paramount of that strange world [the turf], so difficult to sway, and which requires for its government both a stern resolve and a courtly breeding. He had them both; and though the blackleg might quail before the awful scrutiny of his piercing eye, there never was a man so scrupulously polite to his inferiors as Lord George Bentinck."

As for his hero's appearance, Disraeli noted: "Nature had clothed this vehement spirit with a material form which was in perfect harmony with its noble and commanding character. He was tall, and remarkable for his presence; his countenance almost a model of manly beauty; the face oval, the complexion clear and mantling; the forehead lofty and white; the nose acquiline and delicately moulded; the upper lip short."

Contemporary drawings are less flattering, but show a man of good bearing dressed in dandified fashion. Another racing writer, "Sylvanus," described him as he appeared on the Newmarket Heath: "dressed in buckskin breeches—none of your Norway does or West Riding imitation but in the hides of his own stags—with exquisitely made boots of the true orthodox length, and antique colouring on top; a buff waist-coat and reddish brown double-breasted coat, ornamented by the button of the Jockey Club . . ."

By the 1830s and '40s, when Lord George reached his prime, the racing world badly needed some sort of authority. Adam Smith observed that businessmen never gather privately without discussing some sort of conspiracy to restrain trade. He could not have had racing in mind. On the turf he might have found laissez-faire at its purest—leading to deception, failure to pay debts, and even the laming of favored horses.

Sentimentalized accounts of racing history have it that the moral tone on the turf declined as adventurers, sharpers, and the blacklegs en masse descended on racing to pluck pieces from the gentry's betting. Undoubtedly the possibility of arranging to win bets—with a minimum of risk—proved attractive to gamblers from all social strata. But Lord George had enough bad experiences with people he could acknowledge socially. For these more or less equals he saved his most vitriolic insults.

Thormanby tells of an incident during a dinner at Bentinck's club. Lord George saw a waiter about to present a bill to an unnamed captain whom he knew to be a defaulter at the racecourse. Then, according to Thormanby: "Lord George interposed, and in his commanding incisive tones said, 'Waiter, bring that bill to me.' Coolly casting his eye over its items, Lord George said, in a voice heard all over the room and with a severity of tone which made his unfortunate victim wince, 'Before Captain ——— orders such expensive dinners he should pay his debts of honour.' It was cruel and crushing and possibly well deserved, but was it quite the act of a gentleman?"

Rather more serious evidence of widespread nonpayment of gambling debts appears in the rules posted on February 9, 1843, at Tattersall's Subscription Rooms. The regulations set forth fees and conditions for admittance, declared the rooms under the jurisdiction of the stewards of the Jockey Club, and then spelled out at length the one significant rule: that defaulters would be barred from Tattersall's rooms and from the Newmarket racecourse.

A contemporary account (taken from Vincent Orchard's *Tattersalls*) describes some of the defaulters at the rooms. "Defaulters of every description were found from 10 pounds up to 10,000 pounds; several who had lost thousands did not make their appearance at all; others, equally unsuccessful, did attend the room, and notwithstanding their acknowledged integrity, expressed their incapacity of paying their losses. Many came to the room, received all their winnings, and immediately disappeared, leaving their losses unliquidated. Some there are who have paid all, without receiving any; and others who have paid none because they have not, nor do not expect to receive the amount of their successful speculations."

Lord George's wrath rose to its greatest height when swindlers and sharp dealers tried to fix races—or simply held back a horse so that he might win later at higher odds.

On one occasion Lord George finally did have to fight a duel, in spite of his principles. In this case he had paid off a debt on a lost wager—paid belatedly, and grudgingly, and with some insults to the winner, a Squire Obaldeston. Lord George believed the squire had misled him and thereby cheated him, by holding back his horse in an earlier race. That practice, incidentally, has persisted for a century and a half; it is accepted as a fact of racing life, though not always graciously, by those who have just lost a serious wager. Both Lord George and the squire survived the duel. Bentinck fired into the air. As for the squire, he had some fame as a marksman. But a Colonel Anson, who officiated, apparently let the squire know that most of the gentlemen at Newmarket thought Lord George right in the quarrel—and none of them would speak to the squire again if he shot his opponent.

In the case of a horse called Running Rein, an apparent Derby winner in 1844, Lord George clearly acted in the interest of racing as a whole. He thought the horse was what in the United States today would be called a ringer—and what was worse, an older horse running against three-year-olds. He threw all his energies into proving his case, and made it stand up in court. The elaborate system of thoroughbred identification that for the most part prevents ringers from running today can be said to have begun with Lord George's efforts in the Running Rein case.

Before Lord George's time, unscrupulous trainers instructed their riders to cause repeated false starts, among other things, to exhaust a favorite. Lord George introduced the custom of starting horses more or less uniformly by the signal of a flag, and in fact he wielded the flagstaff himself at Newmarket. The flag fall, now symbolic, is still seen at the start of races today, long after the introduction of mechanical starting gates. He also insisted on better identification of horses, for the sake of the viewing public. He tried to force trainers and jockeys to come to the starting line on time. And he pioneered the practice of vanning horses from training farm to racecourse, so that his own stock at least might race fresh.

All this earned for Lord George the title of benevolent despot in racing. But he had a material interest in his own reforms. He himself wagered at the races on a truly massive scale. Disraeli asserted that Lord George's "habits were severely simple and he was the most generous of men." Why then the large wagers? Disraeli said: "He valued the acquisition of money on the turf, because there it was the test of success. He counted his thousands after a great race as a victorious general counts his cannon and his prisoners."

Thromanby took a more prosaic view of Lord George's betting. In 1845, he won, by betting more than £100,000, but his expenses, Thormanby said, were "enormous" and ate up fully half of the total amount won. As another account put it (by T.H. Bird, in his biography of Admiral Rous), it was Lord George's "axiom that, without heavy and successful betting, it was impossible for anyone to make a large stud pay, and that unless the closest attention was given to detail, to trials of horses and to public running, it was impossible to win by betting."

Thus Bentinck's passionate efforts to reform racing could be regarded as protection of his own wagers and, ultimately, of his stables. With all that, at the Goodwood races in 1846, at the peak of his racing career, Lord George abandoned the turf with a single gesture and scarcely more than a sentence spoken. According to all accounts, he offered to sell all his horses and all their equipment for £10,000.

In Thormanby's version, a Mr. Mostyn, meeting Lord George at the breakfast table, said, "I'll take the lot, Bentinck, at 10,000 pounds, and will give you a cheque before you go on the course."

" 'If you please,' replied Lord George, and the bargain was concluded."

According to Disraeli, Lord George had become as deeply concerned about the maintenance of the corn laws as formerly he had been about racing scandals. He devoted the rest of his life, literally eighteen hours a day, to work in the Parliament that he had essentially ignored for the preceding decades.

Two years later, in 1848, Surplice, one of the horses he had sold so abruptly, won the Derby. Disraeli described meeting Bentinck that day in the library of the House of Commons:

> . . . his horse Surplice, whom he had parted with among the rest of his stud, solely that he might pursue, without distraction, his labours on behalf of the great interests of the country, had won that paramount and Olympic stake to gain which had been the object of his life. He had nothing to console him and nothing to sustain him, except his pride. Even that deserted him before a heart, which he knew at least could yield him sympathy. He gave a sort of superb groan.
>
> "All my life I have been trying for this, and for what have I sacrificed it? . . ."
>
> It was in vain to offer solace.
>
> "You do not know what the Derby is," he moaned out.
>
> "Yes, I do, it is *the Blue Riband of the Turf.*"
>
> "It is the *Blue Riband of the Turf,*" he slowly repeated to himself, and sitting down at a table buried himself in a folio of statistics.

Three months later Surplice also won the St. Leger. A week later, during a visit to his father's estate, Lord George set out on foot to visit a neighbor some six miles away. He never arrived. That evening he was found on the footpath, dead, apparently of a heart attack.

Lord George Bentinck appeared frequently in courts, most often as a defendant in actions brought by losers to avoid liability for a gambling debt. He was sued under the Act of 1710, largely ignored for more than a century, which prohibited "excessive" betting and provided a threefold penalty for those, like Bentinck, who tried to collect bets over a small minimum.

On Lord George's most famous appearance, this time to expose fraud in the Running Rein case, Baron Alderson presided as judge. According to Wray Vamplew, the baron remarked in his summation that "a most atrocious fraud has been proved," thus in effect complimenting Bentinck. But he went on with the reproof that he had "seen gentlemen associating themselves with persons much below them in station." The judge concluded: "If gentlemen would associate with gentlemen, and race with gentlemen, we should have no such practices. But if gentlemen will condescend to race with blackguards, they must expect to be cheated."

In actuality, Lord George repeatedly hounded members of his own class as defaulters, both in court and in the subscription rooms. But if he had followed Baron Alderson's precepts, at the very least he would have had to curb the size of his stud and racing stables. Making wagers on a vast scale, as he had to do, required the use of betting commissioners and led to the creation of a circle of bookmakers. Lord George needed them, commoners all, as much as they battened off members of his class.

The new breed of gamblers came from depths of society otherwise unknown to Bentinck and his sporting friends. Among the newly created bookmakers, none stands out as boldly, or was as powerful an adversary for the gentleman bettor, as John Gully, born in 1783 at the Crown Inn, Wick-and-Abson, between Bath and Bristol. Gully started from a low perch on society's ladder. Before he was twenty-one, he had fallen still lower. His father owned the inn at Wick-and-Abson in which young Gully was born. Young John, sturdy and uncommonly strong, was apprenticed to a butcher. When his father died, John attempted to carry on the inn, and evidently failed. He went bankrupt and was thrown into a debtors' jail, London's Fleet Prison. Save for luck, his strength, and physical courage, he might well have died there.

Charles Dickens, who visited his own father in another debtors' prison, the Marshalsea, describes the Fleet in *The Pickwick Papers*. The prison stood well within London, near Farringdon Street. Its interior was dank and filthy stone, dimly lit. Inmates lived, in irregular groups, in store vaults beneath street level. Mr. Pickwick supposed, when he first saw them, that these chambers were "little cellars where the prisoners keep their small quantities of coals." They were in fact places in which some prisoners lived out the whole of their wretched lifetimes. Spread out in the gray stone laby-rinth were a few larger chambers, a handful of more nearly comfortable rooms for favored prisoners, and an open-air, exercise enclosure, whose high outside wall, topped with iron spikes, fronted directly on a city street. The exercise yard played a vital part in Gully's survival and ultimate career.

The horrors of the country's prisons were well enough known in eighteenth- and nineteenth-century England. The first of the great prison reformers, John Howard, did his investigations in the last third of the eighteenth century. Sidney and Beatrice Webb, writing shortly after World War I, in *English Prisons Under Local Government*, cited a few inves-tigative reports but found no overall survey of prisons in the century and a half between their time and Howard's.

A 1759 account of prison life (in *The Gentleman's Magazine*) described conditions that still persisted in the early nine-teenth century when Gully was thrown into the Fleet. From that article's "sonorous language," the Webbs thought that possibly "Dr. Johnson himself" had written the following passage:

> . . . the corrosion of resentment, the heaviness of sorrow, the corruption of confined air, the want of exercise, and sometimes of food, the contagion of diseases from which there is no retreat, and the severity of tyrants against whom there can be no resistance, and the complicated horrors of a prison, put an end every year to

the life of one in four of those that are shut up from the common comforts of human life. Thus perish yearly five thousand men, overborne with sorrow, consumed by famine or putrefied by filth, many of them in the most vigorous and useful part of life.

The plight of jailed debtors particularly moved sympathetic onlookers. Debtors suffered as much hardship as felons (except for those wretches stuffed into rotting hulks—docked and otherwise useless old ships), but they did not receive even the felon's bit of bread.

By mid-nineteenth century reform had begun to relieve some of the miseries of prison life—and sometimes succeeded only in so sterilizing the lives of inmates as to produce a population of the walking dead. Nevertheless, anyone wishing to flee backwards toward freer times, away from reform and the ways of twentieth-century bureaucracy, might well ponder the state of British prisons at the beginning of the nineteenth century. They were the purest expressions of unbridled laissez-faire.

A jail like Fleet Prison was essentially a private, profit-making institution. The jailers, as the Webbs put it, "made rotten public houses of their gaols." The debtor, in particular, remained locked up until he or his friends could settle his debt, and meanwhile he had to pay as best he could for his own keep. The jailers sold liquors, encouraging "riot and drunkenness." Prostitutes in jail were rented to outsiders, who were locked up with them for the night and gave the warder a shilling for the service.

Luckiest of the prisoners were those debtors who concealed assets and drew on them to buy comfort and protection. Professional thieves might have partners who supported them. Convicted felons as a group had a right to "county bread." According to the Webbs, all fared better than "the untried prisoner, innocent witness or destitute debtor, who, if friendless, were within measureable distance of starvation."

The rot and filth of debtors' prison, well enough known in the first quarter of the eighteenth century, were examined in detail by John Howard half a century later, and in mid-nineteenth century still aroused indignation. Thus wrote Sir

Thomas Erskine May, jurist, sometime historian, and for fifteen years clerk to the House of Commons in his *Constitutional History of England*, 1880:

> The ancients allowed a creditor to seize his debtor and hold him in slavery. It was a cruel practice, condemned by the most enlightened lawgivers; but it was more rational and humane than the law of England. By servitude a man might work out his debt; by imprisonment, restitution was made impossible. A man was torn from his trade and industry, and buried in a dungeon; the debtor perished, but the creditor was unpaid. The penalty of an unpaid debt, however small, was imprisonment for life. . . . for an insolvent debtor, there was no possibility of relief, but charity or the rare indulgence of his creditor.
>
>   . . . We read with horror of a woman dying in the Devon County Jail, after an imprisonment of forty-five years, for a debt of 19 pounds.

May cites a series of parliamentary acts that had much relieved the misery of prisoners by the 1860s. Certainly some credit must be given to shame and a sense of decency. A number of people saw a need for socially stabilizing measures. And in part, the safe and comfortable recognized a menace to their very health in the foul miasmas of the prisons. (The Bankruptcy Act of 1861 missed coinciding with Pasteur's germ theory of disease by only a few years.) If years still were needed for general enlightenment about public health, at least some sense of the dangers of congestion in a metropolis preceded scientific understanding. Thus it was known that an entire class of cadets sickened with jail fever, and at least one died, because one member of the class had visited a prison during an epidemic. In the mid-eighteenth century it had been noted that a pestilence swept the prison population so that in Tiverton parish some 1,500 coffins had to be provided; out of a jail population counted only in thousands, the dead totaled 1,700. On an infamous "Black Sessions" day in October 1750 at the Old Bailey, "foul steams" from those jailed spread so that most in the court sickened and of six judges on the bench, four died.

Through all this, some escaped the worst of jail life,

escaped by a discreet word spoken in high places. Douglas Hay asserts in an essay, "Property, Authority and the Criminal Law," in Albion's Fatal Tree, that at least half the death sentences, for example, were not carried out: the accused was someone's retainer, or had done service for a duke, or came from a good family which might be shattered by the sentence.

John Gully, too, came alive from the Fleet Prison, still young and in the fullness of his physical strength. He also had friends—not yet, to be sure, among the gentry. And above all, he had in large measure the qualities that produce survivors in the most squalid of twentieth-century ghettoes: strength, physical courage, shrewdness, and the kind of brain described in other settings as street smart.

One day at the Fleet Prison a man in his late twenties, slightly shorter than Gully, fit and heavily muscled, visited the young prisoner. The man was Henry Pearce, also known as the "Game Chicken," proclaimed the champion prizefighter of Britain. Pearce came from Gully's original neighborhood. Mutual friends evidently had arranged the meeting. Pearce sparred with Gully, presumably in the exercise yard of the Fleet. The champion bruiser found the younger man a fair match. How Gully had learned boxing, no account says (though it is inconceivable that a raw beginner, no matter how strong and agile, could have laid a hand on the best fistfighter in Britain). Somewhere Gully must have learned enough to terrorize the youth of Bath and Bristol. Almost certainly Gully's friends had passed this information along to his celebrated townsman, Pearce.

And Pearce now took up Gully's case with the sporting gentry who esteemed boxing as they did Thoroughbred racing. It was Gully's particular good fortune that in 1805 prizefighting was perhaps the most fashionable of blood sports. Byron, for example, like many of his peers, sought the company of prizefighters and took boxing lessons at the Bond Street rooms of John "Gentleman" Jackson. (It is said that, when chided for the company he thus kept, Byron replied that Gentleman Jackson's manners were "infinitely superior to those of the fellows of the college whom I meet at the high table.")

Quietly, money was raised to pay off Gully's debt and win his release from prison. The same benefactors arranged a fight between Pearce and him. One of Gully's backers was Colonel Henry Mellish, known for betting larger sums, more calmly, than any of his fellows.

Gully and Pearce met in a ring set up at Hailsham, in Sussex, on October 8, 1805—less than two weeks before the Battle of Trafalgar. The Napoleonic Wars, and local opposition, did not prevent a large crowd from watching. According to the sporting writer Thormanby, the crowd included "H.R.H. the Duke of Clarence [afterward William IV] and the cream of England's aristocratic sportsmen."

The men fought barefisted. A round ended when one or the other was knocked down, or thrown or mauled to the ground, or fell from exhaustion. The fight went fifty-nine rounds and lasted an hour and ten minutes. Gully paid for his freedom by absorbing a fearful beating.

According to Pierce Egan's *Boxiana*, the standard source for all accounts of fights in that period, Pearce knocked down Gully in each of the first ten rounds, and then:

Eleventh. Gulley, full of gaiety, made an excellent hit—but the round finished in favour of the Chicken, who completely knocked Gulley off his legs.

Twelfth. Gulley put in a most tremendous blow on the mouth of the Chicken, which Pearce sharply returned, and in closing, they fell.

[By the seventeenth round] The amateurs were uncommonly interested by the reciprocal manliness displayed in this round—and it was the general opinion, that a better one was never contested by any pugilists, and was most certainly, the best fought round in the battle. Pearce, full of gaiety and confidence, nobly opposed his adversary; while Gulley, with an equal degree of valour and firmness, rallied, and made several excellent hits, which were instantly returned by Pearce. Gulley put in two severe hits on the Chicken's left-eye. Gulley reduced the odds considerably—six to four on the Chicken.

[In the eighteenth round] Torrents of blood flowing from Pearce . . .

[In the twentieth] One of the Chicken's eyes so much swelled, that he could scarcely see out of it; and the blood flowing from him copiously—his appearance shy and retreating; which Gulley improving upon, followed the Chicken round the ring, several blows exchanged, when they closed, and fell.

[In the twenty-second round the tide turned again] Several sharp blows upon both sides, when Gulley fell, and, while in the act of fall, the Chicken put in a desperate blow on the side of Gulley's head, which made him vomit considerably.

[In the thirty-third, Gulley] received a terrible blow in the throat, the severity of which brought Gulley down.

From then on, the brutality of the beating Gully received continued to increase, so that by the forty-third round, "Gulley was literally covered from the torrents which flowed down from his ear, and now began to appear somewhat shy—his head was truly terrific, and had a giant-like appearance, from being so terribly swelled, and the effect was most singular, from scarcely any of his eyes to be seen." Still he fell, and rose to fight again, and fell, until finally in the fifty-ninth round Colonel Mellish, who had backed Gully with a £400 wager, threw in the sponge for his man.

Pearce retired from the ring and died a few years later. Gully fought twice more, both times with the "Lancashire Giant," Bob Gregson. He dealt Gregson beatings of the kind he had himself received, and in his turn was proclaimed champion. In June 1808, when he was twenty-five, Gully, too, retired from the ring. He had become the proprietor of a London inn, the Plough, in Carey Street, Lincoln's Inn Fields.

As a fighter, Gully had established himself as a familiar of the gentlemen who raced and bet on Thoroughbred horses. He evidently discovered for himself that judgment counts in predicting a horse's chances in a race. He handled bets for horse owners, as a commissioner, and then acted as bookmaker, offering odds against each horse in a field. Within four years he had done so well, betting for himself and booking bets, that he was able to buy his own first horse, Cardenio.

According to Thormanby: "In Gully's early days what we call 'public money' was almost unknown. The general public did very little wagering, and such a business as that of one of the great Turf Commission Agents of today was undreamt of.

The professional bettor of the first three or four decades of the century laid the odds himself and worked commissions for the big backers. Gully soon had the commissions of the cream of the noble sportsmen . . ."

Gully did so well over the next fifteen years that he became a principal figure at Newmarket. By 1827 he had accumulated enough money to pay Lord Jersey 4,000 guineas for his Derby winner, Mameluke. In fact, Gully by that time was able to endure the loss of something more than £20,000 backing Mameluke in the St. Leger at Doncaster. Turf historians of the period agreed that Gully lost because of the scheming of William Crockford, one-time fishmonger, large-scale bettor, and founder of the gambling club that bore his name. Crockford apparently bribed the starter to allow so many false starts that in the end Gully's horse Mameluke became fractious and would not come close to the flag. When Mameluke's head was turned aside and his chief rival was already seventy yards down the course, the starter did drop his flag and dispatched the field.

Much more often Gully was on the winning side, alone or in partnership with Robert Ridsdale—who, like Gully, had worked as a boy in an inn and, through superior judgment of the merits of a horse and the proper odds to offer a bettor, became wealthy enough to acquire an estate and a racing stable with scores of horses.

Besides Gully, a number of others at the racecourses started in youth as servants or factory hands and rose to a measure of wealth and higher station. Generally, like him, they first made successful bets of their own, and then as bookmakers they prospered by "betting round"—laying odds against every horse in a field in a manner to guarantee a profit, no matter which horse won the race.

Harry Hill fared well after he earned the confidence of Lord George Bentinck by digging out evidence that led to exposure of the Running Rein fraud. According to T. H. Bird, biographer of Admiral Henry John Rous, Hill "was commonly credited with complete control over a number of jockeys, as well as over a number of horses that did not belong to him . . ."

The admiral himself, rulemaker for the Jockey Club and the

dominant figure on the British turf after the retirement and death of Lord George, depended on the bookmaker Frederick Swindell for information about the fitness of horses and any deals afoot. Swindell had cleaned engines in a firearms factory in Derby. He flourished as a bettor, invested in a public house, and became a successful bookmaker. According to Bird, Swindell's will "was proved at 140,000 pounds, and his friends estimated there was at least another 100,000 pounds not shown."

One of the most admired of the bookmakers who followed Gully was William Davis, known as "the Leviathan" because of the scale of his betting operations. He was at first a skilled woodworker, but found his true vocation by booking the bets of his fellow workers. Davis unconsciously anticipated a future in which anyone, of any class, might wager on a horse with a bookmaker. He was surely among the first, if not the very first, to post in a public place, a list of prices on horses in future races. He thereby began to tap a mass market of smaller bettors.

Among all his contemporaries, Gully stood out—partly perhaps by physical presence, or by the occasional flashes of fierce temper (as when he horsewhipped his partner Ridsdale) which recalled his days in the prize ring. Above all, though, he traveled farther upward into the labyrinth of class and social position and was more nearly accepted by those from whose bets he grew rich. He acquired a succession of choice country properties. He invested racing profits in a growth industry of the time—coal mining. He became, in fact, a leading mine owner and operator. Ultimately, having sold his property near the racing center of Newmarket to one of the gentry, he bought Ackworth Park, near Pontefract. There he put a final stamp on a career that, unique as it was, marked the truly revolutionary changes possible for a few during the industrial transformation of nineteenth-century Britain. He won the parliamentary seat for Pontefract and represented his borough from December 1832 to July 1837.

In a preface to his *Laws and Practice of the Turf*, Admiral Rous noted the allegation by a foreign observer that higher and lower classes in Britain had so little in common that they seemed as distinct as different tribes accidentally occupying the same land. Rous retorted: "There is at least one amusement in which all classes participate, one point of contact between all parties and one source of enjoyment to individuals of every rank—namely horse-racing."

Lord George Bentinck and John Gully represented the opposite social poles joined in prominence and authority at the racecourse. Somewhat less obviously, they demonstrated in their persons the vast spread of the most popular and significant form of gambling in the country. That spread attached new significance to gambling, at least in its sporting and recreational forms. And the result was an unprecedented change in the status of gambling in the courts of law.

3

INTERLUDE:
ON THE NATURE OF GAMBLING

IT MAY BE IN ORDER TO EXPLAIN MY USE OF THE WORD *Interlude* here and elsewhere in this book.

I once knew Jess Gitt, the editor of what was then the York (Pa.) *Gazette and Daily*. Gitt was a fiercely independent elderly man who, when young, had been the friend of such political mavericks as George Norris and Gifford Pinchot. When I visited Gitt, I found him in an office on the street floor of his newspaper's building, behind a large plate-glass window. It was the kind of room that, in my experience, newspapers generally used for selling back issues or taking classified ads. An interior stairway led to editorial offices and the more familiar smell of ink and the clank of linotypes.

I asked Gitt why he posted himself thus apart, practically on the sidewalk. He said: "I'm the editor of this paper, and I exercise the right to say what I please on the editorial page. In fairness, anyone who wants to come after me with a horse-whip should know where to find me."

It seems to me that much the same principle might hold for the writing of history in any of its forms. The writer owes it to his readers to let them know where they can find him—find him through his assumptions, derived from those ideas and theories for which he must be his own authority. He may base these on observed fact, but they remain—ideas and theories. As a fair warning, I shall set such passages apart. And it seems reasonable to offer, in the first such passage, some notes on the nature of gambling.

Writers of all stripes, preachers, reformers, and agents of justice, for perhaps a century and a half, have joined forces on the subject of gambling. They have produced a considerable literature. With a few exceptions their works can be sorted roughly into two lots. The first sort treat gambling mainly as a criminal matter. The writers see gambling as a crime in itself. Or they say that it breeds crime, or that it finances criminals.

In the other sort of book, gambling appears simply as vice. Here gambling may even appear amusing or picturesque. But the writers always hint at the threat of impoverishment and, worse, destruction of personality and hopeless obsession.

In either variety of literature, the gambler falls somewhere between wrongdoer and wastrel.

I propose to treat gambling as a normal social function. It is an activity so widespread and pervading, in all ages and all kinds of society, that if the standard views of it are to hold, it must be taken as a massive and infinitely prolonged outcropping of original sin.

I realize that such diverse authorities as Dostoevsky, Freud, and Andrew Carnegie have held forth at length on the sickness of a gambler's soul. Certainly it is easy to find losing gamblers. It is reasonably easy to find some losers who have come to harm. But to say that gambling has caused harm says almost nothing. Harm has also been done, in some cases, by eating cherry tarts, making love, walking in the park, or drinking wine.

Certainly some gambling is associated with crime. Such an association is not unique. Engraving, for example, may be associated equally with a work of art or with counterfeit money.

May gamblers be compulsive? Indeed yes. So may be

persons who reach out to touch each telephone post in passing, or workers who fly into a rage if a single tool at a bench has been turned out of line.

It seems to me that gambling is far too diverse to be neatly docketed. To cast what may be a more revealing light, I propose to examine gambling historically and, finally, as a quite basic function of economic life.

The prevalence of gambling in ancient times was so widespread and is so well known that it scarcely needs documentation. The Greeks, encamped before the walls of Troy, wagered very large stakes on chariot races. Their prehistoric ancestors, in their middens, left knucklebones, which seem clearly to have been used as dice—possibly for augury, but very likely for gambling as well.

Gambling figures equally in the Stone Age cultures of modern times. The British psychologist John Cohen, using material recorded by the Bureau of American Ethnology in the time of John Wesley Powell, remarked with apparent astonishment that American Indians were avid gamblers. (The observation did nothing to change Cohen's point of view; in common with many of his colleagues he, for the most part, regarded gambling as aberrant behavior.)

The primitives in present-day American cities, towns, and villages are the very young. Among boys, at least, gambling in many places is so widespread as to be nearly universal. If this remark seems extreme, let any adult recall how many boys in his own first few grades in school shot marbles ("for keeps"). Of the ones not skillful enough to risk their marbles, how many matched baseball cards? And how many, finally, risked hard currency, lagging pennies to a line? None of these games may be conducted regularly in present-day casinos, but they constitute gambling just the same. In each case, the wager consists of something valuable (at least to the players) in a trial of either skill or pure luck, and the winner keeps the stakes.

Children's rhymes and jump-rope songs have been traced back through several centuries. Their gambling games go back so far that the traces vanish in antiquity. At neolithic digs, archaeologists have found small, round, stone pellets and asked, Are these weapons (too small for slingshots) or are they—marbles? Certainly children in ancient Egypt and Rome played with marbles. Adults, in most times and places, happily left children free to play marbles by themselves. Left alone, children improvised their own rules—which tended to be repeated. Thus in the 1700s boys in England shot at marbles in a ring on the ground, under rules that would have been familiar in back alleys in towns of twentieth-century America.*

Some of children's gambling games fairly closely resemble adult gaming. Boys pitching pennies close to the base of a wall, or to a crack in the pavement, take part in a game belonging to the ancient and international families of bowls and quoits. Even a street name for this pastime, "lagging to a line," resembles the medieval English adult game of "loggatting in the field." This last (defined in the *Oxford Universal Dictionary* as "an old game played by throwing pieces of wood at a stake fixed in the ground; the player . . . nearest the stake wins") also survives in codes of law. It was one of several games proscribed in the first English antigaming regulation in 1388.

It may be suggested that all things juvenile are not necessarily innocent. Children do all sorts of antisocial things, like bloodying each other's noses, and committing public nuisances, and occasionally expropriating their elders' property. True enough: but the point made here concerns prevalence, or normality, as against singular or aberrant behavior. Among the schoolboys I remember, those who matched baseball cards far outnumbered the bullies and brawlers.

---

*Flora Thompson, writing of English village life in the 1880s (*Larkrise to Candleford*, [London: 1973], Penguin, pp. 150–51), gives a timeless description of marbles as a child's circulating medium: "Even marbles, at twenty a penny, were seldom bought, although there were a good many in circulation, for the hamlet boys were champion marble players and thought nothing of walking five or six miles on a Saturday to play with the boys of other villages and replenish their own store with their winnings. Some of them owned as trophies the scarce and valued glass marbles, called 'alleys.' These were of clear glass enclosing bright, wavy, multi-colored threads, and they looked very handsome among the dingy-coloured clay ones." Others, in a more prosperous country, across a gap of time and space, may recall glassies or alleys as common currency, aggies or agates as trophies.

As for the ancients, their literature proclaimed their own vices. They performed every crime imaginable except those requiring high technology. The wise men and lawgivers among the ancients knew about crime around them at least as well as their descendants. And they made laws against crime. Three of the great codes of antiquity will serve as examples. The codes of Hammurabi and Solon, and the Mosaic law, all condemned murder and punished it severely. They dealt sternly with theft, trespass, and deceit. The ancient codes set limits on debt and sometimes forbade it altogether. The code of Solon, in fact, must have turned the hierarchy of early Athens bottomside-up, wiping out mortgages and forbidding servitude for the debtors.

But—none of the codes says anything at all about gambling.

Nowhere does the Holy Bible, bedrock of Judaeo-Christian morality, in either its Old or New Testaments, take a stand against gaming. I have discussed this point with seminarians, but actually Increase Mather did the basic work, and we may assume he did it thoroughly, three hundred years ago, in the Massachusetts colony. He drafted a law aimed at preventing a number of pastimes that might lead to time-wasting. This was understandable enough, in a time and place where survival depended on unremitting hard labor by all hands. But so far as gaming was concerned, Mather's only biblical justification, from Proverbs 16:33, was distinctly weak and vague (for a zealous theocratic legislator): "The lot is cast into the lap, but the decision is wholly from the Lord." (Mather might just as well have argued *for* the casting of lots, with Proverbs 18:18: "The lot puts an end to disputes and decides between powerful contenders.")

In truth, gambling, while old and nearly universal as a pastime, made its way into criminal codes only gradually and rather late. The term *gambling* itself may not have appeared in the English language until the mid-eighteenth century. Earlier statutes referred simply to "gaming." The statutes of Henry IV, in 1409, and Edward IV, in 1477, mention a number of specific games, and it is not clear that all of them were played for stakes. Thus the 1388 statute directed servants and laborers to have bows and arrows and to use them on Sundays and holidays and to cease from playing football, quoits, dice, putting the stone, "kails," and "other such importune games." Mather's seventeenth-century Massachusetts law also banned recreational games.

The early English laws, incidentally, demonstrated the power of what today would be called an arms lobby. The statutes from 1388 to 1541 stressed the need to keep bowmen hard at practice at the archery butts. The 1541 statute was passed on petition of the bowyers, fletchers, stringers, and arrowhead-makers and was called specifically an "act for maintenance of archery and debarring of unlawful games." It spoke of crafty offenders who were "daily inventing new games and plays" and mentioned such games as "logating in the fields" and "slide thrift, otherwise called shove groat." While the law makes scant reference to divine service on Sundays, or to crime or impoverishment, it does cite the possible loss of archery trade to Scotland "and other places out of this realm."

It appears then that society's view of gambling evolved through the centuries. For long periods the lawgivers and moralists ignored it. In modern times the penalties and strictures gradually grew more severe. And yet, the attractions of gambling must have remained fairly constant.

I will briefly suggest a few of the many possible attractions: exercise of ego (in the simple desire to win); combat (denatured, or rendered fairly safe); sheer pleasure in the exercise of wits (in those games requiring thought); testing of fate and the rare delight of peering around corners to see what has not yet happened; and the desire for gain. It seems to me that the economic function of gambling may throw the most light.

Both Adam Smith and Karl Marx wrote of the need for capital in a developing economy. Both considered the possibility of an early, or primitive, society in which capital had not yet been accumulated. Smith, in the *Wealth of Nations*, referred several times to "that early and rude state of society which proceeds both the accumulation of stock and the appropriation of land." He offered no explanation for the first accumulations, though he talked in the same connection of unusual rewards to labor for "superior hardship and superior skill."

Marx used the term *primitive accumulation* in Vol. I of *Capital* and said that in the work of his predecessors, this "plays in Political Economy about the same part as original sin in theology." Marx scorned the idea that differences in diligence, intelligence, and frugality led to the first accumulations. Rather, he said, "in actual history, it is notorious that conquest, enslavement, robbery, murder, briefly force, play the great part."

Both Smith and Marx, and many thinkers of all varieties who came after them, assumed an arcadian simplicity at the foot of the economic tree. On closer inspection, though, it appears that no society is organized simply—the most primitive (or underdeveloped) least of all.

Only comparatively recently did field anthropology and economics join forces to learn something about the operation of primitive economies. In *Capital, Savings and Credit in Peasant Societies* (edited by Raymond Firth and B.S. Yamey), field anthropologists reported findings on economic life among Rossel Islanders, the Tolar of New Britain, pastoral nomads in South Persia, Laotian peasants, and other primitive peoples. It was found that none had a truly simple economy. None operated without currency. In fact, the currency systems were so complex and subtle that in some situations units of currency (for example, shells) had altogether different values depending on the purposes for which they were spent and the social relationships among the people making the exchange. Finally, all of the societies studied made use of debt—though again social relationships made the systems of repayment highly complex.

With currency and a system of debt, primitive accumulation was constantly taking place—leading in Smith's reasoning to sufficient accumulation of stock to permit division of labor, in Marx's to the expansion of capital through the exploitation of labor. Presumably, ability, frugality, or certainly brute force all played parts. But accumulation also took place, with concentrations of circulating media and land as well, in relatively few hands, through the working of primitive systems of debt.

The findings among preindustrial peoples today sharpen the meaning of the ancient codes. The codes attempted in some measure to undo the concentrations of land and enslavement brought about by the exactions of debt. Thus, in the words of Moses (according to Deuteronomy 15:1,2): "At the end of every seven years you shall grant a release. And this is the manner of the release: every creditor shall release what he has lent to his neighbor . . ." Leviticus (25:23) has Moses alleging that God directly instructed him thus: "The land shall not be sold in perpetuity, for the land is mine; for you are strangers and sojourners with me." And in Proverbs (22:7) the Mosaic tone carries over: "The rich rules over the poor, and the borrower is the slave of the lender."

As for Solon, he seems to have banned serfdom, outright, in the lands surrounding Athens. Before he was elected chief archon in 594 B.C., peasants who failed to meet mortgage payments lost both land and personal liberty. Solon, according to ancient historians, thereupon banned all borrowing in which the debtor pledged his person as security. He annulled mortgages. And he set limits on the increase of landholds. It is only possible to guess at the outrage felt by creditors in Athens.

Why then did both Solon and Moses thus attack debt (and in Moses' case, the taking of interest)? What they did by code would require revolution in a modern industrial society. Yet it seems most reasonable to suppose that the great ancient lawgivers were seeking not revolution but social stability.

To the extent that Moses can be accepted as a historic figure (and why should he not?), he must have been the leader of a beleaguered people struggling for survival, literally an army of families making a passage over hostile land. The books of the Old Testament attributed to Moses can be read partly as theology and partly as army regulations (which covered, among other things, the digging of latrines, personal hygiene, and the issuance of rations). He proposed to enforce the regulations, not through courts-martial, but through priestly edict based on statements ascribed to God.

Solon stands as a figure in recorded history more clearly than Moses. Nevertheless, few of his own words have survived. Testimony about the substance of his edicts comes from such sources as Plutarch and Aristotle (in the *Politics*). But this much can be accepted: Solon rose to authority as chief executive in the city-state of Athens after leading his people to victory at Salamis, against the Megarians. Then and for several centuries, until finally Roman armies overran all of Greece, Athens withstood one foreign threat after another. As much as Moses, Greek leaders, from Solon to Pericles, must have had the same interest in social stability. Survival, at least as much as balance of power politics, would have justified the mediation of class interests. Effects of the code of Solon thus persisted. In the face of class distinctions, in spite of the purchase or capture of slaves in battle, a free peasantry still worked lands around Athens—above all, because the code tempered the effects of debt.

Debt, and in particular the taking of interest, continued in ill repute, well past the first Christian millennium in Europe. Then merchant bankers of the Italian city-states gradually found ways around church interdiction of usury. After the Protestant Reformation, only occasional legal exercises in the regulation of interest rates interfered with the central position of debt in capitalist economies.

The legal and moral status of gambling fell as debt (or, more properly, debt formation) was rising to respectability. What makes this exchange of positions the more striking is—the two appear to have much in common as aspects of economic life.

1. At different times the law has impeded or proscribed both gambling (or, in its earlier and more generalized form, gaming) and debt formation and the taking of interest. In seventeenth-century Massachusetts, as in fifteenth-century England, the lawgivers held that gaming deflected working people from good works and useful labor. Later reformers charged that gambling further impoverished the poor and ruined families. In *The Theory of the Leisure Class*, Veblen avoids a moralistic stance, merely

dismissing gambling as "an archaic trait, inherited from a more or less remote past, more or less incompatible with the requirements of the modern industrial process, and more or less of a hinderance to the fullest efficiency of the collective economic life of the present."

As for the burden of debt, it was seen as a means of driving peasants from their land and into serfdom or outright slavery. In either case the law acted to thwart what was seen as a threat to the stability of the social order.

2. Both gambling and making loans at interest serve to increase the velocity of a circulating medium of exchange. In their simplest forms—even among children and in primitive societies—both gambling and debt support attempts to acquire goods which otherwise do not come readily to hand. The ultimate effect of a vast accumulation of debt, seen in twentieth-century inflation, marks an end point in an ancient trend.

3. Both gambling and money lending carry risk. People engaged in either activity take the risk for granted. In fact, they proclaim it. They assume, or hope, that they will be rewarded for the risk involved, by taking in more money than they started with.

It is obvious that in the course of ordinary business there is much overlap between gambling and money lending. Perhaps the overlap shows up most clearly, and very early, in the field of insurance. An oration of Demosthenes records, with a tinge of aristocratic contempt, the manner in which the Greeks of his time insured marine cargo. In effect, the insurer advanced, as a loan, somewhat less than the value of the ship and its cargo. He received back, on successful completion of the voyage, a much larger sum. The margin—the reward for risk, which later might sometimes be called interest, or in some cases, profit—guaranteed that a number of cargoes reaching harbor safely would more than make up for an occasional loss.

Whether the slaves who manned the oars in the merchant galley figured in the amount insured, Demosthenes does not say. In any case, the insurer took a chance, he gambled, on the safe passage of ship and cargo. Just so did the venture capitalists, predecessors of Lloyd's, with whom Samuel Pepys met in London coffee houses to exchange news of ship arrivals. And so, equally, does the modern insurer sitting snug behind a battery of actuarial tables when, in the form of term insurance, he makes a three-cornered bet with you and your estate on the length of your life.

To be sure, interest cannot be explained entirely on the basis of risk, and the more complex the economy the less clearly do interest rates reflect varying degrees of risk (the U.S. treasury notes whose interest rates trebled in less than ten years did not become three times as speculative as investments). And, as ideology increasingly crept into economic discussion in the fullness of the nineteenth-century triumph of the Industrial Revolution, interest was sometimes justified on moral grounds, or sometimes as a reward for frugality, and saving, and doing without. John Maynard Keynes dismissed this last notion brusquely: "It should be obvious that the rate of interest cannot be a return to saving or waiting as such. For if a man hoards his savings in cash, he earns no interest, though he saves just as much as before. On the contrary, the mere definition of the rate of interest tells us in so many words that the rate of interest is the reward for parting with liquidity for a specified period."

In any case, in the course of practical affairs, businessmen have always assumed an ascending scale of risk in their operations and have used the terms *gambling*, *speculation*, and *investment* to represent stages on the spectrum of risk. Perhaps the clearest statement of the case was made by Sir Ernest Cassel, private banker to King Edward VII of England at the turn of the century (my paraphrase is based on an anecdote told by Bernard Baruch in his autobiography): "When I was young, people called me a gambler. As the scale of my operations increased I became known as a speculator. Now I am called a banker. But I have been doing the same thing all the time."

4. In all times and places both gambling and debt have played important parts in original (or primitive) accumulations of capital. In spite of occasional proscription under law, both have sometimes led, for better or worse, to economic growth. That the mechanics of debt underlie the vast and complex securities markets of today is so obvious as to need no elaboration. But gaming also played its part in the unfolding of economic history, starting as it may have done from a dice box in a Bronze Age military camp, or a schoolboys' circle scratched on the ground, or a horseplayers' handbook in a cigar store in the mean streets of a great city. Much of the rest of this book will be, in effect, a series of demonstrations of this process in action.

4

GAMBLING COMES OF AGE: THE FIRST REPRESSION

IN ENGLAND IN THE 1840S GAMBLING FINALLY CAME OF age. It became the subject of full-scale parliamentary inquiry.

The ancients had lightly regulated gaming, or ignored it. In medieval England and colonial America the laws that affected gambling sought merely to keep people at their appointed tasks. And in the first stages of the Industrial Revolution, courts of law, to the extent that gaming matters came before them, heard complaints resulting in one way or another from default by losing bettors.

By the 1840s, though, the taste for gaming had permeated society. It was a society with some shift in class lines, with rapidly increasing town populations, which had survived riots and tensions without outbreak of open political revolution. Its leaders as they governed heard at least a faint echo of tumbrels in the street. And thus the great questions, which made the ancients regulate debt, fastened as well onto gambling. The questions concerned, at root, social stability.

At intervals during 1844, distinguished committees from both Houses of Parliament conducted hearings "to Inquire into the Laws Respecting Gaming." On one subject, the recent spread of gambling clubs, both committees and their scores of witnesses—including police officers, gamblers, and the sporting gentry—almost entirely agreed. Where a generation earlier gambling had been the province of a few clubs, like White's, and largely for gentlemen, a number of new gaming houses had sprung up in London. Their owners represented no very powerful social or political influence.

Gamblers of high and low estate sometimes lost all they had in the gaming houses. William Crockford, the most notorious proprietor of a gaming house in London, had risen from a fishmonger's shop to great wealth, pandering to the craze for, in particular, dice games. Given some changes in costumery and in the rules of the craps table, a present-day Las Vegas gambler might have felt reasonably at home in Crockford's place in St. James Street.

The gaming houses offered an easy target, readily banned, as casinos and gambling houses in most countries have been at one time or another, when the inexorable weight of the house advantage caused such losses as to produce a public outcry.

Rather different was the situation at the racecourse. Betting was done, still in some cases, head to head, or, increasingly, through bookmakers. In either case, the bet seemed often enough a reasonable exercise in judgment. And the major bettors at the racecourse in their own persons represented powerful political interests.

The array of interests stood out clearly enough when Viscount Palmerston interrogated Admiral Henry John Rous during the House of Commons hearings in 1844. Rous was the heart and soul, and lawmaker, of the Jockey Club. His rules sought to prevent crookedness in racing and, above all, default of payment among bettors. As for Palmerston, though he held no cabinet office in 1844, he had already been lord of the admiralty, secretary of war, home secretary, and foreign secretary. Within a few years he would be premier. But he was also, as his colleagues in Parliament knew well, a racing man himself. He bred his own racing stock. His filly Iliona won the Cesarewitch in 1841, and his Buckthorn won the Ascot Stakes of 1853. According to the reminiscences of William Day, who trained horses for Palmerston, the premier, presumably completely unavailable, left the floor of the House of Commons during a crucial debate on Ireland to do a favor for Day's father, John.

The dialogue between Palmerston and Rous might have been an extension of unrecorded conversations between them in the subscription rooms at Tattersall's:

LORD PALMERSTON: You have had considerable experience of betting on the Turf. Do you consider it is honestly conducted?

ROUS: I should say upon the whole it is. The difference is this: there are some gentlemen on the Turf of the highest possible sense of honour; there are others who may not have that same sense of honour, but who will still act fairly; and—there are a swarm of locusts who will come in and bet any sum of money, and never pay.

LORD PALMERSTON: If has been stated by another witness that he thinks there is little honesty connected with the Turf, and it has also been stated elsewhere that a man must be either a rogue or a fool to go on the Turf. Does your experience lead you to that conclusion?

ROUS: I am a confederate in the stable with the Duke of Bedford, the Duke of Beaufort, Lord Spencer, Lord Albemarle, and Captain Spencer; and I am quite satisfied that if any man were to propose to any of these gentlemen to commit an action, or to make any bet with others in a way which might be considered a dishonorable transaction, he would be turned out of the room. In my opinion, men of the highest integrity and the highest honour, are members of the Turf.

MR. MARTIN BLAKE [for the committee]: They are not fools?

ROUS: The Committee are the best judges of that. When I come back to England, I conceive it the most delightful society in the world, and there is no society equal to the society I meet at Newmarket.

Concerning gambling in general and particularly the conduct of the gaming houses, Rous took a different tone:

I think that, in respect to society commercially, the great harm happens to clerks; but I think that, with respect to a rich man, it does not signify whether he loses his money as long as the money is distributed among the public. [Though the poor should be protected, what] should I care what a rich man does with his own? . . .

LORD PALMERSTON: Would you draw a distinction between a common gaming house and such as it is supposed Crockford's was?

ROUS: I should draw the greatest distinction; for the members of Crockford's are persons of a certain station, and, therefore, it signifies very little to the working people and the prosperity of the country, whether those men are ruined. If a man of a hundred thousand pounds a year loses it, the country will be the better for it; but if persons engaged in mercantile or banking establishments were induced to lose money that did not belong to them, the commercial and banking community would be very much injured.

Asked whether he had "heard that persons of station in the country have lost large sums of money [at Crockford's], larger than they have been able to pay?" Rous replied: "I have heard of them losing larger sums than they liked to pay, but not more than they could pay." And he later added: "So far as regards my opinion: I wish Crockford's had been burned down many years ago."

The parliamentary committees, and the witnesses they heard, thus agreed readily on the iniquity of establishments like Crockford's and the plundering of large and small fortunes at the hazard (dicing) tables. Equally, the committees clearly declared their confidence in Thoroughbred horse racing as such. The text of the report of the select committee of the House of Lords began with the statement that:

"The Committee think it desirable that this Amusement [racing] should be upheld, because it is in accordance with a long established National Taste; because . . . [it brings together for a common object] . . . vast Bodies of People in different Parts of the Country . . . [and serves to] promote Intercourse between different classes of Society . . ."

The committee went on, though, to state that it could not "in too strong terms condemn the Practice of excessive Betting which now appears to exist."

Two problems, contradictory but closely related, equally bothered the parliamentary committees: how to regulate what might be excessive betting, and how, whether bets were restricted or not, to proceed against defaulters who refused to pay after losing.

V. G. Dowling, the editor of *Bell's Life* of London, told the committee of the House of Lords that many defaulters won large sums in one year and refused to pay off their losses in the next year, while continuing to live in affluence. Owners of horses, too, engaged in sharp practices, Dowling testified. Some of them bet on their own horses, at very long odds in what amounted to a future book, much in advance of a given race. The long odds (as much as 50 or even 100 to 1) were justified because of the considerable chance that the horse might not run. But if the horse did well in training, and did actually face the starter's barrier in the race, the owner might hedge on the day of the race by betting another sum *against* his own horse—thus guaranteeing a gain no matter what the outcome of the race.

Richard Tattersall, in 1844 the head of his family's auction firm, testified at length before both committees. Though he said he scarcely bet at all himself, and though the firm had no official connection with betting arrangements, the Tattersall subscription rooms were the headquarters for those who bet heavily. Richard Tattersall spoke with the authority and objectivity of an insider who remained aloof from the action himself.

With Tattersall, the committee of the House of Commons came directly to the most knotty questions facing it:

> You say that it would be desirable to legalize betting and to give the power of recovering a bet by a legal remedy in a court of justice?
>
> TATTERSALL: Yes; you cannot now seize a person for a common debt as you used to do. A man would come to my house and buy horses and then laugh at me if I trusted him; formerly, I could arrest those persons, now I cannot and they laugh at me; and it is the same with betting; they bet with a man and lose a good deal of money to him; they say, "I cannot settle with you now; you must give me time;" and they go again and lose and laugh at the

man, and you cannot recover it by any means, but if you could by
law you would have a resource.

Mr. Gibson for the committee pointed to one of the many
kinds of sharp practices that made the members of Parliament wary of legalizing the collection of gambling debts:

> You say that you would legalize betting. In case a man had betted
> against his own horse largely, and then withdrew his horse, he
> could recover that money?
> TATTERSALL: Yes.
> Would not that give a man the power of recovering large sums of
> money, and thereby ruining another, when he himself had been
> the cause of it by withdrawing the horse?
> TATTERSALL: As a man of honour he must pay it if he has the
> means. If a man has not the money he cannot pay it; it is all upon
> honour.

Before the committee of the House of Lords two months
later (in May 1844) Tattersall again acknowledged that many
losers at the racecourse refused to pay, but said legalization
"would save a great many young men." As for tradesmen,
many of them, too, "come and bet beyond their Means, and
compromise, by giving so much, and many never pay. If they
could be pressed for it it would prevent their betting . . ."

But Tattersall did suggest that better days might be coming, for racing and for honorable bettors. He said: "People are
getting more careful; they are afraid of one another. It is in
consequence of Men levanting, and, having got themselves
into Scrapes, Gentlemen will not bet with them. Even in my
little Way, I say, 'You must put down your money.' If those
men could be forced to pay it would be the best thing that
could happen to the Community, even amongst the middling
Class of People."

The hearings of 1844 had little effect at the time. All had
agreed that the "gaming hells" were deplorable, but these
were left to the attentions of local police. Their heyday, in fact,
had passed. The most famous of them, the luxurious Crockford's Club in St. James Street, had lost its virtuoso chef,

Eustache Ude, had faced a revolt of its managing committee of gentlemen, and had finally closed—three years before the hearings. William Crockford, when he appeared before the committee of the House of Commons as a reluctant witness, was retired and near the end of his life.

Racing itself had been endorsed, sanctimoniously if not glowingly, by both committees. Betting was accepted as a necessary part of racing. The committees unreservedly condemned the nobbling of horses, or injuring them, the use of outright fraud and ringers, and all other sharp dealing. But they left these matters in the hands of Admiral Rous and the Jockey Club and the other leading racing people.

One early attempt at legislating against "excessive" betting was passed by Parliament in 1710. The act allowed legal action to recover betting losses greater than £10. Moreover, anyone informing on violators of the 1710 Act might obtain up to three times the amount staked. The law was simply ignored. It remained for the most part a dead letter until the 1830s and '40s when Lord George Bentinck was warring against sharpers and defaulters in racing. Then the 1710 Act was used as a counter blow. In 1843, Charles Henry Russell, who had been warned off by Bentinck, brought a number of suits for damages against members of the Jockey Club. The suits failed, because after the hearings of 1844, Parliament abolished the law of 1710.

One more great unresolved problem sat like an undigestible lump before both committees: What should be done about defaulters? The committees concluded in the end that any legislation could only damage the wealthier bettors. If defaulters could be forced into court, those with money might in fact have to pay. But those with little money or no money could not be forced to pay by any means. And so Parliament let the matter rest.

As a curious by-product of parliamentary inaction, bookmaking came fully of age. A silent consensus was reached among large-scale bettors and the racing gentry. Where the law could not regulate, the problem could be handled by private businessmen, the bookmakers (who would eventually, quite appropriately, call themselves turf accountants). Let them collect from defaulters—or withhold credit.

Until then, the early bookmakers had acted in several capacities. They accepted bets, or booked them, or laid against horses. They bet for themselves. They might become horse owners and racing men, as in the case of John Gully. And often, Gully again as an example, they acted as agents or commissioners, placing what still amounted to head-to-head bets on behalf of men like Lord George Bentinck, who wished to keep their actions secret.

From the 1840s on, the bookmaker assumed his modern role, providing a service for all who wished to back a horse with a wager. He could accept, if he wished, only bets offered in cash. He could, at his own discretion, extend credit. The problem of default between gentlemen had proved insoluble. The bookmaker most likely was not a gentleman and never could be considered one, but the problem of defaulting losers had now been shoved over to him, to be solved according to his judgment as a businessman.

Something of this silent, unrecorded transformation may well have been reflected in Admiral Rous's attitude toward bookmakers. Rous himself in every particular, by rank and character, was an aristocrat. Yet some of his fellows among upper-class racing people accused him of taking the side of the legs, or bookmakers, in their disputes with gentlemen backers.

As a contemporary account cited by T. H. Bird put it:

It cannot in justice be concealed that [E. Rous] was disposed to court popularity with professional members of the Ring. He lent a ready ear to their complaints and grievances, or cannot it be denied that, in more than one instance, he furnished the aggrieved bookmaker, if he chanced not to wield the pen of a ready writer, with a rough copy of a letter stating his complaint, and addressed to the Admiral himself. Upon this letter he then proceeded with entire and unquestioned impartiality to pronounce judgment in writing, with the . . . probability that both letters would find their way into print ultimately.

Also at work, apart from the racecourses themselves, was a major force set loose in the further development of the Industrial Revolution—the rapid spread of railroads in the mid-nineteenth century.

Horse people looked at the railroad expansion with fear and distaste. Thus, in 1844, Richard Tattersall remarked before the House of Commons committee: "There are not so many gentlemen who keep horses, and there are not so many people that have money to bet."

He was asked, "Are people poorer than they used to be?"

"We horse people are. The hunters do not fetch half the price that they used to do."

"Is not the general price of horses in this country as high as it used to be?"

"No."

"Is that caused by the railways?"

"Entirely."

But the rail boom had countereffects as well. Newer courses were built close to lines that fanned out from London. They became as easy to reach as American tracks like Belmont and Aqueduct at the ends of New York subway lines. A crowd of plebeian city workers came out—and patronized bookmakers.

The bookmakers catered to their new clientele in two ways. No longer dealing with a fairly small number of big bettors (presumably well informed), they posted lists of all horses entered in every race, with the odds offered against each. And, to reach city people who might not readily visit the track themselves, they opened betting shops, mainly within London.

Chambers' Edinburgh Journal of July 24, 1852 (quoted in John Ashton's *The History of Gambling in England*), described the betting shops:

"Betting Shop" is vulgar, and we dislike vulgarity. "Commission Office", "Racing Bank", "Mr. Hopposite Green's Office", "Betting Office", are the styles of announcement adopted by speculators who open, what low people call, Betting Shops. The chosen designation is, usually, painted in gold letters on a chocolate coloured wire gauze blind, impervious to the view. . . . Many shops have risen out of simple cigar shops. When this is the case, the tobacco business gives way, the slow trade and fast profession not running well together. . . . A [high] partition runs midway across the shop. . . . By such means visions are suggested to the intelligent mind, of desks, and clerks. In the partition is an enlarged *pigeon* hole—not far off, may be supposed to lurk the hawk—through which are received shillings, half crowns; in fact, any kind of coin or notes, no sum appearing inadmissible. . . . But the betting lists are the attraction—these are the dice of the betting men; a section of one of the side walls within the office is devoted to . . . long slips of paper—each race having its own slip—on which are stated the odds against the horses.

Some of the betting shops (again according to *Chambers' Edinburgh Journal*) were "speculative, May-fly offices, open today, and shut tomorrow—offices that will bet any way, and against anything . . . and should a misfortune occur, such as a wrong horse winning, forget to open next day." Other shops, apparently, took the risk out of booking bets by "buying" horses that were sufficiently heavily backed—and seeing to it that they lost.

The number of shops increased rapidly. The number of losing punters increased, evidently almost as rapidly. And at this point, in 1853, Parliament did act against one form of betting on horses by approving "An Act for the suppression of Betting Houses."

For one brief period, a number of the leading bookmakers responded by posting their betting lists on trees in Hyde Park, so that some sections of the park were said to resemble a racecourse without horses. Bookmaking in the park also was suppressed, by local police action. But bookmaking at the races remained intact. Constables tested it, in gingerly fashion, with no significant effect, until Parliament enacted an 1897 law declaring that the betting rings at racecourses were not "places" in the sense meant by the Act of 1853. As for defaulters at the races, bookmakers were expected to report them to the stewards at a racing meeting to have the defaulters ruled off the course.

Within a number of clubs for the London wealthy, bookmaking continued as before, on the basis of proved credit. The London clerk and other city workers, as a matter of course, also continued to bet with bookmakers. For fully a century they did so more or less surreptitiously, placing bets with "street bookmakers," until finally in 1960 the law recognized a durable reality and legitimized the betting offices of turf accountants all over Britain.

In the aftermath of the 1853 betting shop prohibition, a certain number of bookmakers were uprooted. Some, according to Wray Vamplew, moved across the English Channel. In France they opened new vistas for French bettors and led, at least indirectly, to an invention characteristic of French logic—the pari-mutuel system of betting.

Yet another band of hardy British bookmakers waited a few years longer, then turned westward in pioneering fashion. They followed the *Mayflower*'s path, two and a half centuries later, landing in New York rather than Massachusetts. They looked about at the New World, liked what they saw, and established American bookmaking.

5

SARATOGA, MORRISSEY, AND THE REDCOATS' SECOND COMING

IN 1819 THE ELDERS OF SARATOGA TOWNSHIP, THIRTY-ODD miles north of Albany in the upper Hudson River Valley, faced a decision that would influence the course of gambling in America. In the fashion of most of their nineteenth-century countrymen, they made their decision pragmatically, with a strong prod from economic necessity.

The township, sparsely settled and the size of a present-day county, had given its name to a crucial battle in the Revolutionary War and then had settled back as a summer resort known mainly for its mineral springs. The settlers, largely from neighboring New England, took to temperance, good works, and piety. Visitors who wanted wine with dinner and dancing afterwards moved their trade to neighboring villages and spas, threatening Saratoga with decline. As George Waller, the historian of Saratoga put it, "With this chilling prospect in view, [the elders] agreed that they had no alternative but to arrange a truce with Satan . . ."

Part of Saratoga was declared a special township, to be called Saratoga Springs, with the right to govern itself. Congress Hall, a local hotel, set aside rooms for billiards and brought in an orchestra, paving the way for dancing. Gentlemen could now gamble at card tables in private rooms.

Saratoga rapidly recaptured the summer traffic. In the 1840s the railroad pushed north of Albany and the Springs became a leading summer resort for middle-class and elderly people as well as for the elite. At the same time, poker players began stepping outside their own hotels to look for action in the billiard parlors. In 1842 the first house equipped exclusively for gambling opened for business. According to Waller, the proprietor, Ben Scribner, was a professional gambler, and he set up shop off an alley near the United States Hotel. A few years later a half-mile track for trotters (not Thoroughbreds) offered races for summer visitors several days a week.

Thoroughbred racing, already the major gambling event in Britain for more than a century, would become preeminent among American gamblers, too. But until the American Civil War, the country squires who owned Thoroughbreds entered them in match races. They bet heavily, but only in head-to-head wagers among owners and their friends. They followed along, a century late, in the path of British squires before bookmaking.

According to the generally accepted history of American racing, horse owners matched their mounts more or less formally on the plains of Long Island less than half a century after the Plymouth settlement. Some cities and towns today still have streets which bear the name *Race*. The name is attributed, not to the different kinds of humans but to the racing of horses along dirt tracks long since paved over and dedicated to automobile traffic.

Southern landowners, before and after the Revolution, paid the greatest attention to the running horse. They relied most on horses, they suffered least from Puritan morality, and they had the appetite for gambling of people rich in land and chronically short of cash.

Nearly all the early southern presidents seem to have had at least some interest in horses. William H. P. Robertson cites an entry in a pre-Revolutionary diary of George Washington in which the young planter made careful note of wagers he had lost at nearby horse races.

Almost certainly, the president most deeply involved in buying and selling, racing, and betting on Thoroughbreds was Andrew Jackson. In the days when Jackson was known simply as a backwoods judge, sometime soldier, and land speculator, he fancied a horse named Truxton. He bought him largely without cash changing hands, by assuming the previous owner's notes. When Truxton was matched in a race against the leading Thoroughbred, Greyhound, Jackson and his friends backed their horse heavily. According to the biography by Marquis James, "hundreds of horses" and "numerous 640 acre tracts were staked." One of Jackson's friends, Patton Anderson, bet all his money, the horse he was riding, and fifteen horses belonging to others. At least two of the horses bore ladies' saddles, and it was assumed they belonged to Jackson's wife and her niece. Jackson himself accepted "fifteen hundred dollars of additional wagers in 'wearing apparel.' " Truxton won, and his later winnings were an important source of cash for the president-to-be, at a time when his resources were tied up in undeveloped land which would become the city of Memphis. As a sire, after his racing days, Truxton also figured in an economy short on cash. His stud fee was given as "$30 in ginned cotton."

One of Jackson's duels, in which he killed Charles Dickinson, resulted from a complicated quarrel that proceeded through ritualistic stages of public and private insults but had originated in a dispute over racing debts. In his biography of Jackson, William Graham Sumner called the dispute with Dickinson "a capital specimen of the quarrels stirred up by the gossip and backbiting of men who had too much leisure." Sumner in his time at Yale at the turn of the twentieth century was an accepted authority of folkways. Still, it may be asked if he ever felled a tree, dug a post hole—or staked all his possessions on a horse, to be able to meet the payments due on a land deal.

In the 1860s gambling at Saratoga Springs developed further—to a point where bookmaking was ready to emerge. The Civil War was producing dead and wounded men, and prosperous men, in something like equal numbers. The prosperous turned their faces northward, away from the sounds and smells of war, thronging the streets and hotels and boardinghouses of Saratoga in the summer months. Among them, in 1861, came a tall, powerfully built man named John Morrissey. Morrissey was then thirty years old. Just a few years earlier he had won recognition as the most feared fistfighter in the United States.

Some of the parallels between the careers of Morrissey and England's John Gully are startling. Morrissey's family was, if anything, poorer than Gully's, and more submerged on the social ladder. Morrissey too used his fists to fight his way up from the streets. He too was acclaimed a world champion in the ring. He too became a gambler and a very rich one. And by a final curious twist, Morrissey stood for election, and won a seat in the U.S. House of Representatives.

As a child of three in 1834, Morrissey emigrated with his family from Ireland. They settled first in Canada but left after only a few months, spurred, apparently literally, by starvation, and settled in Troy, New York. The father found enough work to keep the family alive, and in John's case at least, vigorously growing. The boy worked briefly in a wallpaper factory and later in an ironworks. People in Troy knew him chiefly as a brawler and street gang leader. In some accounts Morrissey was described simply as "wild in school" and skilled "in rough and tumble fighting." Elsewhere it was said (among others, by Boss Tweed, many years later) that he also spent several months in jail after two indictments for burglary and assault with intent to kill. In any case, he left Troy at seventeen as a deckhand on a Hudson River Boat. He went ashore in New York City and entered at once on a serious career as a thug.

As a first step he became a runner for a boardinghouse; it was his job to grab immigrants at the docks and bring them in as roomers. His battles with other runners on the waterfront brought him to the attention of Tammany Hall, then and for another century the dominant political organization in New York. New York held its first direct election for mayor in 1834 (until then the mayor had been appointed). In that first election Tammany dispatched bands of toughs to keep all but safe votes away from the polls. The fights that followed between opposed factions were deadly serious. Particularly in the bloody 6th Ward, men died in the streets for trying to vote.

As leader of a Tammany gang called the "Dead Rabbits," Morrissey polished his skills as a fistfighter. When he was twenty-one he somehow made his way across the continent. The gold rush of 1849 was now three years past its peak. Morrissey hunted for gold, found none, and looked instead for a professional fight, in the prize ring. He challenged the leading western fighter, Tom Hyer. When Hyer evaded him, Morrissey fought Hyer's trainer, George Thompson. Back on the East Coast in 1853 he fought Yankee Sullivan. Though Sullivan was a far more experienced and accomplished bruiser, Morrissey beat him in thirty-seven rounds, perhaps with some help from his seconds. He thereupon claimed the heavyweight championship. He had another fight of note, not in the ring but on a New York dock, with a man named Poole. Accounts of the fight differ, but the final outcome was clear: sometime after the bout, Poole was murdered. Morrissey was arrested, but charges against him were dismissed—not surprisingly, considering his political connections. In October 1858, when he was twenty-seven, Morrissey fought in the ring for the last time. He beat John C. Heenan, the "Benicia Boy," in eleven rounds, at Long Point, Canada, and retired with a convincing claim to the championship.

By this time Morrissey held a firm position in Tammany. In factional fights within the organization, he had shrewdly backed winners. He left streetfighting to the younger toughs and, like his seniors among the Tammany Sachems, turned to making money. With ample political and police influence, he opened a succession of gambling houses in New York. As his capital accumulated, he looked about for new fields. Saratoga Springs was flourishing, and gambling there seemed ready to expand. In 1861, as the Civil War was beginning, Morrissey moved to Saratoga to open the resort's grandest casino.

If contemporary accounts can be trusted, Morrissey seems to have been a rougher and more brutal man than Gully. And yet, like Gully, Morrissey as a gambler moved easily among the elite of his time in New York. He became friendly with the richest man in pre–Civil War society, Cornelius Vanderbilt. In fact, Vanderbilt gave him tips on investments, though it is not clear whether Morrissey won or lost by following the Commodore's advice. In Saratoga, Morrissey remained something of an outsider but he was an outsider who could deal intimately enough with the social leaders of the booming resort.

In 1863, Morrissey made his main contribution to sport and gambling in America. That summer, having prospered greatly from his casino and from real estate deals, Morrissey built a grandstand and laid out an adjoining oval track, roughly a mile around, for the running of the Thoroughbred horse. A track near the original site still operates, the country's oldest in continuous use.

In that summer, northern and southern armies groped for each other along roads in Pennsylvania, approaching Gettysburg. Beside the Mississippi River, the armies remained locked, like twined serpents, in siege fortifications near Vicksburg.

For individuals there were lulls in the battles, recorded in some cases. At Vicksburg a young Union officer, John Wesley Powell, who had returned to service after losing an arm at Shiloh, used a quiet moment to note in his journal the varieties of insects he had seen from his emplacement. An even younger officer, the twenty-two-year-old Oliver Wendell Holmes, already three times wounded and marked for life by the war, spent a convalescent leave that summer at his father's home in Boston. He read the casualty reports from his decimated 21st Massachusetts Regiment and contemplated his incomplete education and uncertain future.

And life at Saratoga Springs represented another kind of wartime lull, with side effects of its own. The war had produced surpluses of money so great they could be spent freely, in some cases at a fashionable summer resort. But the fighting had also created a shortage of horses fit for racing.

According to Waller, "Morrissey laid the problem before three turf experts: William R. Travers, a wealthy stockbroker, clubman and New York society's favorite wit; John R. Hunter, a prominent sportsman; and the lawyer, horseman and yachtsman, Leonard W. Jerome, whose daughter Jennie was to become Lady Churchill and make him the grandfather of . . . Winston Churchill."

The three formed a racing association, with Travers as president. They managed to find twenty-six horses fit to run. Horses raced twice a day for four days. *Wilkes' Spirit of the Times* (quoted by Waller) proclaimed the first Saratoga meeting "a great success," which "must have laid the foundation for a great fashionable race meeting at the Springs, like that at Ascot in England, where the elegance and superb costumes of the ladies vie with the blood and beauty of the running horses and the neat but splendid appointments of the various riders."

The next year the association took over the track and relocated it across the road from Morrissey's original site. The 1864 meeting, held as Sherman's armies of the west were closing in on Atlanta, was also a social and financial success. Though Morrissey no longer owned the track outright, he shared in the profits. He acted as chief betting commissioner for the meeting. He must also have remained at least a silent partner in the ownership of the track. At his death in 1878, his holdings in Saratoga were listed as including a three-eighths share in the gambling casino, a one-third interest in the racetrack, and various other buildings and parcels of land in and around the town.

By 1866, Morrissey had so prospered, and his interests had so broadened, that he took one last step paralleling John Gully's career. He stood for and won a seat in the U.S. House of Representatives and held it through two terms. Among other things, the House in which he held a seat passed a Bill of Impeachment of Andrew Johnson and sent it to the Senate for trial. Morrissey's part in the tumultuous debates in the first stages of post–Civil War Reconstruction was so minute that it was not recorded in the *Congressional Globe*. The New York newspapers suggested that he had run for election chiefly to spite the sanctimonious. One account alleged that while in Washington he ran a faro game.

By the 1870s, Morrissey had quarreled with Boss Tweed of Tammany Hall. When Tweed, a ruined man, faced jail and an early death, Morrissey was quoted in the New York *Sun* (September 17, 1877] as saying:

> Tweed . . . acknowledges that he is the most notorious thief that the world has ever seen, and that no man ever did more to make public officers thieves. Why, the community knows but little of this man's transactions. For years he had two mistresses, one of whom lived within a stone's throw of his house in Fifth Avenue, and in the summer as near as his residence in Greenwich. Rumor says that he gave those two women $1,800,000 of the public money which he stole from the city treasury.

Before an investigative committee of the New York Board of Aldermen, Tweed retorted that Morrissey had been "a professional prize-fighter and public gambler—a proprietor and owner of the worst places in the City of New York, the resort of thieves and persons of the lowest character."

In an outburst of self-criticism, Tweed added: "Perhaps one of the worst faults which can fairly be attributed to me, is having been the means of keeping his gambling houses protected from the police." And Tweed listed what he said were criminal acts committed by Morrissey in Troy, alleging that Morrissey had also been indicted for felonious assaults three times in New York, as recently as 1857.

The aldermen suppressed Tweed's reply to Morrissey (though the New York *Tribune* printed it anyway). But one place where Morrissey could never win any kind of hearing, or polite reception, was in his home town of Troy.

Late in his life he attempted to move back to Troy. He offered to buy a lot, in the fashionable part of town, with the idea of building an elaborate home for his wife and himself. No one would sell to him. Morrissey still felt affront as keenly as ever in his life. (When refused entry to the offices of an anti-Tammany politician, he was heard to mutter, sardonically, "No Irish need apply.") He paid off the solid citizens of Troy. Upwind from their homes he bought a piece of industrial land and built a soap factory on it. The factory belched forth a constant smoke screen of vile-smelling fumes, and finally the local social leaders had to buy Morrissey out.

Fashionable Troy nevertheless had a silent, last word on the matter of Morrissey. In 1891 there appeared a large, commemorative volume on Troy's history: *Troy's One Hundred Years: 1789–1889*, by Arthur James Weise. In his preface, the author said, "I addressed myself to the toilsome task of obtaining all that was deemed worthy of preservation, so that little of any great value should be lost irreparably by the fatalities of time." In the best traditions of local history and country weekly journals, the book mentions names copiously. The index records no fewer than four thousand individuals. Still, nothing about John Morrissey—from streetfights, to prizefighting championship, to leadership in Tammany, to wealth from gambling, to association with Vanderbilt, Travers, and Jerome, to a seat in Congress—none of this "was deemed worthy of preservation." The only Morrissey mentioned in the book was one James M., who had been assistant alderman for Troy's 7th Ward at various times in the 1870s.

The longest lasting of Morrissey's accomplishments in his rise from the slums was no doubt the Saratoga racetrack—and the system of betting that developed there.

The horses that ran at the first Saratoga meetings stood in the same Thoroughbred line of descent as Andrew Jackson's Truxton and Ploughboy. But the manner of betting had changed altogether. The bettors now included hundreds, if not thousands, of visitors to the Springs, most of them having no connection with the owners of the horses. For the large bettors, who might wish to get down head-to-head bets or bets on one horse against the field, Morrissey acted as commissioner, arranging the transactions and taking a piece of the action for his service. For others, he conducted auction pools. Each horse in a field in turn was put up for bid. The highest bidder for a horse won the whole pool if his horse won the race. Again, the manager of the pool, Morrissey, took a percentage from the winnings. In a primitive way the auction pool was a first step toward a pari-mutuel system. It had several obvious drawbacks: the public choice, or most favored horse, was most likely to go to the bidder with the largest bankroll; the bidder could not know the odds at which his horse would go off; and, in general, it was impossible for the average bettor to wager as much as he wanted on any horse of his choice. In effect, the manager of the pool, unlike a true bookmaker, took no risk at all. Unlike the bookmaker, he did not quote a price against every horse and book every bet brought to him in the hope that he had so adjusted the odds, and thereby the flow of the money, that he would profit no matter which horse won.

The society leaders who took over the Saratoga track from Morrissey liked the results of the venture enough to set up a comparable track on the outskirts of New York City. In 1865, Leonard Jerome bought the old Bathgate estate in Westchester County, and by 1866 a racecourse later known as Jerome Park was completed there. Jerome's idea was to create something rather like Newmarket in England, with an American Jockey Club to match. In the list of the first fifty life members of the club appear such names as Belmont, Bayard, Travers, Vanderbilt, Withers, Constable, and Dennison. An elaborate clubhouse shaded by a hill on one side of the track faced a grandstand on the other side where the general public could come for a day of wagering at the races. Jerome and his associates drew up a list of rules similar to those devised by Admiral Rous for the original Jockey Club, including the threat of expulsion for defaulting members. As for the general public, a diagram of the track in its first years shows a rectangle marked "betting enclosure."

With the population of a growing city nearby, the betting system used at Saratoga could no longer work effectively. But help was close at hand. The Philadelphia firm of Sanford, Sykes and Eaves may have booked bets on trotting races, as well as on cricket games and regattas, as early as 1866. In New York the first bookmaker of record appears to have been a man named James E. Kelley. He and a group of migrating English bookmakers set up their stands at the New York tracks from 1871 onwards. And racing—and gambling—in America took on a modern shape.

BEFORE THE FALL:
THE FIRST CROP OF
AMERICAN BOOKMAKERS

THE 1870S IN AMERICA SAW A NUMBER OF HISTORICAL rarities: events that might be called genuinely new, without puffery. One novelty, occurring in the midst of an Industrial Revolution that unfolded the more rapidly for having first lagged behind the British source, was the sudden boom in horse racing. Racing in turn produced a form of gambling new in America.

As with steelmills, so with racetracks. What took perhaps seventy-five years in Britain needed no more than ten or twenty years in the post–Civil War United States. The first track for something like modern racing emerged at Saratoga in 1863; the second at Jerome Park, on the outskirts of New York City, in 1867. Almost at once several racing associations were organized in the New York area.

By the mid-1870s Thoroughbred horses were racing around ovals in New Jersey, Maryland, Kentucky, and Illinois. In 1883 racing was sufficiently organized so that a group of Thoroughbred racing associations met at Louisville, Kentucky, while a number of associations, mainly from New York, stayed away. Altogether the number of racing associations probably totaled fourteen, and some of these operated at more than one site. By the 1890s the number of American racetracks had risen well past a hundred (a number roughly equal to the total in the 1980s). By the end of the century, after a further mushrooming growth, the number of tracks rose to more than three hundred, spotted about the country from coast to coast.

Without exception, the spectators went to all tracks to bet on horses of their choice. Early and late, advocates of racing made much of other virtues. Measured tests of speed and stamina were said to help improve the breed of Thorough-breds (and indeed, as centuries of experience have shown, the genetic experiments have worked). Race-goers in America also thought, on occasion, that they succeeded in aping the style of the British gentry. But, above all, gambling was the point of the game. Without a well-organized means of han-dling the wagers of the thousands attending racing meetings, the sport would have lapsed at once into a sporadic arrange-ment of a few match races among land-rich and gambling-minded farmers.

As it happened, by 1875 racing had developed *no less than three different* methods for handling bets. All three worked reasonably well. Among them they quickly attracted so many bettors that within another decade racing had become the country's leading form of gambling—and this at the expense of games already established from the birth of the republic.

Why the rise of horse-race betting? Romantic reasons may be offered, but they fail to convince. The facts do point toward one quite realistic, if crass, explanation for racing's success. It soon enough became clear that while most horse-players might lose, a few could win—on the basis of judg-ment. In the other forms of organized public gambling, everyone fairly soon lost. And this requires a brief interlude of the forms of gambling prevailing throughout nineteenth-century America.

For many Americans in the 1980s, taxes may seem in fact to be as certain as death. Nevertheless, this was not always so. In spite of appearances to the contrary, the art of systematic extraction of taxes took some time to develop. And so, in the infancy of U.S. public finance, in the first half of the nineteenth century, lotteries often served to raise money for public works or the general welfare. Such use of lotteries eventually languished—but not because of moral strictures against gambling. Rather, tax collectors, as they learned the many forms of their trade, brought in more money at lower cost. Lotteries, of course, never disappeared. They reemerged in modern U.S. slums as the numbers or policy racket, and have once more been adopted by some states as a device for capturing stray dollars.

Card and dice games flourished throughout the century. Some of them were purely games of chance. Others, poker above all, clearly required skill, judgment, and psychological strength. The problem with both card and dice games was the ease with which the sharper could cheat innocent victims.

The classic gambling-house card game of the nineteenth century was faro (another European import). An objective view of the rules and practices of faro sheds some light on the plight of the visitor to nineteenth-century gambling clubs and saloons. The story of faro also has something to add to local history in frontier towns.

The game, played with cards on a specially designed layout at a gambling table, has disappeared from American casinos. The reason is easily seen. The rules, with a few minor complexities, called essentially for matching cards, with a 50 percent, or even-money, chance for both player and the bank. The only house edge occurred when the same value card was dealt twice in succession. This house advantage amounted to about 3 percent, but even that figure (low by modern casino standards) was exaggerated. A simple card-counting device on the layout permitted any player capable of thought to reserve his serious bets for the late stages of a game when the odds were no less than even.

How then did this seemingly profitless game spread so widely throughout the saloons and gambling houses of the West? Clearly the professional gambler in a frontier town did not dispense charity. The answer, simply, is that if the game was easy to play and seemed to offer the same risk as matching coins, it also offered the dealer an opportunity to cheat. The case can be put more strongly. In the light of what is known today about casino management and margins of profit, the faro dealer had to cheat—or else the game would quickly have disappeared. This conclusion, obvious enough when the rules of faro are considered, casts a peculiar light on some of the gunfighting heroes of mining camps and rail-head cow towns.

In the specialized literature of frontier gunfighters, whether men like Wyatt Earp emerge as villains or heroes frequently depends (as in the case of Tombstone, Arizona) on which file of two newspapers the writer has relied on most heavily. But in reality it was common knowledge that Earp, for example, when not employed as the town marshal, worked for the owners of gambling halls, or owned them himself. The nature of faro strongly suggests his actual duties. He could not confine himself to pacifying unruly drunks. A fair number of fleeced faro players must have noticed second dealing and other cheating devices in use. If rage overcame caution and the player attacked the dealer, Earp was at hand to protect the sanctity of the faro bank. Earp's friend Bat Masterson not only defended the faro bank with his fast gun: he was accounted an uncommonly skillful dealer himself. In 1883, Masterson lived in Trinidad, Colorado, and supported himself at the faro tables. In March 1883, Masterson ran for town marshal. The editor of Trinidad's *Daily Advertiser* wrote:

> Mr. Masterson has the advantage over Mr. Kreeger [his opponent] of being a bank president.
>
> There are now two bankers running for city officer—one on each ticket—Mr. Taylor of the Las Animas County Bank, and Mr. Masterson of the bank of Fair O. Both have large numbers of depositors—the one of time depositors and the other receives his deposits for keeps.
>
> Mr. Masterson is a professional gentleman and stands high for proficiency in his profession. It is for the voters to say— professional or nonprofessional.

Many Trinidad voters seem to have visited Masterson's faro bank and come away poorer. They elected his opponent marshal by a vote of 637 to 248.

Crooked dealers, marked decks of cards, loaded dice, and

rigged roulette wheels could be found in any decade, and for that matter in any century. But by the end of the 1800s some knowledge of cheating had spread throughout the United States. Increasingly, gambling houses and casinos found it most profitable to concentrate on those games that, even if played honestly, assured the house a constant and high rate of return. Faro, which if played honestly gave the sharp player an even chance, dwindled. In Nevada today, for example, no one plays faro.

As for Thoroughbred racing, it afflicted its followers with its own varieties of cheating. Still following in the English model, crooked owners and trainers interfered with horses ("pulled" or "stiffed" them, in the language of a later generation), or brought in outright ringers for the sake of betting coups. For all that, a large proportion of suspicious horseplayers constantly watched out for race fixing and prevented enough of it to make the sport, from its infancy, a test of judgment. A large majority of players lost. But a few, then and later, did win. They won consistently enough, and grandly enough, to attract public attention and thus encourage a growing number of bettors to try to follow their example.

Some of the names of reputed nineteenth-century bettors remain just that—names, attached to anecdotes and legends. In some cases, genuine lives can be documented. The Dwyer brothers, Mike and Phil, grew up in Brooklyn, the sons of a butcher. Within the first ten years of establishment of the New York tracks, they had won such large sums that they bought horses of their own and competed with owners of established wealth. By 1883 the Dwyer stable was said to have won more purse money in a single year than any other in the world (England included).

In 1886 the Dwyers organized the Brooklyn Jockey Club, with a track of their own at Gravesend, near a fair grounds where trotting horses had run. The brothers quarreled in 1890. Mike, the more ambitious, formed a new partnership with Richard Croker, the Tammany boss. They shipped horses to England to race there. Mike was first snubbed, and then ruined—and never recovered from the disaster of his invasion. His health collapsed. For the last five years of his life he could only visit racetracks in a wheelchair. But in an obituary after his death "of erysipelas or cancer" on August 19, 1906, the *Thoroughbred Record* saluted Mike Dwyer as "the heaviest and for sixteen years the most successful turf plunger the American racing world has ever known."

A year earlier, a younger and possibly more successful horseplayer also died. He was George Smith, known at racetracks and in racing history as Pittsburgh Phil. When he died in 1905 he was only forty-three. Different accounts give the cause of his death variously as tuberculosis or repressed emotion. At any event he had early premonitions—and large sums to spend. One biographical sketch carries a photograph taken in a Pittsburgh cemetery, which shows an elaborate monument he commissioned for $30,000 as his own memorial. Pittsburgh Phil's estate, as his heir, a nephew, told the writer Clem McCarthy, amounted to more than a million dollars. Phil first worked cutting corks in a Pittsburgh shop, but he found that he could make more betting on baseball games than he earned with a cork-cutter's knife. Then, still a youth, he discovered horse racing and with it his true vocation. He quickly displayed his talent as a horseplayer in the poolrooms of Chicago. Later he did battle with the bookmakers' ring at every major track in the country, from New York to San Francisco. Evidently his entire fortune came from horse-race betting.

Indispensable for all bettors at the races, whether for the few outstanding winners like the Dwyers and Pittsburgh Phil or for the large majority of losing players, were the three systems of handling bets. All three operated as early as the 1870s. They were: (1) auction pools; (2) bookmaking; and (3) a French importation, known first as the "Paris-Mutuals," or "French pools," or, eventually, the pari-mutuel system as it is correctly called today.

The auction pools after John Morrissey's time at Saratoga remained cumbersome. They favored the largest bettors who could always outbid the rest of the crowd for outstanding horses. Generally, they prevented the average bettor from wagering whatever amount he wished on the horse of his choice. Still, with all its disadvantages, the auction pool proved a hardy plant. It cropped up from time to time even in the twentieth century. During the closing decades of the nineteenth century, it proved a mainstay of betting shops in cities away from the racetracks. The billiard tables in those shops provided entertainment that was incidental to the main business of betting. But the shops became known as pool halls, and the word *pool* thereby attached itself to some of the cue-and-ball games.

The bookmaker at the new American tracks followed in the path of his British forerunners. In essence he booked your bet, for any amount, on any horse in a race. Since this temerity put him in imminent risk of disaster should he be overwhelmed by bets on an apparently unbeatable horse, he regulated the flow of money into his book by judicious raising or lowering of the odds he offered. Was too much money being bet on a highly favored horse? The bookie lowered the odds until the promised return, even on a minimal risk, seemed so low that the bettors turned to other, marginally attractive, choices. Or, was a horse being treated with disdain by every passing bettor? The bookie raised the offered odds until they attracted at least a few backers. And overall, he reduced his entire list of odds sufficiently to guarantee himself a profit no matter which horse won. In practice this sort of continuous adjustment was far from mechanical. It demanded keen judgment and rapid calculation, and the bookmaker engaged in continuous battle with his most astute clients.

As for the French import, it appeared at a handful of American tracks no later than 1875. The French pools (or pari-mutuels) were invented by Pierre Oller, a Parisian who had made his living selling perfumes, and lottery tickets, while occasionally booking private bets. He devised a ticket-selling and calculating apparatus that permitted those attending a racecourse to bet among themselves in any amounts they wished and on any horses they wished. And yet the operator assumed no risk. In the simplest form (where the bettors are only trying to pick one horse, the winner of a race), after the race the operator first takes out his own commission. The rest of the pool goes to holders of tickets on the winning horse. They get back the amount they bet, plus shares of the remainder of the pool proportionate to the size of their original bets. The more the bettors wager on a given horse, the lower the payoff if that horse wins; the profit is cut into more and therefore smaller bits. If little has been bet, the fortunate winners enjoy a high rate of return. The bettors, in short, have determined the odds on each horse by their own actions. The operator of the pari-mutuel system can view the proceedings calmly and with detachment: he takes his cut, with no risk, and without setting odds.

Anyone who has attended any American racetrack since 1940 has encountered Oller's invention. The state controls the system. It cuts the pari-mutuel pool from the top and divides the take-out among tax collectors, track management, and the owners of successful horses. The pari-mutuels have changed only in growing larger and more complex. But it took more than two generations for the system to establish itself. In its first years the bookmakers and poolroom operators nearly killed it.

Inevitably, the three methods of betting battled for survival. A poolroom in a city might coexist with bookmakers at the track. They appealed to different customers. At the track, though, every dollar bet through the French pools was a dollar withheld from the bookie.

The bookmakers drove the infant pari-mutuels from the New York tracks before they could fairly start. Thirty years later it was difficult to find one of the mutuel machines stowed away in a warehouse as a relic. At the newly established Churchill Downs, in Louisville, Kentucky, the bookmakers had not yet made an appearance, and the French pools had a slightly better chance. The Louisville track, site of what was to become America's best-known race, the Kentucky Derby, opened in 1875. The first spectators at the track made their bets by bidding for horses in auction pools. In 1878 a Frenchman known as Professor Drommel installed four of Oller's machines for conducting French pools. The new machines attracted little business, and by 1881 they had disappeared, at Louisville as well as in the East. In that year the Dwyer brothers brought some of their horses to Churchill

Downs. According to the memoirs of Colonel Matt J. Winn, in later years the head of the Louisville track, the Dwyers complained bitterly that Churchill Downs had no bookmakers. Auction pools, they said, were "hick stuff." The next year, 1882, the Dwyers consented to run their three-year-old colt, Runnymede, in the Kentucky Derby, but they insisted that they be allowed to bring with them a party of bookmakers. The bookies thus installed took over the betting at Churchill Downs, though in 1884 and again in 1886 they, in effect, went on strike against the track in a dispute over fees to be paid for the betting concession.

The bookies prospered wherever they could set up their pitches. But their progress was neither easy nor automatic. A handful of the keenest horseplayers walked about the betting enclosure, watching for what they called overlays—good horses that a bookmaker underrated and therefore held at too high odds. The players pounced on overlays and bet heavily on them. If enough overlays won, the bookmaker faced ruin.

Many years later, in 1934, mortality was still heavy among the more unwary bookmakers. According to Fred S. Buck, who became the first chief of legalized pari-mutuel betting in New York: "In 1934 in New York State seventy-one bookmakers were operating at the beginning of the racing season. During the season a total of 175 were approved, but at the close only fifty-nine were operating."

The bookies of the nineteenth century did what they could to overcome the hazards of their trade. They paid stables for information about the condition of horses. They posted their own clockers along the rail at morning workouts. And on occasion they interfered directly in the running of a race. Some horsemen alleged that the bookies themselves, in some races, entered horses that had absolutely no chance of winning. Then they offered spectacular odds against these "plow horses . . . with cockleburrs in their tails"—as a contemporary writer described them—thereby tempting the gullible into hopeless wagers. For practices of this sort, in 1880, the tracks at Jerome Park and Sheepshead Bay moved to ban the books and replace them with auction pools. But the bookmakers quickly enough made their peace with the New York society leaders. For wealthy horse owners who wanted to bet, the bookie offered one great advantage—secrecy. A bid in an auction pool was a public gesture, even when made by a commissioner. In practice, it was the poolrooms, operating miles away from the tracks, which clashed most openly with the wealthy clubmen who dominated most Eastern-Coast racing.

The name Cassatt serves among other things to demonstrate that art is long and life is brief, and a fine painting on the wall may outvalue securities in a bank vault. Mary Cassatt is well known as one of the first truly distinguished American painters. In her lifetime, though, she was far overshadowed by her brother. Alexander J. Cassatt was the president of the Pennsylvania Railroad. A Philadelphian, he owned estates, and a racing stable, and generally had social position in keeping with his corporate rank. In the late 1870s, A. J. Cassatt, in combination with August Belmont, Pierre Lorillard, James Gordon Bennett, and D. D. Withers, bought the Monmouth racecourse, near Long Branch, New Jersey. Over several years they improved the Monmouth plant and made it fully comparable to Saratoga and Jerome Park. But Cassatt enjoyed racing at Monmouth for less than a decade before he and his associates were embarrassed into shutting down the track. The poolroom operators of New York City played a large part in that discomfiture.

The year 1889 had been a difficult one for Cassatt. Several of his best horses suffered injuries. What was worse, Monmouth found itself in competition with what it regarded as outlaw tracks which had sprung up elsewhere in New Jersey. Cassatt and his associates decided to close Monmouth after racing on August 15. On that day, though, his horse Eurus won the Monmouth Handicap. What happened as Cassatt led Eurus from the winner's circle is told by Cassatt's biographer, Patricia T. Davis:

> While he was still receiving the congratulations of his friends, Cassatt was arrested by the New Jersey state authorities. The charge on the summons accused him, under an old state blue law, of "running a disorderly house" at the Monmouth race track. This

shocking charge, especially repugnant to a man of Cassatt's dignity and reserve, implied only one thing: In the parlance of the times, a disorderly house was a brothel. What could be more abhorrent to a man like Cassatt!

The authorities also arrested Cassatt's associate, D. D. Withers, but they released both on the posting of $200 bond. According to the *Livestock Record* a man named Thomas Cruchen filed the complaint against the two magnates. Without doubt, Cruchen acted on behalf of the poolroom operators of New York City. Besides carrying on a battle with tracks they regarded as outlaws, the Monmouth directors had cut off the telegraph lines that flashed the names of winning horses to the poolrooms. Trackside bookmakers paid a fee to the track. The off-course poolrooms paid nothing.

A spokesman for Monmouth, J. N. Galway, accused the poolroom people of acting out of spite because of the cutting of the telegraph lines. Told of the countercharge that Monmouth feared use of the wire might keep some of their customers away from the track, Galway replied: "Pool room customers are not the sort of people who go to race tracks. They could not afford it."

Among other things, the Monmouth incident demonstrated, vividly enough, the importance of a racing wire for off-course bookmaking of all sorts. Any bookmaker's profit depended on the volume of bets. A fast wire service from track to betting shop encouraged immediate reinvestment of winnings. The wire might easily double the action, or handle, in a betting parlor.

The poolrooms were natural enemies of the managers of tracks; with trackside bookmakers matters were more complicated. Owners and bookies bargained hard. Racing associations in the late 1880s refused to do business with organized combinations of bookmakers. Yet the two parties needed each other. In effect they made common cause with antigambling forces in putting down the poolrooms.

Thus Anthony Comstock, self-appointed guardian of public morals and organizer of the New York Society for the Suppression of Vice, turned his attention as well to the perils of gambling. He picked the poolrooms as his targets, not the racetracks. He contributed an attack on "Pool Rooms and Pool Selling" to the *North American Review* in November, 1893. He spoke of a "horde of nearly one hundred boss gamblers, with their touts, [who] flocked from one track to another." What evidence he presented came largely from the hearings of the Bacon Legislative Committee held in Brooklyn in 1887. A year after Comstock's article appeared, the New York State Legislature passed the first significant law aimed against racetrack betting.

The U.S. economy in 1894 was in turmoil. It had recovered hardly at all from the business panic of 1893. As bankruptcies continued throughout the year, foreign investors called in loans or sold their holdings for gold equivalents. The U.S. Treasury was staggered by the drain on its gold reserve, unchecked by several bond issues of its own. By February 1895, the Treasury's gold reserves had dropped to $41 million and the decline continued at the rate of $2 million a day.

At this point, President Cleveland "negotiated with J. P. Morgan and a group of bankers for a loan of 3.5 million ounces of gold, to be paid for in 4 percent United States bonds. It was agreed that half the gold should be obtained abroad . . ." It was further agreed that the bankers would use what influence they had to check further withdrawals. And, lo!—their influence proved great indeed. The gold withdrawals stopped. Foreign investment flowed back into the United States. Effects of the 1893 crisis finally passed, and business blossomed again.

The episode has many features of interest. For one, J. P. Morgan, who consented at the last moment to come to Washington to save the country's financial system, was also considered by many to be the principal architect of corporate trusts and monopolies and thereby the most flagrant violator of the Sherman Anti-Trust Act. For another, the chief among the bankers who joined in Morgan's rescue mission (and the one who went with him to Washington) was August Belmont. Almost certainly Belmont's special influence resulted from his intimate relationships with the Rothschilds abroad.

And it was Belmont, earlier in 1894, who looked upon the disorder in American horse racing, and in combination with several dozen of his wealthier sports-loving friends, applied something like the idea of a trust to the turf. In January 1894 they established the American Jockey Club in very much its modern form. The Jockey Club, of course, could not suppress the continued spread of new tracks. So far as it could, it did regulate the sport and its betting. And in the key state of New York it quickly acquired exclusive control of licensure for jockeys, trainers, and owners. It maintained that hold for more than half a century.

As if to prove that the idea of monopoly need have no class barriers, the bookmakers at the New York tracks in 1895 set up an equally exclusive organization of their own, the Metropolitan Turf Association, known generally as the Mets. The Mets limited their membership to two hundred. They sold places in the betting ring as seats were sold on the New York Stock Exchange.

In 1894 again, as a sign of growing maturity among bettors who wanted serious racing information, Frank Brunnel of Chicago started a paper to be called the *Daily Racing Form*. He sold it in 1922, but with only minor interruptions the paper has been issued continuously from its start. It rather quickly produced racing charts that are completely recognizable today. Thereby it made available to all serious students of the bookmakers' odds much of the same information Pittsburgh Phil had stored in a remarkable memory or noted in his own records. Brunnel, incidentally, was another of the English immigrants who turned his knowledge of the sport to advantage in America.

On a lesser scale (merely as a mark of sophistication in chicanery), some would-be race fixer in 1894 invented an electric shocking device, which later generations regarded as peculiarly the property of crooked jockeys. The 1894 contraption, which worked through spurs, was a complicated version of what racetrackers today call a joint, or battery, or buzzer.

And finally, also in 1894, horse-race betting saw passage of its version of a Sherman Act. The New York state legislature passed the Percy-Gray Law, aimed at severely restricting betting. The law forbade off-track bets. It also tried to limit on-course betting to head-to-head wagers between individuals, but here the legal draftsmen evidently faced a dilemma: some of the elite of society owned and raced horses, had always bet on them, and could hardly be stopped now. In any case, to complete the parallels, the Percy-Gray Law proved about as ineffectual as the Sherman Anti-Trust Act.

The mushrooming of racetracks around the country picked up again with the recovery from the panic of 1893. According to William Robertson's tally (based on *Goodwin's Official Turf Guide*), a peak number occurred in 1897—with 314 tracks having some racing in the United States and 43 in Canada. Admittedly some of the meetings at these tracks were brief. Nevertheless, the total was roughly three times as great as the number operating in the 1980s.

As for bookmakers, they continued to post their odds, perhaps more discreetly at the track and with more concessions to local police off the track. Among the leaders at the eastern tracks, differences of style and temperament emerged. The differences make it impossible even to guess at the sums of money the bookmakers won, though it is obvious that the risks for all were great and the winnings for some even greater. Some of the bookies appeared to be quiet, conservative men, content with the edge given them by a balanced book (the equivalent of a commission, its size depending on whether they moved their whole price line up or down). Robertson quotes an 1894 article in the New York *Herald* that cited Ed Burke and George Kuhnsman as men of the quiet sort. Some, like Ike Hakelburg and Saul Lichtenstein, were respected for their all-around judgment and speed in calculating. A few were feared most as gambling bookmakers. These were not satisfied merely to pay off the winners and pocket a somewhat greater amount from the losers, to show a profit (vigorish, vig, or juice, as the margin came to be known). All bookies watched each other every moment between races. All sniffed about for every scrap of racing information. But the gambling bookies specialized in picking up information from clockers and their agents in stables. If the gambling bookie thought he had picked a winner in a race, he might hold that horse out—accept no bets on him—and raise the rest of his price line to make the odds on other horses more attractive. Obviously this involved great risk: the horse held out might lose. Then the bookie might have to pay off more bettors, at higher odds, on the actual winner. But if the bookie's selection won, he pocketed every dollar bet with him. Among gambling bookies singled out by the *Herald* were Riley Grannon, Billy Mackin, Orlando Jones, and "that grizzly-haired, stubbly-mustached veteran, Ike Thompson." Thompson was another of the wandering Englishmen. Of him the *Herald* said, "There is no bookmaker around the ring more closely watched than Thompson. He is on the inside of a great many good things, and when the gang sees him marking up the price against the favorite, or 'killing it', as the term goes, and holding out a longshot, the most of them follow suit through a sort of blind instinct. They know very well that something is in the wind."

According to several accounts, Grannon made a head-to-head bet with "Pittsburgh Phil" Smith on the match race between Domino and Henry of Navarre (over a mile and an eighth, at Gravesend, September 15, 1894). The amount wagered is variously given as $50,000 or $100,000—a staggering sum in either case, in pre-1900 dollars. No one ever counted the money. The race ended in a dead heat. It can only be said that both men could afford the bet. Grannon in particular might have sought it—though such a large bet, on a race between horses so closely matched, does not square with what is known of Smith's methods.

It should be noted that, early and late, the sizes of reported bets have been subject to gross inflation. Comstock's article in the *North American Review* quotes an assertion that on a racing day at Brighton Beach in the 1880s, just eight booths handled pools totaling $80,000, or $10,000 per booth. The number is remarkable. An equivalent betting terminal at an American racetrack a century later handles about $10,000—and this with much faster electronic equipment and a longer racing day by far, to say nothing of vast inflation of prices.

The poolrooms continued at the turn of the century too. Without further resort to harassment of tycoons, poolrooms once more established a wire service. In 1905 the Metropolitan News Company of Louisville set up its own racing information service, speeding race results from New York tracks to more than 450 poolrooms around the country. The *Thoroughbred Record* (cited in *Hoofprints of the Century*) estimated that Metropolitan News would "clear from $800,000 to $1,000,000 annually from the traffic."

Finally, as stories of fixed races, stiffed horses, and betting coups multiplied, bookmakers continued to prosper. Some used their winnings to establish tracks of their own, or to buy into older racing associations. As a result, some tracks refused to operate at all without their own chosen ring of bookies. Thus in Kentucky, in 1908, the State Racing Commission ordered use of pari-mutuel machines at Latonia, some ten miles south of Cincinnati, across the Ohio River. Controlling director at Latonia was Louis A. Cella of St. Louis. At a meeting of Latonia directors Cella said the track could not afford to operate without bookmakers. Cella was a man of much power and wealth; at his death ten years later his fortune was estimated at more than $10 million. He owned theaters and much real estate in the St. Louis area. He had owned all or pieces of racetracks up and down the Mississippi Valley. But it was generally assumed that Cella had made his start toward wealth as a bookmaker. Certainly Cella stubbornly defended the interests of bookmakers at Latonia. The Cincinnati *Post* published detailed figures showing that with pari-mutuels, revenue to the track itself had increased 40 percent over a similar period in the preceding year when bookmakers handled the betting. Cella's response: "If bookmaking don't go the track will be closed."

Latonia did shut down. When it reopened in the fall of 1908, the bookmakers were back at their stands—and the state promptly revoked the track's license.

In a dispute over bookmakers versus pari-mutuels it could be said that Louis Cella was prejudiced or, at the least, an interested party. But many heavy bettors, who had never themselves booked the bet of anyone else, also preferred dealing with a bookie. Perhaps they disliked the impersonality of the mutuel machine. Certainly they valued the privacy of a bet with a bookie. They thought they could profit from the right to be paid at the odds prevailing when they got the bet down, not the closing odds paid by the pari-mutuel system.

On the other side it could be argued that the sport could only benefit from the machines' objectivity. No one running the machines had reason to care who won the race. Therefore no one was likely to interfere in the running of the race. The mutuels reduced betting to a fair contest among the players themselves.

Whatever the merits of either case, the argument was about to be set aside as meaningless. At the moment of its greatest expansion and success, horse-race betting faced a wave of moral uplift. Reform threatened to wipe out bookmaker and poolroom operator, track manager, horseman, and bettor, all with one blow.

The epidemic of antigambling fervor seemed to catch the racing and betting industry by surprise. Yet the signs of the coming disaster were clear—for example, in the uncomfortably moralistic tone adopted by some of the biggest bettors the track had known.

In 1907, James R. Keene was one of the wealthiest men on Wall Street, an insider's insider. He also owned perhaps the most successful racing stable in the country. In an interview with the *Thoroughbred Record* (cited in *Hoofprints*), he talked at length of his horses, and then said: "It is not the sum that the horse may earn, it is not the possibility that he may be employed for speculation that makes him desirable. Racing for gaming is not sport."

No doubt Keene genuinely admired and loved the fine horses that raced under his colors, among them Domino, Colin, and Sysonby. But he also had a well-deserved reputation as a heavy bettor. When Bernard Baruch was in his early twenties (as he recalls in his autobiography), he was able to perform a service for Keene. He acted as a "beard" for Keene—that is, he carried a great wad of money, amounting to several thousand dollars, to a New York racetrack where one of Keene's horses was running. Baruch circulated among the bookmakers, betting the money on Keene's horse a little at a time, to avoid jostling the odds. The horse won, and on the way home Baruch was more anxious than ever, with his pockets now stuffed with winnings. Nor was Keene a conservative financier who relaxed by risking a wager on his own horse. He was above all a speculator, and as he told Baruch, he speculated in the spirit of a hunting dog that chases yet another rabbit.

Toward the end of 1907 the *Thoroughbred Record* wrote about Keene again. At this time the Jockey Club was trying to curb the huge bets of plungers like John "Bet-a-Million" Gates. Apparently Keene helped carry the Jockey Club's message to Gates. The *Thoroughbred Record* reported:

> It is known . . . that James R. Keene tried to get John W. Gates to cut down his betting. On this occasion Keene called Gates aside, and in fatherly tones said: "John, wouldn't you have as much pleasure betting $1,000 on a horse as when betting $20,000?" Gates looked him in the eye and replied: "Mr. Keene, would you have the same pleasure if you bought 100 shares of stock instead of 100,000, and they went up ten points?"
>
> This was too much for Keene. He smiled at Gates, shook his head, and walked away. . . .

For a better understanding of what was about to happen to American racing and betting in 1908, it may be necessary to look more closely at the reform movement that was sweeping the country.

7

INTERLUDE:
AN ESSAY ON REFORM

IN THE AFTERGLOW OF NOSTALGIA, THE UNITED STATES in 1900 seems a place of industrial vigor and opportunity for all, in a time of fun and simple pleasure. For some, it was all those things. But for many others it was none of them. What those others saw, flowing as if through a safety valve at the top of a social cauldron, was a thin stream of reform.

The Populist platform of 1892 asserted that the country had been "brought to the verge of moral, political and material ruin." According to the Populists, corruption dominated politics, newspapers were muzzled, and all the while "The urban workmen are denied the right to organize for self-protection, imported pauperized labor beats down their wages, a hireling standing army, unrecognized by our laws, is established to shoot them down and . . . [the] fruits of the toil of millions are boldly stolen to build up colossal fortunes for a few . . ."

Behind the Populist platform could be heard the muted voice of a rural majority. During a third of a century of poor farm prices and high rail rates, as Richard Hofstadter put it, "farmers had found little sympathy in the federal government and had won no great measures of legislative policy designed to give them relief."

Hundreds of thousands of newly employed industrial workers fared, if anything, worse. They organized greater and lesser strikes (in 1877, 1892, and 1894, for example). All the strikes were broken, forcibly.

And yet—if the Populists failed to cheapen money enough to ease the farmers' debts, they did become a force within the Democratic Party in 1896.

Did freight rates remain high? At least an Interstate Commerce Commission, from 1887 on, took the first steps toward railroad regulation.

Did corrupt political bosses continually regain power, no matter how often exposed? At least the Pendleton Act of 1883 began the building of a federal civil service. And, after 1903, most states gradually passed laws requiring political parties to nominate candidates by primary elections.

Perhaps twelve-hour days in foundries, or the unchecked dangers of picking at veins of coal underground, seemed grim but inevitable parts of industrial life. At least some could dare to think of the children. All the censuses from 1880 to 1910 revealed the same fact about child labor: of all children between ten and fifteen, one in six worked, generally putting in as many hours as the adults. In steelmills, water boys worked through the whole night. But by 1900 at least a few states were trying to limit the work of children. The National Consumers League (organized in 1899) and the National Labor Committee (from 1904 on) took up the fight for a federal child labor act. And in 1916 they succeeded—only to have the law thrown out by the U.S. Supreme Court. They succeeded again in 1919, and again the high court declared the welfare of children alien to the United States Constitution.

It may have seemed impossible to protect immigrants from exploitation in sweat shops (just as it seemed impossible to protect wage rates from the flood of cheap labor). But the U.S. Immigration Commission in 1907 was able to investigate "Importation and Harboring of Women for Immoral Purposes." And Congress in response passed a White Slave Traffic Act in 1910.

A National Tuberculosis Association was organized in

1904; the first American Conference for the Prevention of Infant Mortality was held in 1909; and in 1910, Kansas City seems to have set up the first Board of Public Welfare.

If steps like these seemed timid, they did try, by regulation, to improve what could not be stamped out. And if, in the language of the 1980s, *regulation* seems an ugly word, it is worth a backward look at the savagery of life, in the industrial prime, before any regulation.

But reform came in curiously mixed packages. It sought more than relief from the clearest evils of exploitation. Religion in the nineteenth century governed higher education and much of the language of public policy. Some reformers busied themselves most, or even exclusively, with the state of their neighbors' souls. They knew, absolutely, that only thrift, abstinence, and hard work could save the soul. Reformers of this stripe outdid all others. The godless had numbers enough, but they lacked friends at court. The godless rich (those, for example, who gambled and drank wines and whiskey) could ignore reform. The godless poor could not avoid it.

Comstock wrestled mightily with obscenity and had himself appointed a postal inspector. The censorship he created, like a ghostly shroud, so far outlasted him that in the 1930s the United States was still deprived of all but bootlegged copies of some of the world's literary masterworks.

Moral reform's greatest triumph came with the prohibition of liquor, achieved with the 18th Amendment and passage of the Volstead Act in 1919. More than a century of prayerful agitation and political organizing paved the way for Prohibition. Pious women most often took the lead in the long campaign. Many of them, not quite ready to do battle with men for their own franchise, took their first political action in the temperance fight. Along the way several states passed Prohibition laws of their own.*

---

*Maine adopted prohibition at mid-nineteenth century. Georgia, as another example, in a burst of piety led by the Woman's Christian Temperance Union, passed a prohibition law in 1907. The leader of the WCTU in Georgia, Mary Harris Armor, was called the "Joan of Arc of Temperance" and the following verse paid tribute to her:
"Georgia lifts her heart in gratitude sublime
To Him who sent her a gift so divine—

The campaign against gambling started later and proved easier. Communities that wanted to shut down small-scale gambling did so with local ordinances. As for horse-race betting and bookmaking, at the peak of the reform movement laws in a few key states stifled them.

By the late decades of the nineteenth century, gambling was receiving bad notices from some business leaders. Magnates like Andrew Carnegie reasoned from their own success that hard work and virtue had been rewarded. Unlike many of his peers, Carnegie also felt that virtue required him to pay back some of the acquired wealth in good works. Among other things, young people in small towns across the country first read books in the free libraries he endowed. But he decried stock jobbing and any gambling aspect of business. As for the social and recreational forms of gambling, they were beyond sufferance.

When Carnegie's protégé in the steel industry, Charles Schwab, visited Europe, newspapers reported that he had been in a party with Baron Henri de Rothschild and had gambled at Monte Carlo. Carnegie sent J. P. Morgan a clipping of the newspaper story accompanied by the following note:

> I feel in regard to the enclosed as if a son had disgraced the family. What the *Times* says is true. He is unfit to be the head of the United States Steel Co.—brilliant as his talents are. Of course he would never have so fallen when with us. His resignation would have been called for instanter had he done so. I recommended him unreservedly to you. Never did he show any tendency to gambling when under me, or I should not have recommended him you may be sure. . . . I have had nothing wound me so deeply for many a long day, if ever.

Morgan himself was a more complicated case. He, too, showed lofty disapproval at the mention of gambling. Bernard Baruch thus felt Morgan's displeasure. Still in his early

This woman toiling on in faith through heat and cold
To free her native State from curse of liquor's gold!"
—*History of the Georgia Woman's Christian Temperance Union*, by Mrs. J. J. Ansley, Gilbert Printing Co., Columbus, Ga., 1914

thirties, Baruch had already made his first millions as a stock speculator. He approached Morgan about a possible investment in Texas sulfur. "We could buy the whole property outright, including royalties, for $500,000," Baruch told the older man. But then, according to Baruch's own account, he made a fatal error: "I added that I was willing to 'gamble' half of this sum from my own funds.

" 'Gamble' was a poor choice of language. I should have said 'invest.'

" 'I never gamble,' replied Mr. Morgan, with a gesture that signified that the interview was over and the venture closed as far as he was concerned."

Possibly Morgan had other reasons for not wanting to deal with Baruch. At any rate, his attitude toward gambling had many shades of coloration. Morgan crowned his career as a trust builder with the assembly of U.S. Steel (buying out, along the way, both Carnegie and the gambler of gamblers, John Bet-a-Million Gates). Then, when it came time to offer U.S. Steel shares on the New York Stock Exchange, at a suitable price and without rocking the market, Morgan called in James R. Keene—that premier racing man and bettor—to do the job.

Even Morgan's own practices may have been questionable, in spite of his frigid declaration to Baruch. If Richard Canfield's account can be trusted, Morgan sometimes visited Canfield's gambling house at Saratoga. And according to racing historian Dan Bowmar III (as quoted by Robertson), Morgan, along with W. C. Whitney, Thomas Hitchcock, E. D. Morgan, and of course August Belmont himself, was a principal backer of the construction of Belmont Park in 1905.

Where public statements and private actions did not square, horse racing was the victim. Left undefended by its own friends of high station, racing, and in particular the bookies, quietly went under in the wave of reform in 1908.

As a student at Brown University around 1880, Charles Evans Hughes sometimes indulged in gambling. He and his friends played poker—using matches instead of money. In due course Hughes went on to become one of New York's leading lawyers, an investigator for commissions bent on reform, and governor of New York. In the bitter gubernatorial campaign of 1906, he crushed the political hopes of William Randolph Hearst.

Administering the affairs of New York state proved more difficult than running an inquiry into the insurance industry. Democrats opposed Hughes as a matter of course. But so too did many of the upstate county bosses in his own Republican Party.

In the spring of 1908, Hughes took on a campaign which he could win—against gambling. Originally he gave the issue low priority. Hughes, as his biographer, Pusey, said, "was not opposed to horse racing and did not take a puritanical attitude toward betting." But, having been balked on such issues as reform of the state's insurance department, Hughes let himself be drawn into an all-out fight on the Agnew-Hart Bill, introduced at his suggestion. The bill, banning horse-race betting, both on and off the course, barely passed. A state senator, deathly ill, staggered to the Capitol and cast the deciding vote.

For two years racing dragged on at the New York tracks. Arrested bookmakers tested the law in court. Then in 1910 the legislature tightened the grip on racing. It passed a Director's Liability Law—placing track managers in jeopardy if they permitted betting on their premises.

Finally in 1911 the New York tracks shut down. Some stables shipped their best horses to England and for the time being, New York bookmakers looked for other work—or left town. Some racing states, including California and Louisiana, followed New York's lead. The two most important racing states that allowed the tracks to stay open were Kentucky and Maryland.

Other immediate effects of the Agnew-Hart Law were less clear. Governor Hughes had referred to horse-racing betting as "this source of misery and vice." Comstock some years earlier had said "thousands are infatuated" by the poolrooms and "lose their all." Still, poverty did not notably abate in New York with the demise of horse racing. On the other hand, antigambling legislators did not benefit greatly either. Senator George B. Agnew himself lost his bid for reelection in 1910, though he ran in a district presumed safely Republican.

As for the long-run effects of New York's shutdown of racing:

So far as doctrine is concerned, perhaps the most interesting antigambling statements were made by an Englishman far removed from the debate in Albany, New York. John A. Hobson in his own person united the two kinds of reform. As an economist at the turn of the century, he presaged the welfare economists a generation later and in some degree the work of John Maynard Keynes. As a moralist, he was offended by the very idea of gambling. He acknowledged difficulties: some games involve skill, and if much skill, then "the game ceases to be classed as gambling." But this reasoning did not excuse the most popular games and sports, horse-race betting among them.

Pure gambling, by its appeal to chance, Hobson said, "stands condemned as a formidable enemy of education and of intellectual order." By exposing gambling's irrationality, Hobson said he "implicitly exposed its immorality also." He opposed exploitation, and theft—but, "a bad system, the worst of systems, is less derationalising than no system. So the habitual exploitation of the poor by the rich—though substantially irrational in the mode of acquisition of property involved, is less demoralising than the abandonment of the determination of property to pure chance."

Gambling might not seem to be as unjust as theft, fraud, or "sweating," but in Hobson's view it is worse because "it plunges the mind in a world of anarchy," breaks down the rules of civilization, and causes reversion to "savage or pre-human man."

Nothing in the debates that took place in American legislatures, law courts, or police stations either supported Hobson or refuted him. He stood at the exit from a nineteenth century in which the world and the universe around it, and man within it, answered to reason and predictable, mechanical law. The answers would be longer in coming. Or, perhaps the answers were coming at that very time, but from an unexpected source: the notebooks, and blackboards, and laboratories of a handful of the most advanced physicists in the world, Einstein among them. They were discovering that universal law may exist, but it contains indeterminacy within it. Our lives are a tissue of probabilities, variously calculated. And though they could scarcely have heard of James R. Keene, or he of them, they might have sympathized with his assertion that "our whole lives are a speculation."

As for Charles Evans Hughes, he went on to a U.S. Supreme Court appointment in 1910, to a run for the presidency in 1916, to the secretaryship of state under Harding in 1920, and returned in the end to Supreme Court as chief justice.

Racing, of course, continued, and so did betting on horses. At Churchill Downs, in Louisville, Colonel Winn brought in pari-mutuels to handle the action when bookies were outlawed. Given this much headway, in a generation the pari-mutuel system would take over the on-course betting in every state where racing was legalized.

The New York tracks remained the most important in the country. They resumed operation after only a two-year break. And the bookmakers returned to the New York tracks. The state courts ruled that a bet made by word of mouth between two individuals did not violate the Agnew-Hart Law. By a masterful stroke of hypocrisy on a grand scale, everyone agreed that all bets at the New York tracks were oral. The elite, the impoverished, and the outlawed, track management and horse people, state officials and police, all joined in a solemn pretense that no law was being violated. Only twenty-five years later, when California and other large states derived substantial revenue from the pari-mutuel system, did New York rouse itself and install its own pari-mutuels. And only then did the most fortunate bookies lose their favored positions at trackside.

As for bookies in general, they continued their business. But after the New York shutdown, since booking bets in most places became illegal, they operated as outlaws—outlaws accepted as such by their neighbors and sometimes by policemen and politicians.

OUTSIDE THE LAW

BEFORE 1908, BOOKIES SOMETIMES BROKE LAWS. OCCA-
sionally they went to jail. Still, their neighbors did not regard
them, as a whole, as crooks. After passage of the Agnew-Hart
Law in New York many bookies continued to enjoy good
reputations. But from 1913 on, the shadow of outlawry hung
over them, and by far the best-known individual bookmaker
who ever lived came to be called the Emperor of the Underworld.

Arnold Rothstein is remembered as the most notorious
gambler of his time and as the man who fixed the World
Series of 1919. In truth, he was willing enough to fix any
event he could, but close students of his life and works agree
that he probably did not actually fix the 1919 Series. He
merely profited from the fix.

Rothstein's lawyer, William J. Fallon, said of him: "Rothstein is a man who dwells in doorways, a gray rat waiting for
his cheese"; Gene Fowler, Fallon's biographer, called Rothstein "Broadway's pawnbroker and fence"; Rothstein's biographer, Leo Katcher, described him simply as a man with a
ceaseless itch for money, and more money. Rothstein concentrated on accumulation as intensely as any businessman who
ever lived, whether working legally or illegally.

With all that, and with the nearly countless rackets Rothstein had a hand in, it is nevertheless a fact that he started his gambling career as a runner and collector for a bookmaker. He started accumulating a bankroll with his own handbook. He made enough as a bookmaker to set up his first gambling club, and for the rest of his life he continued to book bets from time to time.

The inner circle of New York bookmakers in the early 1900s moved en masse to Saratoga for the summer racing. They journeyed on a train known as the Cavanagh Special, named for their arbiter, John Cavanagh. In 1904, at the age of twenty-two, Rothstein rode the Cavanagh Special. He then made the trip to Saratoga every year until 1909, when he married Carolyn Greene, a beautiful young woman who had appeared in a Broadway show. The Rothsteins' witnesses were Herbert Bayard Swope and Swope's fiancée. Swope, then twenty-seven years old himself, was already known around New York as a flamboyant newspaperman. Within another decade he had become the executive editor of the New York *World*. He was variously referred to as the intimate of presidents, as one of the three or four leading newspaper people anywhere, as an awesome and erudite talker, and, also, as the younger brother of the chairman of General Electric.

When asked about his connection with Rothstein, Swope replied that a reporter should get to know potential news sources. In fact, though, the two men shared an absorption in gambling. Swope loved horse racing all his life and bet heavily. In his later years he became racing commissioner of New York state and only reluctantly agreed to forgo betting. Swope and Rothstein played together in a high-stakes, floating poker game, which, according to Swope's biographer, E. J. Kahn, moved about among hotels and restaurants and was known as the Partridge Club. Other players included the oil mogul Harry Sinclair and the owner of the New York baseball Giants, Charles Stoneham.

Eventually, at a time when he was heavily in debt to Rothstein, Swope decided he could no longer afford to be seen with the gambler. But their strangely mixed circles overlapped on one more notable occasion—during the Becker-Rosenthal case, which dragged on from 1912 to 1914. Charles A. Becker was a police lieutenant who was a key figure in New York graft. Herman Rosenthal ran a gambling house and acted generally as Becker's payoff man and his link with criminals. When the two had a falling out, Rosenthal turned stool pigeon and incriminated Becker. Becker hired four gunmen, who murdered Rosenthal. After much prodding from the press, a reluctant police force arrested the gunmen, and in due course they, and Becker, too, were convicted of murder and executed. The case made Swope famous. His stories in the *World* were generally credited with forcing the arrests and trials.

For Rothstein, the case was, more quietly, another opportunity. He slipped into the murdered Rosenthal's place, and for the rest of his life was the man to see if a crook with money wanted to buy something from the law. With every transaction, something of value stuck to Rothstein. Thus he owned a piece of the great lightweight fighter Benny Leonard as a payoff for helping Leonard's manager get a New York license.

When Rothstein set up his own first gambling club in 1910, he was already making use of political connections. His sponsor and protector in that case was Tammany leader Tim Sullivan. The political boss charged a fee, too. Rothstein had to take on a lesser Tammany figure as a kind of silent partner. The club prospered. Rothstein then bought out his partner and went his singular way, unencumbered.

Over the fourteen years between 1914 and his own murder in 1928, Rothstein bankrolled, organized, and profited from half a dozen rackets and many legitimate businesses for good measure.

He operated a number of gambling clubs in the New York area.

He personally supervised the highest-stakes floating poker and crap games in New York.

He was a pioneer in large-scale rumrunning, after Prohibition. He also left bootlegging early, when he spotted too much competition.

For a price, he took either side in labor disputes, supplying thugs and political protection for the higher bidder.

He fenced stolen bonds on a million-dollar scale.

At the time of his death he had so many millions invested in narcotics smuggling, with shipments yet to be made, that he may actually have been pressed for ready cash.

Nothing about money reveals its origins. It flows as naturally as water downhill, toward legitimate business. Always a moneylender, Rothstein dealt as readily with ordinary businessmen as with racketeers. His family was middle-class. Through a brother-in-law, he became a partner in the Longchamps restaurants. He brokered insurance policies, using his political influence to bring in clients. He owned real estate on Long Island and, by Leo Katcher's count, at some eight locations in Manhattan. According to a New York *Times* estimate, after his death his equities in the real estate alone had a value of more than $3 million. With all that, Rothstein never lost his interest in horse racing and always kept his hand in large-scale bookmaking.

In at least a few cases the money he won on single races mounted into the hundreds of thousands of dollars. He operated a racing stable of his own. In the 1921 Travers Stakes his horse Sporting Blood beat Harry Payne Whitney's stakes-winning mare Prudery in what amounted to a match race. According to Katcher, Rothstein got down more than $200,000 in bets on his own horse—at favorable odds—after a prominent trainer, Sam Hildreth, first entered his own horse, Grey Lag, and then, conveniently for Rothstein, scratched him from the race.

As a moneylender with a large bankroll, Rothstein was in a position to back other bookmakers. And this led him to pioneer in what would later become a key part of bookmaking nationally: layoff betting. If a bookmaker found he was overloaded with bets on one horse (or on one team, or one fighter), he could protect himself by laying off some of the surplus, with Rothstein, thereby acting as a bettor himself.

The one summit Rothstein never attained, though, was respectability. Unlike John Gully and John Morrissey before him, he never reached high office. Perhaps he did not want it.

The respectable rich who governed racing at Belmont Park barely tolerated him. Broadway gamblers, on their way to being sentimentalized by Damon Runyon, borrowed from him and also sneered at him; whatever their sense of style and background may have been, his did not please them.

And, by the summer of 1928, Prohibition had spawned a new and tough breed of outlaws, hungry and violent, who competed with Rothstein in the rackets. Possibly that summer he was overextended in his multimillion-dollar drug-smuggling operation. He had too many uncollectable debts out. And he had gambling losses of his own. His losses on a single day at Belmont late in May totaled more than $100,000. In a high-stakes poker game that went on for two days early in September, he was the only heavy loser. His markers added up to a total well into six numbers. Weeks passed and still he had not paid up. His personal life, too, seemed in a decline. The young actress he had married nearly twenty years earlier in Saratoga now moved to divorce him.

That summer Gene Fowler worked as a public-relations man for Tex Rickard, the fight promoter. In his biography of Jimmy Walker, Fowler quoted Rickard as saying: "It's my guess that Rothstein will be shot before the year is out. He's been asking for it. They tell me he's been mightly slow lately makin' good on some big losses in the floating card games."

A little later, Fowler said, he got a tip from one Johnny O'Connor at the *Morning Telegraph* office that Rothstein would be shot. Fowler told the *Telegraph*'s publisher, Joe Moore, of the tip. Moore replied, "Even if Rothstein gets killed, we won't print a line of it."

On November 4, 1928, a gunman whose identity was never established shot Rothstein. Two days later Rothstein died. George McManus, a gambler and bookmaker who had organized the September poker game and whom the winners held responsible for collecting from Rothstein, was tried for murder—and acquitted. The police investigation was notably vague. Rothstein's records evaporated and three groups of heirs began a battle over his estate. The identifiable items were valued at more than $3 million. Drug shipments allegedly arranged by the murdered gambler were seized. The value set on them was more than twice the amount of the legal estate. Most of the debts owed to Rothstein could never be collected. In one case the estate did sue, and collected $40,000—from Frank Costello, in a few years to be regarded as one of the half dozen most important figures in organized crime.

Nearly ten years later Arnold Rothstein's brother, as his executor, filed an accounting with the New York Surrogate. He listed no assets and asked that the estate be declared bankrupt. But the major legacy had already been paid. The murder had badly shaken the ties among Tammany politicians, police, and criminals. It led to investigations (most notably by the Seabury Committee) and to the election of Fiorello LaGuardia as a reform mayor of New York in 1933.

After World War I many bookmakers continued to practice their trade, more or less illegally, but quietly. In Brecht's words, they tended to lead two lives: one in darkness (bookmaking), one in sunshine (some other calling, often in sports). No matter how hard they tried, none could have had a career as lurid as Rothstein's. Instead, several jumped the gap to respectability, using their winnings in other businesses.

John Cavanagh continued to preside over the sanctioned hypocrisy of a trackside bookmaking ring in the service of the wealthy sportsmen who raced at the key New York tracks. His occupation was listed as "stationer," and, according to racing historian David Alexander, the rest of the ring taxed themselves to give him a $50,000-a-year retainer. (It may be recalled that in those days the chief justice of the U.S. Supreme Court was paid $15,000 a year.) In fact, Cavanagh did supply his colleagues with notepaper and pencils. In his more serious job, all sources agree, Cavanagh immediately settled all betting disputes at the track before matters became so ugly they could not be overlooked by the law.

When Louis A. Cella died in 1918 he was described in a racing magazine as a "race track magnate, theatrical owner and one of the richest men in St. Louis." His obituary noted his ownership of racetracks and much other real estate. It did not mention his past association with bookmaking.

Barney Schreiber, another midwesterner, was referred to in the racing press as the owner of a stable. He was that, but he too had his start as a bookie.

Bill Kyne is best known as the man who directed the campaign to return legal racing, with pari-mutuel betting, to California. He also founded the Bay Meadows racetrack. But, according to his biographer, Herb Phipps, he too booked bets when young and learned his craft as an apprentice to Barney Schreiber. In 1920, when he was thirty-three, Kyne made a brief appearance at the New York tracks. Unfortunately for him, that season Man O'War was winning races like the Lawrence Realization Stakes, at a mile and five-eighths, by a full eighth of a mile over the runner-up. Kyne was the only man at the New York tracks who continued to lay odds against Man O'War. He went broke so rapidly that he had to telegraph a friend in Butte, Montana, for $5,000 so that he could settle his debts and get out of town.

When E. R. Bradley died at Lexington, Kentucky, in 1946, the *Thoroughbred Record,* also of Lexington, reported: "Internationally renowned, Colonel Bradley owed much of his fame to the unparalleled success of his extensive thoroughbred racing and breeding interests." In fact, Bradley horses had won the Kentucky Derby four times. He had built his Idle Hour farm into a 1,300-acre showplace, valued in his estate at more than $2.5 million. The *Record* noted, too, that Bradley had made a fortune in Chicago real estate and had "extensive newspaper interests."

A briefer and possibly more pertinent description might have read: Bradley was an unusually successful professional gambler and former bookmaker. He was born in Johnstown, Pennsylvania, in 1859, and as a youth worked in the steelmills there. He went west, presumably had a number of adventures as prospector and Indian scout (none of them documented), but above all became a skillful gambler. The stake that he ran into a fortune in Chicago real estate he accumulated as a bookmaker at racetracks the length of the Mississippi River Valley. In the 1920s, when his own racing stable was already flourishing, he still owned and operated a gambling casino at Palm Beach, Florida, the fashionable Beach Club.

A number of bookmakers invested their winnings in real estate. According to the account of Toney Betts (for years the racing writer for the New York *Daily Mirror*), one such bookie at the New York tracks was known as Kid Rags. Kid Rags (his name was Max Kalish) prospered booking bets both on and off the racecourse. He used his savings to build a Manhattan apartment house, Betts said, at 875 Fifth Avenue, near Sixty-ninth Street—an address generally unknown to ragpickers.

Some bookies added to their reputations and sometimes to their incomes by jumping into sports promotion. The classic case here is Tim Mara. (The case is classic at the very least because A. J. Liebling chronicled Mara's life in the September 18, 1937, issue of *The New Yorker*.)

Mara was born in 1886 and grew up in the streets of Manhattan's East Twenties. His father had died before the boy was born. Mara quit school when he was thirteen, but by that time he had already developed a newspaper route that took him along Broadway and through Union Square to several hotels in the area. As a newsboy, young Mara delivered papers to bookmakers and politicians, among others. The bookmakers seemed to him the most fortunate of men. Among the politicians, local Tammany leader Mike Cruise grew fond of the boy and helped him, then and later. Mara started as a Tammany Democrat, remained one, and by his middle-age was a national figure in Democratic politics.

While he was still in school, Tim sometimes carried bets for hotel guests to one or another of the bookmakers he knew. Win or lose, he stood to earn a tip—from the bookie if the horse lost, from the visitor if the horse won. He took on a job at regular wages for a legal book bindery. But he continued to run bets between his steady customers and the bookmakers. Within a few years, with more experience and some savings, he faced the problem that sooner or later confronts anyone who carries bets for others: Should he stick the money in his pocket and book the bet himself?

Mara chose, when still young, to pocket the whole bet if it was small—with the risk of having to pay off if the bettor won. Thomas W. O'Brien, a retired bricklayer known at racetracks as Chicago O'Brien, helped him make the decision.

O'Brien bet so heavily, and won so often, that his presence terrorized the betting ring and killed the odds on any horse he liked. He therefore wagered through beards, or agents. Young Mara became one of Chicago O'Brien's favored agents. His commissions from O'Brien bets gave him enough capital to risk booking some of the bets he carried. Mara continued to accumulate capital, and by 1921, when he was in his mid-thirties, he managed to make a place for himself among his seniors in the betting rings at the New York tracks.

When Mara sat for his portrait by Liebling in 1937, he was a settled man, just past fifty, outgoing and gregarious, a social and political leader among his colleagues. He was at ease with himself and his place in the world. By this time he had invested in a coal and fuel business. And his most valuable investment without doubt was his ownership of the New York Giants football team. In 1925 the franchise had been offered to him, as a man with excellent connections in both the political and sporting worlds. Though he was a large, robust man, Mara had never played football. Ignorance of the game was no handicap. The franchise proved enormously valuable, just as a number of other sporting franchises were for other professional gamblers.

A few years earlier Mara could hardly have talked freely about himself and his business. But in 1934 bookmaking at the track had been semilegalized in New York. Bookmakers could drop the pretense that bets were oral transactions and could post odds on slates. A naturally expansive man, Mara now talked freely about the way bookmaking was organized.

A bookmaker with Mara's status, working at a favored site in the enclosure at Belmont, paid a fee of $90 a day to the racing association. He paid separately for his share of John Cavanagh's stationery. Depending on the amount of action they handled, bookmakers in the enclosure employed crews of from five to eight assistants. These included a sheet writer, who recorded all bets; a cashier to handle money changing hands; a ticket writer, who kept a special account of bets made on credit; a caller, who called out the amount of the bet, the odds offered, the name of the horse, and the badge number of the player; and, finally, at least two outside men, whose jobs included spotting the odds offered by other books, gauging the action of important or heavy bettors, and when necessary laying off bets or betting for the book itself.

Anyone familiar with present-day racetrack betting will note at once that this considerable crew did by hand—as rapidly as possible, to increase the book's total handle—what the great banks of state-run pari-mutuel machines do electronically. The basic difference still remains: the pari-mutuels pay off at odds determined by the collective action of all the bettors at the track during the whole interval before the race is run. The bookmaker, before pari-mutuels, had to use his own judgment to set odds; he paid off at odds offered at the moment of the bet; and, if he made a mistake in judgment, he could be ruined.

If his nerve and his judgment did not fail him, the bookmaker at trackside stood to profit handsomely. Mara's handle (the total volume of bets handled by the book) averaged between $10,000 and $15,000 on ordinary days and might total as much as $30,000 on a holiday. A bookie's profit depended on his vigorish (vig, take-out, or juice; the percentage of the handle remaining after the winners were paid). The vigorish varied from book to book, depending on two factors. The bookies, even in a well-organized ring at tracks like Aqueduct or Belmont, were to some extent in competition. For example, to attract a customer or to make one of his regulars happy, Mara sometimes raised his odds a point—on a horse he thought had little chance. Obviously, if he was wrong, he paid out more and profited less. Second and more important, bookies were more or less daring. No book was ever perfectly in balance, or round, with odds so nicely adjusted that the amount paid out would be exactly the same (as with pari-mutuels) no matter who won. The bookie always, to some extent, took a position, allowing himself to hold a disproportionate volume of bets on one or another horse. The ones who tolerated the largest bets, without laying them off with other books, made the greatest profits if their judgment was good—or went broke.

Overall, though the number cannot be exact, it appears

that the vigorish came to a little more than 10 percent of the handle. Out of this, the bookmaker met his payroll and other expenses. The remainder was profit. Numbers cited by Fred S. Buck suggest that a successful and well-placed bookmaker at the New York tracks might net between $150,000 and $170,000 a year, an attractive sum during the 1920s and the Depression years of the early '30s.

As a matter of course, the bookmakers whose names have survived were the most successful and the most visible. Thousands of others operated less profitably, or not at all profitably, and the overwhelming majority of those did business away from the track.

In the 1930s, Captain Frederick W. Egen, a retired New York City policeman, classified the off-track books from a law-enforcement point of view: At one end of the scale, a single bookie operated a handbook alone. He picked up bets on the street, or went looking for his customers at home or on the job. Or he worked from a "spot," possibly on his own regular job, and bettors came and went in haste, leaving behind written notes with their bets.

Several steps upward on the bookmaking ladder came the wire room. No players were allowed in a wire room. All business was set up over the telephone. A wire room might be the property of a single bookmaker or of a partnership. Employees included sheet writers, who recorded bets and results, and runners, who met bettors at arranged spots to pay off or be paid. It should be noted in passing that the wire room proved itself a hardy plant. While the name is no longer used as such, it is closest to the form of bookmaking that operates most widely in the United States today.

At the top of the heap for off-track bookmaking—because it was the most profitable—was the horse parlor or horse room. If the bookmaker here profited most, he was also most vulnerable, and therefore had to have the most intimate ties to police and politicians. The customers came to a horse parlor, as many as sixty to a hundred of them at a time, and could stay during the running of a day's races. Blackboards carried lists of horses, riders, odds, and results. Players bet and cashed tickets at a cashier's cage. The horse parlor of the 1920s descended directly from the poolroom of a generation earlier, and it had to be nearly as publicly known if customers were to find their way there.

Operators of a horse parlor went through drills of hiding equipment in case of police raids. Courts, in turn, required more evidence than a mere gathering of presumed horseplayers indoors. Acceptable evidence included scratch sheets with amended odds noted by hand, or tally sheets showing details of individual bets. But gathering such evidence was largely a stately dance. A horse parlor had a fixed location and the schedule of a racetrack. It seems evident that any illegal horse parlor (and a large majority were illegal) could be shut down and nailed tight within a week if the local police force wished.

Thus, whether working at trackside or hustling for petty stakes on street corners, the bookmaker followed his chancy trade along lines laid down by custom. He obviously needed political influence to run his business and to stay out of jail. He needed helpers and he needed organization.

He also needed one other, less obvious, kind of help at the start of each working day. He needed a sensible price line, or set of odds, to offer on each horse running at the tracks he was covering that day. Some simple arithmetic will serve to demonstrate this need.

Suppose the bookmaker's first customer wants to bet $10 to win on Morning Lark, in the fifth race at Belmont that afternoon. Assume that ten horses are running in the race and that they have equal chances of winning. Assume finally that exactly equal amounts are bet on each horse (and why not, since the horses are equally swift or slow). If the bookmaker sets odds of 9 to 1 on each horse, he will break even, no matter which horse wins (the losses of nine losers will pay for the winnings of one winner). To avoid this sort of stalemate, the bookmaker offers 8-to-1 odds against each horse. Now eight losers pay one winner, and the tenth bet profits the bookmaker, or provides him his vigorish. This simple process is, in fact, the basis for a profitable or balanced book.

But life seldom provides simple problems. Suppose actually when the first customer offers to bet his $10 on Morning

Lark, the bookmaker realizes with a pang that Morning Lark has been rounding into form splendidly, would have won his last race going away save for foul luck, and has had a brisk workout since then. Of the ten horses, he seems to have much the best chance of winning. Unless the bookie is bent on charity (and ultimately on his own ruin) he must drop the odds on Morning Lark sharply to deflect greedy players and shunt them toward other choices.

Now suppose the hypothetical bookmaker notices another horse in the same race, Midnight Visitor. His stable sources have told him that Midnight Visitor is sore and unlikely to run well. But the bookie knows Midnight Visitor is popular with local players because he has won bets for them in the past. He must set odds on Midnight Visitor high enough to attract action but not so high as to cause suspicion. And thus he must proceed through the entire field, and through the fields for all the other races on the card, working out odds that subtly blend the horses' chances and the public's opinions so that the most money is bet on horses with low odds, the least on the longer odds, in such fashion as to guarantee the book a profit no matter who wins. Of course the odds will be shifted by the course of the betting, but the opening odds, or morning line, can be of crucial importance.

Some bookies made this line for themselves. Most had a pricemaker do it for them.

The title of pricemaker had no official standing, but the job was real enough for all that, and to this day the good pricemakers are remembered and honored by those who understood their talents. Russell Brown, an eighty-year-old senior official at tracks in the Pacific Northwest in the 1970s, was thought to have been the keenest pricemaker in the West in his youth. In New York in 1937, when A. J. Liebling was pursuing Tim Mara to his lair in the Turf and Gridiron Club, he was writing at the same time about a seventy-six-year-old veteran of racing named Augustine J. Grenet.

"Tex" Grenet was born of a French father, in Texas, in 1861. His family sent young Grenet east, to Manhattan College. He had been around horses since early childhood. Around 1880 a bookmaker at Jerome Park hired Grenet as a sheet writer, with the task of rapidly balancing the book as betting progressed. He succeeded brilliantly. Working for bookmaker Dave Johnson, and later for another leading bookie, Sol Lichtenstein, Grenet became the best-paid sheet writer at the major tracks. For several years he made book himself, and at one time he owned a string of a dozen horses. But Grenet had already revealed several unique abilities. He had an encyclopedic knowledge of horses and their ways. He had an apparently flawless memory for every happening in races and around racetracks. And he had remarkable speed and skill as a calculator. Liebling credits him with having used this mix of talents to invent pricemaking. Considering the British headstart of more than a century in bookmaking, it might be safer to say that Grenet reinvented this wheel. But certainly he was able to work out a sensible and effective price line at a time when the other bookmakers were still fumbling with the problem, often with disastrous results when sharp bettors pulled off betting coups. In 1892 he proved his skill graphically: he devoted himself full-time to pricemaking and sold his numbers to the trade.

For the next forty-odd years, Tex Grenet watched every race at every major meeting, gathered in every scrap of stable information, and hired the best clockers at the track to time workouts. His prices, if interpreted shrewdly, achieved a neat balance between the horses' abilities and the bettors' leanings.

By the mid-1930s, when the New York bookmakers at trackside enjoyed a few years of nearly legal prosperity before the coming of pari-mutuel betting, Grenet's list of customers in the ring had dwindled. Younger pricemakers had learned the art and cut into his business. Bookmakers' own sense of the odds had grown more sophisticated, and in any case all members of the ring avidly watched each other.

But Grenet had another source of income. Even more than the big-time bookies at the New York tracks, the off-track bookmakers, and particularly those in other cities, needed his services to stay out of trouble. A man who kept busy all day walking about the racetrack, observing and calculating, could scarcely even have considered the huge task of flashing numbers, regularly and on time, to hundreds or possibly thousands of separate horse parlors, wire rooms, and handbooks around the country. For this purpose a wire service was needed. And, in fact, by the 1920s one had been created, a consolidation or monopoly based on several earlier wire services, rounding out a national system of bookmaking in the decade after World War I.

9

THE RACING WIRE AND THE RISE OF MOE ANNENBERG

HORSE-RACE BETTING HAS GIVEN A LIVING TO MANY. Some have grown downright prosperous from it, most often at the expense of bettors. But the national congeries of horseplayers and bookmakers, and the varied thousands who serve them and the running horse, all joined hands to create just one great fortune: the Annenbergs'.

Considering his accomplishments, remarkably little has been written about Moses L. Annenberg. For whatever it is worth, that skimpy body of writing, much of it invidious, offers no evidence that he had an interest in racing as such. No anecdotes picture him visiting the track, or making bets, or investing in horses, or for that matter, gambling at all. One sketch, by his sworn enemy, Elmer L. Irey, investigator for the U.S. Internal Revenue Service, suggests that Moe Annenberg enjoyed playing pinochle with cronies or trusted employees.

As a young gold hunter in California, Collis P. Huntington, one of the Big Four who founded the Southern Pacific Railroad, discovered that the way to wealth was to sell equipment to other gold hunters. Moe Annenberg made the discovery that a truly important American fortune could be built through the sale of information—one kind for horseplayers and another for bookmakers.

Toward the end of his life, Annenberg's fortune proved to be something of an affliction. Except for a few weeks during which he was terminally ill, he spent the last two years of his life in a federal penitentiary. But his son, Walter H. Annenberg, carried on the family enterprises and increased their value. The younger Annenberg entertained presidents of the United States, including Richard Nixon and Ronald Reagan, and served as Nixon's ambassador to London. Walter Annenberg's entry in *Who's Who in America* (1980–81) lists his many honorary degrees and foreign decorations, and a dozen clubs to which he belongs. It makes no mention of his parentage.

Horseplayers riding, say, on a subway to Aqueduct in New York, recognize one another at once by the racing paper each carries. The paper's name, in tribute to one of the most effective monopolies ever built in the face of the Sherman Act, is always *The Daily Racing Form.* It is not merely a totem, or bit of tribal insignia. Unique among serious gamblers, the horseplayer depends heavily on his analysis of information encoded in the *Racing Form*'s dense columns of numbers in the past performances. A poker player who brought a book with him to the card table would expect laughter. A blackjack player who laid a counting device beside his cards in a Nevada casino would be astonished if he were not summarily thrown out. At roulette wheels in Europe, aged devotees sometimes fumble with endlessly long rolls of numbers, hopelessly seeking to find an imperfection in the wheel. With horseplayers, too, the search often fails. But the player has no hope at all unless he buries himself in the published information. A handful of players do have enough knowledge, astuteness, and discipline to win consistently. They are impervious to flashes of intuition and they use stable gossip cautiously. Mainly they depend on superior understanding of a rather remarkable depth of information about the past performances of perhaps eighty or ninety horses on a day's card.

This need for information may cast a revealing light on some of the charges made about horse-race betting, early and late. For the moment it is enough to suggest only that vast profit awaited someone shrewd and strong enough to grab a monopoly in its sale.

If the horseplayer needed information, the bookmaker was doubly dependent. He needed to know what the player knew. And then, in the 1920s and '30s, he needed a source of information of his own which could make the difference between a handbook and a horse parlor. If he worked alone with a handbook, the bookie could only hope to scrounge a meager living. With a horse parlor, the bookmaker increased his action manyfold and became downright prosperous. The difference was so overwhelming that the bookmaker equipped to use it, like the hopeful horseplayer, paid willingly for the information he needed. The specific information that might enrich a bookmaker, came, of course, through the racing wire. It flashed scratches, rider changes, and, above all, results, to the horse parlor. It permitted the player to spend a whole afternoon at the betting place, reinvesting any bets he happened to win, usually to the ultimate benefit of the book.

In about ten years, from 1922 on, Moe Annenberg managed to fashion a monopoly in both kinds of racing information. With possession of the monopoly, Moe and his heirs crossed the line of mere wealth and entered the sparse ranks of the very rich.

Moe Annenberg did not invent the racing wire—nor did John D. Rockefeller invent petroleum. For at least a third of a century before Moe looked over the field and found it fertile, a number of telegraph systems had been used to speed race results to poolrooms and horse parlors. It will be recalled (chapter 6) that, as a result of a dispute over a racing wire in 1889, the poolroom operators of New York used their political influence in New Jersey to bring about the arrest of the president of the Pennsylvania Railroad. And the wire generally made handsome profits for its various owners. Thus in 1905 the *Thoroughbred Record* estimated that the Metropolitan

News Company of Louisville, which took over a service to New York when political pressure temporarily forced Western Union to abandon the business, might net between $800,000 and $1 million a year from the traffic.

Another agency, the Payne Telegraph Service of Cincinnati, also served poolrooms with racing information in the first years of the twentieth century. Mont Tennes of Chicago in turn bought the Payne Service. According to a Chicago Crime Survey, Tennes dominated gambling and, in particular, bookmaking in Chicago in the years before World War I. Among other things, he retailed the information from the Payne Service to individual books—at a daily rate of $50 to $100, according to one estimate, with an added arrangement to cover bookmakers' losses in return for a piece of the action.

In 1910, Tennes shut down the Payne Service. In its place he set up an organization of his own creation—the General News Bureau. The General News Bureau became the dominant racing wire in the Midwest. It remained so well into the 1920s, and by that time Moe Annenberg had entered the field.

Annenberg's biographical sketches agree that he was born February 11, 1878, in a village near Insterberg, East Prussia, a few miles from Poland. In common with many poor Jewish immigrants, Moe's father, Tobias, preceded the rest of the family and settled in Chicago in 1882. The family clearly had little in common with prosperous German Jews already settled in the United States. In fact, they emigrated in the first year of the exodus following the Russian pogroms of 1881. Moe came to Chicago with the younger children of the family in 1885, when he was seven. Tobias worked as a junk peddler and the family moved into a flat over a junk shop. Moe went to work almost at once, first as a Western Union messenger boy. He worked in a livery stable, sold newspapers, and as he grew older, tended bar. He married when he was twenty-one. Sometime in his late teens, through his older brother Max, he seems to have gotten his first job in newspaper circulation.

Many years later Annenberg's enemies charged him with much of the blame for use of thugs in the newspaper circulation battles in Chicago in the early 1900s. The newsboy wars, they said, paved the way for the racketeering of the 1920s. In passing, let it be said that, depending on the source, many individuals have been singled out for blazing the trail that Al Capone followed. One so honored was the gambler Mont Tennes.

Without doubt, Annenberg, still in his early twenties, was in or around the fighting. He associated with, and may have hired, some very tough men. He himself was evidently tough, physically and mentally. But much of the case against him breaks down readily.

If anyone started the newspaper circulation war, it was William Randolph Hearst when he raided the Chicago market with his own publications around 1900. Each Chicago paper in those days had its own newsboys. The newsboys had their own corners. Hearst's people had to do battle to offer their papers for sale. Before the war was over, thugs had been hired on both sides. The thugs smashed newsstands, beat the vendors, and some people were killed.

The fighting reached a climax around 1910. According to a more or less official history of the Chicago *Tribune* by Lloyd Wendt, the *Tribune* gained the upper hand in October 1910 when it hired *Max* Annenberg, "much the best circulation manager in town," away from Hearst's *Examiner*. Wendt continued: "Rough methods were employed by all sides, despite the fact that the Hearst circulation manager was Max Annenberg's brother, Moe. Vendors were threatened and beaten. At least some of the drivers and dispatch riders employed by the newspapers later found employment with gangsters in the Prohibition era—one of them being Dion O'Banion, who had worked for the *Examiner*. But it was the editorial content of the rival publications and their promotion and services that in the long run would determine the victors in the circulation struggle."

Burton Rascoe, in his memoirs of newspaper days in Chicago, *Before I Forget*, also speaks of both Annenbergs in the circulation fighting, and supplies more details, but only about Max: "[Hearst's Chicago publisher, Andrew M.] Lawrence sued [Max] Annenberg for breach of contract, and when the case came before the courts the contract was held invalid because it stipulated that Annenberg had been hired by the Hearst organization to commit unlawful acts."

Rascoe first met Max Annenberg "sometime in 1914:"

> ... [he] was already a power and something of a pet in the *Tribune* offices—a burly barbarian, endeavoring with conspicuous success to live down his reputation as a roughneck and at the same time to enhance it. . . . He was alert and alive, physically courageous. . . . He had no respect for the law, and therein, in Chicago at the time, he showed his intelligence; for the whole social and political organization of Chicago was so shot through with corruption, graft and thievery on the grand scale that there was scarcely a wealthy family in Chicago which was not deriving a considerable portion of its income from lawlessness of some sort—rents from gambling places and houses of prostitution, expropriation of public lands, profits from jerry-built slums or industrial highbindery.

All this about Max, and it may at least cast some light on the atmosphere in which Moe Annenberg lived and worked: But what of Moe himself? The fact is that the brothers quarreled in 1906 or 1907. Before 1908, Moe had moved with his young family to Milwaukee; his son Walter was born there that year.

In Chicago, Max had been the major figure. Moe worked for him, for ordinary wages; when he arrived in Milwaukee, still in his twenties, he started his own newspaper circulation agency. He was a frugal man, but he had been able to save so little that he had to raise $1,500—half of it by pawning his wife's jewelry—to get the business started.

Moe Annenberg's news agency flourished. He invented a series of devices for attracting attention to the papers he represented. As a demonstration of his energy, shrewdness, and aggressiveness, he also reinvested savings as fast as he accumulated them—in taxicabs, restaurants, bowling alleys, and drug stores. He continually picked up parcels of real estate. Years later, when he had long since moved on to other places, his holdings in Milwaukee real estate were still valued at $3 million.

In 1917, Arthur Brisbane started a Milwaukee paper and hired Annenberg as its publisher. Moe accepted the job—on the condition that he be able to keep his other businesses going. Two years later Brisbane sold out to his own employer, Hearst. Hearst not only retained Annenberg; he brought him to New York as head of circulation for all Hearst publications.

It was in New York in 1922, at the age of forty-four, that Annenberg heard the *Daily Racing Form* was for sale. In the fifteen preceding years, Moe had established a reputation as a rising star in newspaper circulation and publishing—to be sure, on the yellow side of journalism. Not one anecdote about rough tactics figures in his rise in Milwaukee. Among other things, it was a quiet city. At the least, Annenberg adapted to its ways. He had no special knowledge of gambling, at the racetrack or anywhere else. It seems reasonable to suppose that as a prosperous, middle-aged, and energetic businessman, he simply judged the *Racing Form* to be a valuable property, languishing in the hands of its founder, Frank Brunell.

Later critics implied that Annenberg entered the racing information business as something of an outlaw. Clearly he did, without scruple, sell his products to horseplayers and later to bookmakers. But it would be hard to argue that anything he had ever seen, as a hard-boiled and realistic businessman, could have caused him to draw a tenuous line of greater or lesser morality among the multitude of business opportunities.

With two partners, Joe Bannon and Hugh Murray, Annenberg bought the *Daily Racing Form*. The transplanted Englishman, Frank Brunell, who started the racing paper in 1894, sold out for $400,000. Within four years, by 1926, the paper had so prospered that Annenberg quit Hearst and for the rest of his life was a publisher in his own right. Within a short time, too, Annenberg decided he could fare better without partners. The partners resisted and took the matter to court. Annenberg wound up paying $2,250,000 for sole ownership —a decent profit for the partners and, as it turned out, a bargain for Moe. It may be asked why the partners sold at all, and the answer in general is that like all the great monopolists, Moe was hard on partners. More specifically, he bought another racing paper, the *Morning Telegraph* of New York, and used it to compete with the *Racing Form* and thereby bleed his partners. In the end, Annenberg owned every racing paper and scratch sheet of any consequence in the country.

In 1927, Annenberg took his second step toward dominating racing information. This time he bought a half interest in the General News Bureau from Mont Tennes. As an eventual result, Moe consolidated the bookies' racing wire and helped give a final shape to American bookmaking as it was before World War II.

Tennes by this time was feeling his years. He sold his shares in the General News Bureau to a man named John L. Lynch and to two nephews of his own. These then became the partners whom Annenberg shucked off on his way to the second monopoly.

In his book *The Tax Dodgers*, Elmer L. Irey of the U.S. Internal Revenue Service recounted how Moe achieved the second monopoly: "Again Moe and his new partners couldn't get along, so Moe set up another company to compete with General News. He called it the Nationwide News Service. Thus the following interesting picture was arrived at: General News, whose general manager was Moses L. Annenberg, was locked in deadly struggle for survival with Nationwide News Service, whose outright owner was Moses L. Annenberg."

According to Irey's figures, General News Bureau in 1933 showed a profit of nearly $1.2 million, while Nationwide had no profit at all. By 1935, General News Bureau showed a $46,000 loss, while Nationwide News Service now showed a profit—to the extent of $1.1 million.

The partners sued. Moe claimed in defense, Irey wrote, that he was "engaged in an unlawful business and therefore no court had jurisdiction." The partners settled out of court for $750,000.

It may be noted that the partners who were squeezed out of the *Racing Form* received three times as much. Either the cost of out-of-court settlements was going down (in a Depression year) or, just as likely, Irey erred in calling the racing wire immensely more valuable than the racing papers.

The rest of the consolidation of the racing wire was never so neatly recorded, and may in fact never have happened. According to articles by John T. Flynn in *Collier's* magazine, in 1929 there had been something like seventeen racing wires in various parts of the country. It is clear that Annenberg took over many of these—but he would not have needed all of them, and as fast as one small-scale operation was stamped out, another might well have sprung up.

A racing wire profited largely by fast transmission of racing results. Any handful of operators, with some boldness and a minimum of ingenuity, could find ways of signaling results to confederates outside a racetrack. (To this day—in the 1980s—patrons may not make telephone calls from racetracks.)

The *Racing Form* monopoly rested, and still rests, on a firmer base. It hired the chart callers stationed in booths on the roofs of racing grandstands all over the country. From these charts it built up a backlog of past performances. The tracks themselves and the racing industry accepted the convenience of having an outside business perform this indispensable and complex service—and they still accept it. Anyone hoping to make a serious crack in the racing information monopoly would first have to find and train a new corps of chart callers (no easy task). The would-be trustbuster then would have to find a chart format different enough to defeat copyright laws, and at the same time he would have to educate horseplayers to use the new form. And finally he would have the sticky task of obtaining permissions from track managements all over the country (because the system must be nationwide: horses may run in New York one week and in California the next).

A weakness of the racing wire proved to be its dependence on the long lines of the American Telephone and Telegraph Co. In March 1936, T. G. Miller, an A.T.&T. vice-president, testified before the Federal Communications Commission that the phone company was supplying lines for two racing wire services. Nationwide News Service sent its racing information to outlets in two hundred cities in thirty-five states and three Canadian provinces. Interstate News, a subsidiary of Nationwide, went to twenty-three cities in six states. Altogether, by 1940, according to both Flynn and Irey, using the same materials, the Annenberg system had become A.T.&T.'s fifth-largest customer.

Nationwide alone paid the phone company $555,000 in 1935. Guesses about the profit the wire service derived from this investment vary wildly. Even guesses as to the number of bookmaking outlets went from lows of two thousand to highs of fifteen thousand—an understandable discrepancy, considering the vast difference between a lone handbook operator on a street corner and a horse parlor complete with wall charts, loudspeaker for the call of a race, and a cashier's window. The weekly cost of a service may have varied from $20 to $400.

Annenberg's own profit can at least be called—very large. Figures later released seemed to put his income substantially above $2 million a year in the 1930s.

The rest of Moe Annenberg's career can be summarized briefly. In 1935 he established a newspaper in Miami, Florida. In 1936 he bought the Philadelphia *Inquirer*. He acquired various other general-interest publications, and one of these grew into the most widely distributed weekly in the country, *TV Guide*. He established residences in New York, Pennsylvania, and Florida, and a ranch in Wyoming. His other business interests spread as well. But in 1939 he was indicted for income tax evasion. He went to jail in 1940. And he died of a brain tumor in 1942, just a few weeks after his release from prison.

After the indictment, Annenberg dropped the racing wire. (It was taken over by one of his employees, James M. Ragen, a veteran of the Chicago circulation battles.) The rest of Annenberg's business interests he preserved intact, and his son Walter carried them on and enlarged them. But what caused Moe Annenberg's personal downfall?

Some accounts loosely assert that he profited hugely from an upsurge in American racing, which in turn brought the law down on him. To be sure, he profited. But what law? And what upsurge in racing? Taking the twelve years from 1922 (when he bought the *Racing Form*) to 1934, the total of racing days at all American tracks did slowly increase—reflecting gradual relegalization of racing in a number of states. But the gross annual purse distribution (the sum of what horsemen competed for, related directly to the sum of what horseplayers bet) remained mainly stagnant over the twelve-year period. The gross distribution increased gradually from $9.1 million in 1922 to $10.8 million in 1924—and it was still only $10.4 million in 1934. As a point of comparison: by the beginning of the 1980s, the gross distribution had increased *fortyfold* and approached half a billion dollars (outstripping inflation many times over).

Was there another moral resurgence in the 1920s and '30s? Did this threaten everyone whose livelihood was connected with horse-race betting? Seemingly, the disaster of Prohibition had lessened the risks. Racing and betting on horses were once more subjects for which the general press could allow defense (at least in those states that had made tracks legal). In an interview in the Miami *Herald* (during a visit in March 1925) Clarence Darrow said:

> I have greatly enjoyed visiting the track. Most people come to Miami to be amused, and I know of no better source of amusement. . . . The few people who hold out objection to racing always remind me . . . of why the Puritans abolished bear-baiting —not because it was cruelty to the bear, but because it was pleasure to the onlookers. . . . A lot of people seem to think that a bet on a horse race is a sin. . . . One is encouraged to buy real estate on the chance that the value will go up, or to take a chance on the price of grain or stocks and bonds rising, and no one thinks anything of it, and yet there is no comparison as to the amount of money lost or won.
>
> All business involves a large element of gambling. . . . Practically all one's life is a gamble. In fact, if the speculative element were removed there would be little left to live for.

Of course laws against bookmaking remained on the books. Police sometimes enforced them. But sale of a service to bookmakers broke no existing law—whether the seller was Moe Annenberg or A.T.&T. And so for twelve years Annenberg grew richer and nothing seemed to bar his way. Then in 1935 the U.S. Internal Revenue Service suddenly took an interest in his affairs.

As Elmer Irey put it: "Moe's gaudy lawsuits, in which he and his various partners engaged, attracted our attention and called for a routine check of his books early in 1935."

It would be idle to estimate the number of people—even the number of rich people—who visit the law courts annually without bringing on an IRS investigation lasting five years.

What Moe Annenberg certainly did in 1935 was invade the Miami newspaper market. He set up a new paper, the *Tribune*, and ran headlong into competition with the existing Miami papers, the *Herald* and the *News*. In his late fifties, and now for the first time publisher of a metropolitan daily of his own, Moe competed as ferociously as ever. He built circulation from scratch with violent attacks on city officials. The opposition replied that he really was trying to protect his customers, the local bookies. Candidates backed by Annenberg won the 1937 city election—and Moe left town, having sold his *Tribune* to John Knight of Massillon, Ohio. For what it is worth, one of the opposition newspapers, the *News*, was published by James M. Cox—who had run for president in 1920 with a young Franklin D. Roosevelt as his running mate. At the least, Moe Annenberg had attracted national political attention.

Meanwhile, in 1936, Moe had attracted even more national attention, perhaps a decisive amount. He entered the Philadelphia newspaper market, buying one of the country's older and more conservative papers, the *Inquirer*. Once more he set out to build circulation, and once more he used methods that had worked before. He closed with the enemy, heaping invective as he went. But now the enemy was strongly political. Never a notable political figure in the past, Annenberg in Philadelphia emerged as a staunch conservative and strong opponent of the New Deal. He did battle, in particular, with one of the few clearly pro–New Deal publishers, J. David

Stern of the Philadelphia *Record*. And he attacked Stern's political friends, including some of Pennsylvania's leading Democrats.

Let it be said that Moe Annenberg did build the circulation of the Philadelphia *Inquirer*. In two years he increased daily circulation from 180,000 to 345,000, while Sunday circulation went from 669,000 to more than a million.

But in the 1938 elections Moe's violent attacks on the Democrats brought equally violent counterattacks. And now his enemies had federal power behind them. Among others, Secretary of the Interior Harold L. Ickes stopped off in Philadelphia to remind voters in passing of bookmaking, the racing wire, and the Chicago circulation wars of long ago.

In his diary entry for October 16, 1938, Ickes noted that the Republican candidate for governor had challenged him to come into Pennsylvania to debate issues. "I told Judge James that I would try to rearrange my schedule in order to accommodate him," Ickes wrote, "but that if I did I would discuss the issue of Moe Annenberg."

The angers did not fade. More than a year later Ickes's diary item for December 10, 1939 described the roasting he had received in Washington at that year's Gridiron Dinner (given by an inner circle of Washington correspondents). He thought his own treatment was the "meanest of the evening." After naming some of the newspaper people who seemed pleased to see him roughed up, he added: "And Moe Annenberg, who was also an honored guest, must have been overjoyed."

Moe himself had more to worry about than an unpleasant sketch at a dinner of the Gridiron Club. The Pennsylvania Public Service Commission investigated use of phone lines for the racing service. A grand jury was called to investigate gambling. A legislative inquiry also picked over the bones of gambling enterprises. The federal IRS investigation picked up its pace. And now, finally, a federal grand jury was called to look into a series of charges against Annenberg and his associates.

The U.S. Department of Justice searched for clear violations of law in the conduct of Annenberg's businesses. An antimonopoly approach was considered—and set aside on somewhat metaphysical grounds. Would courts be willing to punish monopoly in a presumably outlawed business? Justice Department lawyers thought of ingenious arguments to put the racing wire in the class of an illegal lottery (because horses were identified by number and no one truly knew what number would come up). But they found no solid base in existing law. And so, as they had in the case of Al Capone, and soon would again in the case of Atlantic City gambler Nucky Johnson, the federal lawyers fell back on income tax violations.

From 1935 until May 1939, according to Elmer Irey's account, the IRS investigators poked at Annenberg's books and files with distressingly few results. They outlined a general theory of their case. Otherwise, they turned up a few items scarcely worth mentioning—an expense account padded here, a personal medical expense charged to business there. And then, Irey claimed, his team enjoyed a true harvest of good luck. Someone in Annenberg's organization (until then a reasonably effective group) moved nineteen metal boxes of records into the room set aside for the IRS team. The boxes contained the publisher's most important private records. Irey said the transfer was a fortunate mistake. What Annenberg called it, and what steps he took to find out what had happened, can only be imagined.

The records in the boxes made the case against Annenberg. The federal grand jury in Chicago brought in an indictment on August 11, 1939. The indictment charged Moe with having evaded $3.3 million in income taxes for the five years from 1932 through 1936. With penalties and interest of about $2.3 million, the total of more than $5.5 million was the largest in the history of tax evasion cases, the government lawyers said. The jury had sat nine weeks on the tax evasion parts of the case. They heard 227 witnesses and nearly twelve thousand pages of testimony. To bolster the local district attorney's staff, the Justice Department brought in a special corps of assistant attorneys general and no less than fifty auditors.

Among others indicted was the publisher's son Walter. The elder Annenberg said: "I regret keenly that the government has found it necessary to place the blot of an indictment on the name of my son, Walter, who has never been in a position to and could not possibly have any knowledge of any matters whatsoever pertaining to taxes. I likewise regret the indictment of my associates, who, I am certain, had no intention whatever of violating the law."

After months of negotiations, on April 23, 1940, Moe stepped out of a crowd of codefendants and pleaded guilty to one count of income tax evasion. The chieftain took the fall for all the rest. Besides his personal tax liability of $5.5 million, the IRS had come up with another sum of $3 million due from the Annenberg companies. The parties agreed to a money settlement of a round $8 million. As Irey put it: "Moe's barristers gulped, thought of the high probability that a trial might disclose even a greater debt, and accepted. We were pleased by the figure because we were certain we could prove no more liability and might fail to prove as much to a jury composed of mere mortals and not mathematical geniuses."

But money alone did not settle the case. Moe Annenberg was sentenced to three years in jail. He had spent nearly two years at the federal penitentiary in Lewisburg, Pennsylvania, when he was released on June 11, 1942, gravely ill with the brain tumor that killed him. He died in Rochester, Minnesota, five weeks later.

Two questions can be asked about the Annenberg case: How many self-made men who had grown rich in a hurry could stand up to five years of working over by crews of IRS investigators? On the other hand, even within that small group, how many could be so delinquent in their taxes that they would settle for a bill of $8 million?

Another decade would pass before any of Moe Annenberg's business dealings in themselves could be called illegal. And so another question must be raised, this time one of civil liberties: Is it legitimate for a government to use its taxing power not for revenue purposes but as punishment for someone it cannot otherwise indict for crime? And finally, why did the government want to nail Moe Annenberg? Certainly the sale of racing information, whether to the public or to bookmakers, was the least of it. During Moe's rise and sudden fall, racing grew more acceptable, not less. It seems reasonable in the end to suppose that Annenberg was punished not for outlawry but for being in too great a hurry to become the exact opposite of an outlaw—someone not merely rich but powerful, a mover and shaker among other conservatives of wealth and power. Some gods do indeed punish hubris.

As for the racing wire, it continued in various forms for another twenty years. Yet it had already passed its peak when Annenberg dropped it in 1939 before going off to jail. Neither the Internal Revenue Service nor federal law caused the wire service to start its decay. In fact, passage of a federal law against the racing wire would not come until after the congressional hearings of the early 1950s. What happened simply was that racing and pari-mutuel betting were legalized in California in 1934. Pari-mutuels replaced bookmakers at the New York tracks in 1940. Kentucky and Maryland, Louisiana and Illinois had long since made the switch. By 1949 nearly all states with any interest in horse-race betting had paved the way for pari-mutuels. Bookmaking was undergoing a radical transformation—away from the racetracks. By the time it was banned, the racing wire was already a relic.

But for some it was a bloody relic. James M. Ragen lived only seven years after succeeding Annenberg in the wire service. In 1946, Ragen was operating what was now called the Continental Press and was a partner in Midwest Racing News, in place of the old Nationwide. In April 1946, Ragen took shelter in a police station, saying survivors of the old Capone gang were trying to kill him. For two years, he said, he had refused to let them into his business.

On June 24, although he was driving down a Chicago street protected by two former policemen, Ragen was badly shot up by unidentified gunmen concealed beneath a tarpaulin in the back of an old truck. He died some weeks later of complications following the gunshot wounds.

Chicago officials suggested that Ragen's murder may have had something to do with difficulties he had been having in

California, New Jersey, and New York. Ragen had said he was leaving, in a safe deposit box, two additional affidavits about the gang plot against him. After Ragen's death, State's Attorney William J. Tuohy said the new material covered the same ground as the first statement. In any case, all the documents, Tuohy said, "are now hearsay and have no legal merit." And there the matter rested until Congress banned the racing wire outright.

10

LAYOFF BETTING: ERICKSON AND COMPANY

SOMETIME BETWEEN 1940 AND 1950, THE FEDERAL GOV-
ernment reached a position on gambling (for reasons to be
explored later, in chapters 11 and 13). During that decade the
government had much else to consider, including the conduct
of an anti-Fascist war. Concerning gambling, it made progress, like a glacier, slowly.

Such pastimes as poker, craps, and bingo clearly fell under
the authority of local police. The U.S. Department of Justice
therefore concerned itself with horse-race betting.

Until then, the attorney general had officially held himself
as aloof from gambling as a choirboy, except to enforce the
lottery laws of 1890 and 1895 and a minor law having to do
with gambling ships. But horse-race betting was now held to
be in part an interstate matter. Two things could make it fall
under federal jurisdiction, according to government doctrine:
the national racing wire, and—layoff betting.

U.S. Attorney General J. Howard McGrath appeared before
the McFarland Committee (a subcommittee of the Senate
Commerce Committee) on April 17, 1950, to open testimony
on a bill to prohibit interstate transmission of gambling
information. McGrath said, in connection with layoff betting:
"[Among other things] the bookmaker needs a means of rapid

out-bound communication, usually the telephone, with other bookmakers or persons financing bookmakers, in order to balance his book and protect against severe loss when the betting becomes heavy on any particular entry. This hedging process is known as the laying off of bets."

From this starting point, a path led through a multitude of committee hearings, investigations, and trials. The bookmaker who engaged in layoff bets became something of a national figure. He may have booked all kinds of bets with impunity for thirty years, though he broke the law daily. If the layoff label could now be pinned on him, he faced an early appearance in court and probably a stay in jail.

All this must have heaped aggravation on the pain of the unlucky layoff bookie—because some of the information about layoff betting was plainly wrong, and much of it at least suspect.

An interlude about sources:

Since much of this book has concerned people operating on the dark side of the law, material about them may have been as scanty or unreliable as the subjects themselves could make it. Still, their traces have been clear enough. They necessarily dealt with other, less close-mouthed people, and sometimes evidence was brought into courts of law.

In regard to the racing wire, third-party testimony provided a lifeline back to reality. Both American Telephone and Telegraph and Western Union kept vast quantities of records. Both companies were neatly pinioned between their semi-outlawed customers and the government. Therefore they had too much at stake to diddle with their numbers.

But with the so-called layoff bookies, a new problem arises. From 1950 on, abundant testimony about them was offered by agents of the law. But how accurate is such unsupported official testimony?

Did earnest Justice Department lawyers inform themselves by getting bets down with bookies, by holding Jersey sheets in their hands, and by deciphering past performances in a *Daily Racing Form*? Or did they simply start with a point of view and listen to supporting opinions?

It seems clear that the Justice Department believed, as Attorney General McGrath said, that the layoff bookmaker mainly accepted bets from other, generally lesser, bookmakers who held too much action on a horse (or a team, in a sporting event). In this view, the layoff bookie served as a sort of cement to hold bookmaking together as a national system. Evidently, the Justice Department people had convinced themselves that layoff bookies were the royalty of their trade, that they broke laws and did so in interstate traffic, that they stood at the edge of a partially glimpsed underworld empire, and that they might lead on to the heart of the underworld syndicate—if only the clues were followed. In a number of hearings, the government accepted material which supported that viewpoint. It disregarded what did not fit.

I find it necessary to question some parts of the official view. To restore something like realism to the picture, it seems to me necessary to apply logic to the nature of bookmaking itself.

Certainly some bookies accepted bets from other bookmakers. A bookmaker who accepted many such bets doubtless had a large bankroll and merits the title of layoff bookie. Beyond this point, evidence for the official view thins out.

One of a group of New York police officials testifying before the McFarland Committee in 1950 made a matter-of-fact observation: Why go out of town to lay off a bet? Why indeed? Particularly in a town like New York, surely the bankrolls, somewhere, among bookmakers, were large enough. Surely among people in the same trade, in the same town, credit ratings were well known. But this bit of simple reasoning interfered with the notion that layoff betting had to be interstate betting. Neither then nor later was it taken up by the senators.

In other cases, was the smaller book laying off with the larger? Or, was a smaller-scale operator borrowing from a larger one, who underwrote him for a piece of his action? There is every reason to believe that this often took place fifty years ago; it still happens today. A loan is not a bet. But, again, the fact interferes with legal doctrine.

As a practical matter, how often did the bookmaker know,

at the last minute, that his book was badly out of balance? On close inspection, early and later, it turns out that no book is ever in perfect balance. More than that, nine out of ten bookies do not want a perfectly balanced book. They think they can profit more if they take a position—if they are carrying too many bets on a horse they feel has no chance of winning. If they were wrong about the horse, they might suffer, but then it would be too late to think about layoff bets. Furthermore, how many last-minute bets could really get through via long-distance phone connections? Surely not enough to create the neat, self-adjusting system postulated by the attorney general of the United States.

Did the Justice Department visualize a bookmaker as a sort of illegal pari-mutuel window? At the mutuel windows all bets are accepted as a matter of course. The bookmaker has at least the advantage of his illegality: he does not have to accept every bet. All bookmakers, including the legal horse and sports books in Nevada, have limits—surprisingly low limits. Suppose a bookmaker accepts no bets over $1,000 (a rather large limit). If someone offered him a $5,000 wager, he would look at the bettor as if he were mad. Why would he reach for a phone and start making long-distance calls to find someone who wants to book $4,000 worth of the bet? Such a bet could not profit him in any way. One exception should be noted here. Bookies had favored customers, and still do. As a service, they might try to oblige such a customer. In this rather narrow area, the official doctrine of layoff betting does hold good.

But the layoff bookie may never have heard of the customer. Presumably a layoff bookie has as protective a streak of suspiciousness as anyone. He cannot assume the customer is a certifiable loser. Suppose the bet comes from Philadelphia, the layoff bookie sits in Cincinnati, and the horse is running in Chicago. The man from Cincinnati automatically asks himself the questions that would occur to any horseplayer in the world: Why this sudden long-distance interest in Fool's Gold running in the sixth at Arlington Park? Is it a stable connection? Is the horse very sharp, and is a coup being arranged? Nothing requires the layoff bookie to accept the bet, either. But he does have one other recourse. He can call a connection of his in Chicago and ask that the $4,000 be laid off again—at Arlington Park itself, through the pari-mutuel machines. Then, whether the horse wins or loses, the layoff bookie earns a commission.

New York Deputy Police Inspector John Flynn described the opposite kind of case to the McFarland Committee. "Some people in Florida," he said, "called New York in an effort to spread around money so that it would be bet at various places throughout the country, some in Chicago, Cincinnati, and other places. So that the money itself would not find its way back into the pari-mutuel machines, and lower the winning odds on the horse . . ." That is to say, the Florida people may have burned a number of bookmakers elsewhere in the country. This could hardly be tried often, and in any case sounds not at all like a national, self-adjusting layoff system.

In all this, the official assumptions appear to be based on information roughly twenty-five years old. In the 1920s, as racing very slowly recovered from its 1910 Ice Age, horses frequently were running at only one or two tracks at a time. And bookmakers handled the betting at those. Gamblers and people knowledgeable about horses and racing had to bet, if at all, with bookmakers far from the track. A San Francisco gambler in 1925, with knowledge of the horses running in New York, backed his opinion with a bookmaker in his own town. And, without mutuels, the bookmakers were dependent on their own pricemaking skill (or on experts like Tex Grenet). Under such conditions, the volume of betting away from the track may have exceeded the amount booked in the track's betting ring. As for the amount of layoff betting, that cannot be estimated.

By the 1930s and the onset of the Depression, however, state after state legalized racing, in every case taxing pari-mutuel betting. By the late 1940s, legal pari-mutuel betting on horse races was fully national. Players bought mutuel tickets at tracks from California to Washington, southward from the New England states, New York, and New Jersey to Maryland, Kentucky, and Florida, north from New Orleans to St. Louis, Chicago, and Cleveland. Come-back bets—sent by messenger to the tracks themselves to lay off excess action and reduce odds—became commonplace. To be sure, the come-back money flowed through interstate channels. At the time, at least, it did so legally, causing bookmakers and bettors to pay state taxes whether they intended to or not.

One book in the considerable library devoted to the Mafia and underworld syndicates, David Leon Chandler's *Brothers in Blood: The Rise of the Criminal Brotherhoods*, alleges that a national clearinghouse for gambling information was talked about as early as 1947. The author states:

> In [1947] Frank Costello, Meyer Lansky, and Sam Carolla met several times in New Orleans. . . . One project they agreed on was to create a national communications center in New Orleans to transmit financial information. Such a clearing-house would, for instance, make it possible for the bookmaking syndicate in New York to know instantly if a horse, ball team, or what have you was being heavily wagered elsewhere in the nation. Any break in the betting patterns would indicate a fix or an attempt to swindle the syndicate.

The statement raises more questions than it answers. Who witnessed the meeting? What came of the project? Did people in 1947 (in the pre-computer age) truly expect "to know instantly" about transactions all over the country? With all that, it is at least interesting that the mobsters were said to be concerned, not with promoting layoff betting, but with protecting themselves from layoff swindles.

In fact, a certain amount of shopping for prices was going on in the national betting markets at the very time of the presumed Costello, Lansky, and Carolla meetings. The authority for the statement is James J. Carroll, the leading betting commissioner of St. Louis, in testimony before the McFarland Committee. Senator Tobey asked Carroll, "How would you describe your profession?"

> MR. CARROLL: I am a pricemaker. . . .
> SENATOR TOBEY: Then you set the odds on different sporting events?

MR. CARROLL: I set my own odds. Pricemaking is the business of arriving at a figure where one can wager an event will happen and, for a differential, wager the same event will not happen.

The senators found this concept puzzling. Carroll illustrated with an example from the Kentucky Derby, which was to be run a few days after he testified. Carroll said:

Well, for example, Hill Prince is 3 to 1 that he does not happen, and I will take 4 to 1. Well there are many people who think 3 to 1 is too small. Someone might bet me 3 to 1. I will bet someone else at 4 to 1. I have a profit of 20 percent. For every dollar I take in, I make 20 cents.

Translated, what Carroll said was this: He would book a bet on Hill Prince, laying $3 of his own capital against $1 of the bettor's. But he would make a bet of his own, with another bookmaker presumably, if he found odds of 4 to 1. Suppose his own bet amounted to 80 cents. Suppose now that Hill Prince won the Derby. Carroll owes his customer $3. But the second bookmaker, the layoff bookie in this case, owes Carroll $3.20—leaving him with a net profit of 20 cents. If Hill Prince lost (as in fact he did, coming in second to Middleground in the 1950 Derby), Carroll lost his own 80-cent win bet. But then he collected his customer's $1. Either way, Carroll made a net profit of 20 cents.

One of the senators (Homer Capehart of Indiana) wanted to know how it was possible to arrive at the price differential. Carroll went on:

Well, Senator, this is the way it is: There are many bookmakers who call me for a price, in the hope of making a profit. If I say that I will lay 2½ to 1, they try to bet the same event will not happen at 2¼ to 1 . . . and so on and so forth. It is a matter of shopping.

The senators turned downright respectful when Carroll told them how he had managed his bets on the 1948 presidential election (in which Truman had upset Dewey). Carroll said:

I had Truman 8 to 1, and Dewey 1 to 15. He explained further: I had contacted a number of people who were bettors, and I told them I wanted to bet . . . on Truman; what price would they lay? And they say from—first quote I got was 10 to 1 [the price rose to 15 to 1 and even 20 to 1]; and I thought if I could have the public bet me at 8 to 1 [and now at the lower odds, Carroll was betting against Truman], take it in and bet it to these other operators at 10, I, of course, would have a certain profit.

And in fact he did.

Evidently impressed with this display of political acumen, the senators several times asked Carroll for odds on a Florida senatorial primary soon to be held. He said:

I really would not know. The same procedure would be followed by someone who would be familiar with the Florida election, and if I started to bet on either side I would say, "Well what will you lay me?" And if they would lay a price that Mr. Smathers would be elected, or Mr. Pepper, then I, of course, would try to sell the opposite side at a profit to myself. My opinion on that election would have absolutely no bearing on it whatsoever. . . . It would just be a question of a profit.

While Carroll had called himself a pricemaker, he was also known as a betting commissioner. It would be idle to try to trace the metaphysical line separating him from bookmakers. The title of commissioner carried a riper, fuller sound. Carroll may have felt it offered him some legal protection. In any case, he had earned it with forty-five years of service to the gamblers of his area, in the course of which he had built a business with forty employees. And no, he said, no one from a national crime syndicate had interfered with him: "I have never had one of them come to try to exact any tribute or harass me or bother me in any way, shape, or form, and in fact I just do not know the gangsters whom the newspapers are talking about."

Carroll acknowledged that he received a wire service, Pioneer News, presumed to be a subsidiary of Continental, the successor to Nationwide. For this service he paid $350 a week. He called the wire service "valuable under the method of operating today," but, he added, "without it, it would be just as easy to operate." He had operated without it in the past, he said, and as for the future, the next decade proved Carroll right once more.

Yes, he did extend credit to his customers, Carroll said, and yes, debts were sometimes hard to collect, and then he surprised the senators by informing them that, "I do get Dun and Bradstreet."

Finally one of the senators asked Carroll what he would propose, for control of horse-race betting, if he were sitting on the committee himself. Carroll answered: "Legalization in my opinion is the only answer, with the right of racetrack management or operators to conduct branches in the area in which they operate." In this respect, the public consensus evidently began to catch up with Carroll's opinion some twenty-five years later.

In general, the committee seemed to handle Carroll fairly gently. He and his lawyer were allowed to reserve some of their testimony for an executive session (presumably to safeguard business secrets, although the record was published anyway). Sometimes the committee allowed them to go off the record altogether. Conceivably Carroll benefited to some degree from being a Missourian, in a time when the president of the United States was an ex-senator from Missouri.

Another well-known gambler and bookmaker who was called before the McFarland Committee, Frank Erickson of New York, did not fare so well.

Erickson appeared before the McFarland Committee two days after Carroll (on April 28, 1950). Rather more to the point, he appeared just one day after his fellow New Yorker, Frank Costello. In the course of his own rather uneventful testimony, Costello mentioned that he supported himself through his investments. One of those, he said, involved oil exploration in Texas, and he had learned of that deal through a friend. Who was the friend? A man named Erickson.

Senator McFarland asked at that point: "Was that Frank Erickson?"

And Costello's lawyer replied, "Yes."

Considering Costello's reputation at the time as the "prime minister" of organized crime, Erickson was virtually guaranteed a rocky start before the committee. And, in fact, he was shown none of the consideration given to Carroll. The senators repeatedly threatened him with contempt. And his own testimony ran a ragged course, studded with lapses of memory and refusals to speak but then veering to startling admissions.

Frank Erickson was born in New York in 1895. He said his parents, too, were New Yorkers, but for at least some years of his life he apparently lived in an orphanage. The few sketchy accounts of his life agree that he worked as a busboy in a Coney Island restaurant and that he probably first met bookmakers there. One story told about him sounds suspiciously like stories told about many successful bookies. As a youth he supposedly carried a bet for a restaurant customer to a nearby poolroom. He found the horse had already lost. He pocketed the bet, and set out to cultivate a trade as a bookmaker's runner, booking bets for himself when the time seemed right.

According to Toney Betts, Erickson served in World War I and then went to work with Elmer (The Eel) Peters, who headed a Brooklyn subsidiary of the racing wire and published the *H. O. Scratch Sheet* (the initials standing for Harry O'Connell, described as a "big dealer on the phones in New Jersey"). In the early 1920s, Erickson may have helped move betting commissions for Colonel E. R. Bradley. By that time, too, he most likely had made a connection with the redoubtable Arnold Rothstein.

According to Martin A. Gosch, a movie producer who interviewed Charles (Lucky) Luciano in depth, for a possible film:

Rothstein had taken on Erickson to handle his high-level bookmaking business, which dealt only with such big-stakes bettors as Harry Cohn, head of Columbia Pictures, and other corporate and financial executives. While Rothstein handled poker games where there was no limit on bets and, on his own, had begun to move into the narcotics business . . . Erickson dealt with the horseplayers, even accompanying them to the tracks around the city and personally handling their bets so that the regular track odds would not be affected.

Gosch's account would have Harry Cohn old enough and successful enough to make large bets at the New York racetracks in the mid-1920s (Cohn was a major film producer during, and after World War II), but in essentials, Leo Katcher in his life of Rothstein bears out the Erickson connection. After Rothstein's death, Katcher said, his layoff betting operation "would be taken over by Frank Erickson, who would be forced to share it with the syndicate headed by Lucky Luciano and then Frank Costello."

By his own testimony, Erickson had worked with Costello and had done so for many years. Later evidence taken from his own files showed Erickson sharing a variety of investments with not only Costello but with others of the mob elite, including Meyer Lansky and Joe Adonis.

According to Betts, Erickson was already using wire rooms in New Jersey in the 1920s. He was still doing so in the 1940s and '50s. Material taken from his files showed a large number of phone calls to New Jersey numbers established as bookmaking outlets. He had continued to live in New York, so the New Jersey calls put him in interstate traffic from the start. Clearly his later operations in Florida and in large-scale layoff betting with other bookmakers around the country had to be nationwide. He was called paternalistic to his employees, picking up medical bills and paying good wages. His runners in New York took 40 percent of the profit and were carried if they had losses. Altogether, he was said to have a staff of about fifty—not too different in scale from Jimmy Carroll of St. Louis. Again according to Betts, Erickson also went out of his way to do favors for his better customers. He gave them Christmas presents (on a graduated scale according to the size of their bets), and sometimes even wiped out debts at Christmastime. His customers, incidentally, bet on horses most of the time, but not always. To accommodate them he also accepted their bets on sports events, but, as insiders put it, "gave away" those bets—laid them off with other books.

Through all this Erickson had had several brushes with the police but had never gone to jail. Once, when picked up for "vagrancy," he indignantly drove up to the courthouse in an armored car and dumped $100,000 worth of bonds on the judge's bench. Seemingly, when he went to Washington to appear before the McFarland Committee in April 1950, he stood at a peak of success and prosperity. Actually, he never recovered from the effects of the hearing and was to one extent or another a hunted man for the rest of his life.

Apparently Erickson first met his lawyer, a Washington man, on the day of his appearance. He showed no signs of counsel or coaching. He sometimes refused to answer questions, after some prompting from the chairman standing "on his constitution" or on his "constitutional rights." Just as often he did answer questions.

After first refusing to say that he was a bookmaker, Erickson said he had been one for thirty years.

After refusing to give some details of his business, Erickson said he made about $100,000 a year. Throughout, incidentally, he revealed the extent to which the Annenberg case had made bookmakers wary of the Internal Revenue Service. Erickson's office evidently contained reasonably good accounting records—and these were used against him in later proceedings.

He avoided questions about his volume of business but then said that he handled between $20,000 and $40,000 a day—a handle that squares reasonably with a staff of fifty and a profit upwards of $100,000 a year.

As for layoff betting, one of the presumed targets of investigation, he said, "I accept bets from whoever cares to bet." And his further answers, though vague, suggested plausibly that layoff betting represented no more than a third or a quarter of his total business.

Through all this, Erickson presented the aspect of a large, corpulent, rather sharply dressed businessman, balding and round-faced, with the expression of an injured kewpie doll. But his injuries were only beginning.

Three days after Erickson testified in Washington, detectives sent out by New York District Attorney Frank S. Hogan raided Erickson's Park Avenue offices. The detectives carried off what was described as a truckload of records. Naturally enough the bookmaker protested the seizure—and made matters worse. In a hearing two weeks later, District Attorney Hogan justified the seizure by revealing documents that showed business dealings between Erickson and, not only Costello, but Jo Adonis, Meyer Lansky, members of the Purple Gang of Detroit, and Vincent (Blue Eyes) Alo.

By the time the Senate's Special Committee to Investigate Organized Crime, under Senator Estes Kefauver of Tennessee, arrived in New York in March 1951, Erickson had become one of the most silent of witnesses. He refused to say what he had done for employment after leaving school in the fourth grade. When one of the senators (Charles Tobey, a veteran of the McFarland Committee) reproved him for speaking in too low a voice, Erickson said, "The last time I spoke to you, Senator, I spoke too loud."

But silence could no longer help Erickson. In the next two years he served two prison terms for bookmaking—one on Riker's Island in New York, the other in New Jersey State Prison. In 1953, to complete a tour of jurisdictions, he served six months in a federal penitentiary for income tax evasion. In 1954 he paid New York state $328,000 in back income taxes. And still the investigations went on, almost as a matter of routine or police reflex. He was brought in for questioning at the time of the murder of Albert Anastasia in 1957. In 1959, when the district attorney was looking for a mob link in the promotion of a heavyweight title fight between Floyd Patterson and Ingomar Johansson, Erickson was brought in once more. He died in March 1968 at the age of seventy-two. At his death, nearly every other substantial bookmaker in the country could have said, There but for the grace of God might I have gone. With some help from political timing and his clear relationship with Frank Costello, it almost appeared that Erickson had focused the law's attention on himself, thus doing penance for his whole calling.

Obviously, bookmaking would continue after Erickson's troubles began. But the bookmaker's trade would be much changed. It would be changed less by Erickson's trials and the continued Kefauver hearings and other proceedings than by profoundly altered circumstances.

In the late 1930s and '40s the physicians of Baltimore and Washington, D.C., not surprisingly, sometimes encountered women patients who had unwanted pregnancies. A certain number of the physicians felt sympathy when the women pleaded for abortion. If religious scruples or fear of trouble with authority did not hold them back, they solved the problem with near unanimity by writing out for each patient, on a blank piece of paper, a Baltimore address with an unlisted phone number. At that address lived a physician who may be called Dr. McX.

Dr. McX was an outlaw. He had had excellent training. He maintained high standards of practice. But he confined himself entirely to abortions. He did the procedures in the Baltimore house, in a well-equipped surgical suite, assisted by a loyal, friendly, and competent staff.

If necessary, a patient might stay overnight in one of the upstairs rooms of the house. Most of the women went home in a few hours. The comings and goings were quiet and stirred up no interest. McX was as careful as he was skillful, and he avoided every possible complication. In the rare cases where complication could not be avoided, McX somehow managed the occasional hospital admission without scandal.

By unwritten, unspoken agreement, masked when necessary by mock ignorance, McX carried out a social role. He provided an escape hatch, when they wanted one, for the upper echelons of medicine in two cities, and for many other community leaders and authorities as well. No experienced policeman or politician could pretend not to know of McX's practice.

I do not mean in any sense to equate the desperate problems of women, badgered often both by the law and an indifferent healing art, with the situation of gamblers and the shrewd bookmakers who handled their action. But, as exercises in outlawry and social acceptance, the high-grade abortionist and the old-fashioned betting commissioner offer at least some interesting parallels. In the years between the two world wars, and into the beginning of the 1950s, both kinds of outlaws were accepted and used by a society that on the face of it condemned them. Unwritten rules preserved their services at least for those with the price and the right connections. And both services came to an end, though for somewhat different reasons, at about the same time.

A few years after World War II, Dr. McX was arrested. And no one came to his aid, he later told people. Bitterly, he referred to the service he had done his respectable colleagues. His considerable savings and investments buffered his unhappiness; he closed his offices and faded from public view.

What is perhaps more important, no one stepped forward to take his place. The situation was repeated all over the country. Whatever else may have accounted for the peculiar moral climate of the early 1950s, medical full employment was certainly a factor. In the past, a hungry doctor, if he disliked the abortion law, was more willing to consider breaking it. With a full waiting room, he took no chances. Within another decade, social pressure forced a change in the law. But, in the interval, when the anguished patient reported to a respectable physician that she was caught, he shook his head in sympathy—but left her to the care of filthy harpies close to home or grim butchers south of the Mexican border.

In much the same way as Dr. McX, and at about the same time, the old-fashioned bookmaker, who was important enough a political cog to bear the title of betting commissioner, also faded from view. The political forces that drove out the betting commissioner in one town after another will be described in chapters to follow. Meanwhile, of course, gambling continued. And the newer forms of bookmaking are with us today.

11

INTERLUDE: THE MAFIA—
AN ESSAY ON
FACT AND FICTION

AN ORGANIZATION THAT BLENDS SECRECY WITH POWER
and violence works irresistibly on the imagination—like a
mental form of catnip or blister beetle. Its historians commit
all sorts of excesses, tossing facts about like confetti.

In the post–World War II United States, the secret body that
has probably excited more fancies than any other has no
agreed-upon name and can only barely be proved to exist. It
goes under such names as the Mob, the Syndicate, the Outfit,
Cosa Nostra, and, most often, the Mafia.

Official language modestly restricts itself to such colorless
phrases as *organized crime,* hinting at something more lurid
—Cosa Nostra or Mafia, perhaps—at the core of the underworld.

Now, organized crime assuredly has existed for a long time
and on a grand scale. It could be defined meaningfully as any
professional undertaking to break the law, involving more
than two or three people. Counting, for example, every small
group devoted to the cultivation and sale of marijuana, or
business theft by computer, or the numbers racket, or the
handling of stolen auto parts, the total number of people in
organized crime would certainly reach well into the tens of

thousands, or even perhaps hundreds of thousands. Any pretense at a census would be ludicrous.

The Syndicate or Mafia is said to have no more than five thousand members, organized ritualistically into a couple of dozen families. That it can arouse so many imaginations may be attributed to its alleged forms of organization. These need only be summarized (considering the millions who have seen the film *The Godfather* or read one or another Mafia paperback):

1. The Mafia is believed to be a secret national organization controlled by a ruling commission.
2. The national body supposedly is made up of families, each headed by a boss, or *capo*.
3. In all accounts, the bosses appear as powerful and ruthless criminals; violence, including threat of death, figures in every Syndicate racket.
4. It is an article of faith that Mafia members are Italo–Americans.
5. Allegedly, the families borrow oaths and rituals from the Sicilian Mafia.
6. Mafiosi are presented as immensely rich. In every investigation they move on to new triumphs; unlike ordinary businessmen they seem to suffer no setbacks.
7. Syndicate rackets include all forms of gambling, narcotics dealing, prostitution, loan sharking, extortion and shakedowns of employers, labor racketeering and manipulation of union funds, and systematic pilferage.
8. It is granted that mob money flows into respectable business, but it is never cleansed in the passage; instead, the respectable business partners are dirtied by the connection.

Some of these statements seem to me partially correct. Some, in my opinion, are dubious. Proof of any one of them is difficult. Why then venture into such a quagmire?

For better or worse, the possibility of a national crime syndicate in the background has to be considered in any history of bookmaking and related gambling. The alleged connection was asserted the first time the federal government took notice of what came to be called the Syndicate.

The "Black Hand" and the Mafia have appeared in fiction all through this century. Novels and movies, at least since the 1930s, featured Italian-named criminals in the Chicago gang wars. The Internal Revenue Service and the Bureau of Narcotics went after individual criminals or gangs. But the Justice Department as a whole, and the FBI, had little to say about a national crime syndicate.

Then on April 17, 1950, U.S. Attorney General J. Howard McGrath broke the silence when he went before a subcommittee (under Senator Ernest W. McFarland of Arizona) of the Senate Commerce Committee to present "a bill to prohibit transmission of certain gambling information in interstate and foreign commerce by communications facilities." In the course of his presentation, McGrath (formerly a senator from Rhode Island himself) took part in the following colloquy:

SENATOR MCFARLAND: There is one other question, I want to ask now. Senator Capehart referred to a national crime syndicate. Are you prepared at this time to testify that there is such a syndicate in existence?

MR. MCGRATH: No, I am not.

SENATOR MCFARLAND: Do you have evidence?

MR. MCGRATH: We do not have evidence that there is any such thing. That is not to deny that there are large scale, big business operations built around illegal undertakings, such as horse racing and gaming.

SENATOR MCFARLAND: I was, of course, referring to a national syndicate.

MR. MCGRATH: I could not, with any degree of fairness or honesty, say that we know, in the Department of Justice, that there is any great national syndicate presided over by any great czar. We feel that there are, in major cities, the largest cities of the United States, fairly well-organized groups that engage in activities such as control of gambling and horse racing.

In less than ten years the government position changed radically. Justice Department people and some local officials they worked with still clung to the notion that horse-race betting was the heart of the conspiracy. But they had at least raised their sights. The outlines of something like a Mafia now emerged in their testimony.

It is relatively easy, I believe, to demonstrate that book-making and horse-race betting never played the major part in syndicate operations. But it may be more realistic to touch first on some of the other questions about the Mafia which inevitably arise.

THE ETHNIC SMEAR

Attorney General McGrath may not have been ready to say a national crime syndicate existed, but the caricature of Italo-Americans as racketeers was already ingrained. The members of the McFarland Committee (on April 27, 1950) applauded a chief of police from Youngstown, Ohio, who testified, among other things:

> So you see there is a sort of web. You will find that a lot of these Italians, especially Sicilians, call each other cousin, as if they are all related. That is an Italian phrase, but they are really all related to a certain extent, especially that group of Sicilians familiar with the Mafia or Black Hand Society tactics, which still has quite an influence. . . . That may not be known to men who are not Italians unless they go into it pretty deeply, so they do not recognize that influence.

It is obvious on the face of it that the estimated membership of the Mafia could scarcely equal one-tenth of one percent of the foreign-born and second-generation Italo-American population (1970 census). Rather more important is the ethnic progression that has worked its way through the slums of American cities. Progress out of tenements is reflected with a nice precision in the names of boxing champions. At the turn of the twentieth century these were largely Irish. Then Jews took over the boxing titles. Hard on their heels came the Italians. By the 1950s and '60s, blacks and Latinos largely held the titles. For each group the prize ring was a way of escape. As other routes opened, and families moved out into better neighborhoods and better jobs, athletic young

Irishmen, Jews, and Italians found the sport less attractive. Their places were taken by the next wave moving into the slums.

Something very similar took place in the rackets, though the names were not as publicized. It was the luck of the Italo-Americans to come to the fore at the moment when the supreme victory of the moralists, Prohibition, was creating great wealth for outlaws. The money they accumulated from bootleg liquor multiplied their influence.

VIOLENCE

Of course, racketeers have always committed violent crimes. And again realism demands something of a backward glance. Violence for hire has figured in U.S. industrial history practically from the beginning of the republic. In fur trapping (after the speculators' lobby did away with the reasonably humane factory system), violence against Indians was the key to the trade. In the second half of the nineteenth century, fights between rival gangs marked the race for oil pipelines to the seaboard. Armed miners fought underground at Butte, Montana, in the battles over competing copper claims. From the railroad strikes of the 1870s well into the twentieth century, strikes were fought with rifles. At the Ford Motor Company plants in the 1930s, gangster muscle beefed up the so-called service department to keep out unions as long as possible. Harry Bennett, Ford's chief of security, had mob connections of his own—and exerted a powerful influence on his boss. Gangsters figured in fights of the 1920s and '30s in New York's garment trades.

The Italian-named gangsters were as violent as any others. But surely they did not stand alone. It is at least interesting to note that in some of the crucial battles within the Mafia (reasonably well documented, particularly in the 1930s) the hired gunmen who committed the actual murders were Jewish. It is also worth mentioning that most of those killed were other gangsters. This need not be interpreted as a peculiar form of morality. The mobs fought over control of sources of money. Why kill outsiders for nothing? If extortion, for example, was the racket, fear promoted it, but death ended it. All accounts agree, sometimes plausibly, that more or less national meetings followed outbursts of killing.

THE COMMISSIONE

A turning point in the writing of Mafia history came in the late 1950s when Joseph Valachi told federal authorities that he had worked for the mob for many years. Valachi's testimony set loose a Mafia hunting industry within government. According to Justice Department lawyer William Hundley, interviewed by Ovid Demaris for his book *The Director: An Oral Biography of J. Edgar Hoover:*

> Everybody had different theories as to why the FBI really had to be brought into organized crime kicking and screaming . . . Some of them said he [J. Edgar Hoover] didn't want to put his agents into a position where they could be corrupted. . . . Others said that he got himself locked in because he got in a big pissing match with Harry Anslinger over at Narcotics. . . . and Anslinger had the Mafia coming up out of the sewers the same way Hoover had the Communists coming up out of the sewers. So Hoover got himself locked in saying there was no Mafia.

After Valachi began to talk, according to Hundley, "the FBI did a pretty good job with him. . . . Then when Valachi went before the McClellan Committee . . . that's when you see J. Edgar Hoover as the complete bureaucrat. He came out and said he knew all this stuff before . . ."

Among other things, Valachi introduced a new Mafia or Syndicate vocabulary to the country. Through him the Outfit became known as Cosa Nostra. And it was he who spoke of a Commissione, or council of nine to twelve elders who ran affairs nationally.

One problem with Valachi's terminology—which accelerated the Mafia boom—is that it may have consisted of his own terms, or those of people close to him. A more serious problem is that it led believers to assume that his scheme for Cosa Nostra organization was something as neat and stylized as a management chart drafted at a school of business administration.

Thus with the Commissione: It is probable that it existed. It is improbable that a loose national council had any serious control over powerful individual racket bosses in a big city. In any event, on the few documented occasions when a genuine crisis brought the gang bosses together in something like a national meeting, what assembled was not a council of a handful of leaders but something more like a convention.

One such gathering seems to have taken place in Atlantic City in May 1929. George White (a federal policeman in agencies other than the FBI) told newspapermen, long before the days of the McClellan Committee, that Frank Costello emerged as the master diplomat of the Atlantic City meeting. Lucky Luciano's biographers show him as the leader at Atlantic City. In any version, it seems the meeting did take place. Evidently the convention did rationalize the bootlegging trade, and it pointed to the political dangers of promiscuous killings in the battles for territory.

THE APALACHIN MEETING

The best-documented national meeting of the Syndicate, or Cosa Nostra, took place near the small upstate New York town of Apalachin on November 14, 1957. A New York State trooper had been keeping an eye on the country home of an alleged Mafia man, Joseph Barbara. The trooper observed a number of large cars converging on Barbara's place. Apparently, too, Barbara had made an unusual number of motel reservations and had ordered special supplies of choice meat. The state police set up roadblocks. It is alleged then that the people at the meeting scattered into the woods and were picked up in their flight. The bag of those taken in for questioning totaled fifty-eight (presumably some got away on foot; one Justice Department rumor had it that as many as fifty of the visitors eluded the net). Those detained represented a large part of the presumed Syndicate leadership. Among them they had an impressive number of police rap sheets. They also carried substantial amounts of cash—an average of about $6,000 each. It is noteworthy that the arresting officers reported they found no weapons.

Civil liberties aspects of the Apalachin affair caused no great outcry. The visitors had obviously done nothing at Barbara's home; they had just arrived. The authorities could only guess at what they were proposing to do. But a number were brought to trial anyway. They were charged with a conspiracy to obstruct justice by refusing to say what they planned to do in Apalachin. Actually they did explain their presence. They said they were old friends of Barbara. He had been ailing, they claimed, and they had stopped by to cheer him up. Since the visitors had come from as far away as California, Texas, and Florida, and represented every major city, the authorities did not accept the story. They pressed the conspiracy suit, and obtained convictions—which were thrown out on appeal.

Naturally, a number of explanations of what was supposed to be discussed at Apalachin did eventually surface. Albert Anastasia had been shot to death in New York not quite three weeks earlier. A problem of succession and restoring order necessarily followed. According to Valachi and others, Vito Genovese was bidding to become the boss of bosses. According to Joseph Bonanno (as reported in *Honor Thy Father*, Gay Talese's remarkable account of the Bonanno family), other subjects up for discussion included disputes over narcotics traffic ("erratic Cuban and Puerto Rican gangsters and undisciplined youths," in Talese's words, evidently made the Dons uneasy). Some families, too, were under fire for taking in too many new members.

CRIME AND BUSINESS

But if the Apalachin meeting was aborted, it made one substantial contribution to the description of the Syndicate. Newspaper accounts as a matter of course listed the men taken in, supplied details about their alleged backgrounds, and in each case stated the subject's presumed business. Included were soft-drink distributors, automobile distributors, garment manufacturers, olive-oil importers, and in one unhappy case a taxicab-fleet owner who in the preceding year had been named Man of the Year by a club connected with the Buffalo, New York, police department. In short, Joe Barbara's friends represented a cross-country sampling of successful Italian-named businessmen.

Crime experts made light of the business connections. The men hauled in clearly were outlaws; the respectable businesses were covers. But were they?

Among the more ignored aspects of the story of the Mafia, or Cosa Nostra, or call it what you will, are: the effects of money as it tends to accumulate, and the drive toward respectability.

In several accounts of the lives of mob leaders, the same story occurs: the boss used influence (or friendship, in one case I know of) with a congressman to gain a West Point appointment for his son. The act sounds very like countless stories of immigrant parents who wanted solid careers for their children.

Official writ frequently addresses today's problem with information that was only relatively accurate a generation ago. In regard to the Mafia, the assumption is—force and lawbreaking beget more force and lawbreaking. But it is also true that force begets money. And money begets more money and rules for its own protection. The Knights Templars and Knights Hospitalers were fierce bodies of religious soldiers when founded in the early twelfth century. Christians saw them as defenders of the faith; Mohammedans, presumably, as bloody maurauders. By the fourteenth century both orders had ceased to be a military force and both had become rich. The Templars, before greedy monarchs destroyed them, were among the chief moneylenders of Europe.

No one has ever called the mobs a religious or moral force. But they do demonstrate the same transition from effective violence to wealth. With them, too, wealth acquired calls for a more conservative and defensive posture—in short, respectability.

All this, of course, is also theory. But some evidence supports it.

Francis A. J. Ianni, a sociologist, performed the feat of approaching a family within the Syndicate in much the style of a field anthropologist. By chance, he met someone related to the family. They became friends. Gradually Ianni learned more about his new friend's associations. Through the friend, Ianni met members of what he calls the "Lupollo" family in his study, *A Family Business*. Eventually, with at least tacit consent (and trust), he became a systematic observer of the so-called Lupollos. Ianni says they were not "a notorious family." But he added, "Within the Italian–American community however, and to the police and federal agencies, the family is known to be involved in crime. I found them friendly and open."

Ianni notes that "criminologists" are likely to say that going into legitimate business "permits underworld figures to evade income-tax prosecution, and provides a respectable 'front' behind which to continue their dirty work."

For himself, he offers a possibly simpler and more straightforward explanation: "the desire that [the criminal] and his family play a legitimate, respectable role in the American community."

When he actually came to grips with the Lupollo family history, Ianni found that the family's movement "toward legitimation . . . seems to have been a steady trend for forty years, and the main motive in the growth of the family empire."

As for how far "legitimation" can go, Ianni concluded: "In 1970, forty-two fourth generation members of the . . . family could be identified. Their movement toward legitimation seems almost complete. Only four of the twenty-seven males we traced are involved in the family [criminal] business."

Another writer, Annelise Graebner Anderson, also studied a model Mafia family, using for it the fictitious name "Benguerra." Unlike Ianni, she drew her material largely from government files and apparently has confidence in its reliability. But she too found that: "The group's legitimate business activities are not generally predatory and cannot be characterized as an aggressive effort to achieve profits through illegal means. The use of violence in legitimate business is minimal, and corruption only occasional."

Since 1950, when the Justice Department began taking a cautious look at what might be a national crime syndicate, material about the Outfit has piled high. Much of it has come from police files. And much police investigation proceeded on the assumption that nationwide gambling, bookmaking in particular, was the heart of the matter.

Considering the tendency for any official prophecy to fulfill itself in its reports, it is truly astonishing how little evidence of mob control of bookmaking has turned up. In fact, it might be said that investigation started at the top—with Frank Costello, a self-proclaimed associate of the bookmaker Frank Erickson—and has worked its way down ever since.

Valachi, a key informer and one of the most heavily used, strongly affected the language which describes the Syndicate (life does imitate art). He is quoted at length about the organization and the people in it in Peter Maas's *The Valachi Papers*. But he makes only a few passing references to bookmaking—as, in Maas's own words, a standard remark about Costello's "huge bookmaking operation."

The Cavalcante wiretaps, another source of mob information, loosed a flood of insider's gossip about the Mafia. But, again, little if anything was said about the details of bookmaking.

Ianni, reporting directly on his observations, said that the Lupollos knew people in bookmaking, but they themselves were involved in the numbers racket. His record shows meticulous detail about numbers but practically nothing about bookmaking.

As for Anderson's model Mafia family, the Benguerras, they too pass lightly over bookmaking. For them, "numbers gambling and loansharking are the two illegal industries that generate [the] most . . . illegal income."

Another study, this one done by Peter Reuter and Jonathan B. Rubinstein in 1978, suggests some reasons for the weakness of the evidence linking bookmaking to a national crime syndicate. Of course bookmaking exists. It has been here all along. But the very nature of the business works against its being taken over and centralized by anyone.

Reuter and Rubinstein also made extensive use of police materials. But they took an independent look at the records of gambling operations and conducted long interviews with "informants active in bookmaking and numbers."

They concluded: "Most bookmakers are just that—

bookmakers; perhaps not the worthiest of citizens but certainly not the terrifying mobsters of whom we are told. They have few involvements in other criminal activities such as narcotics trafficking or fencing."

Yes, bookmakers are involved with loansharks, according to Reuter and Rubinstein, but as customers themselves. They make little use of violence. Nothing suggests that they are part of a "coercive cartel." And as for the alleged layoff system, New York bookies, at least, do deal with others in New Jersey, but they "do not have regular dealings with bettors or bookmakers in other parts of the country."

Certainly, after repeal of Prohibition, the same racketeers did move into gambling, where and when they could. It was a natural use of money to make money. Costello, besides his obvious connection with Erickson, had an equally obvious connection with slot machines and casinos. Mobsters were early on the scene in Las Vegas. Both Costello and Erickson evidently did business with the dominant bookmakers in Miami. If some accounts of the Chicago mobsters, post–World War II, can be believed, they retained considerable control over bookmaking in their area.

But overall, the numbers game was far better suited to the Mafia than bookmaking. The numbers form of lottery calls for a large volume of very small bets, no betting judgment of any kind, but a substantial bankroll to pay off when numbers happen to hit several times running. Appropriately enough, because the numbers game centers in slums, it is in the numbers business that blacks and others low in opportunities are taking over from the older, now prosperous mobs.

With all this, it is still not possible to rank gambling as a whole either high or low among the various sources of Syndicate income. No truly convincing evidence has ever backed up the official assertion that gambling provided the greatest amount of illegal income for the Syndicate. It would be interesting to see what choice a well-informed mobster might make if offered control of all bookmaking from Chicago to New Orleans or management of all Syndicate-influenced union health and pension plans over the same territory.

About Costello himself some questions remain. He evidently was a gambler by choice and temperament (though not, himself, a bookmaker). But for that matter so was Albert Anastasia. Valachi remarked in passing: "Besides Albert was losing heavy at the track, he was there every day, and he was abusing people worse than ever on account of that."

The fact is that Costello used his first national appearance, before the McFarland Committee in 1950, to proclaim himself a gambler. A clue to his reasons may be found in his colloquy with Senator Homer Capehart.

After Costello had professed ignorance on a number of questions, Capehart then said: "We read in the newspapers often about Mr. Costello, and many of the witnesses . . . have connected you either directly or indirectly with what they term many undesirable things. Why do they do that? Can you explain?"

Costello said, "The only way I can explain it is . . . that newspapers have a great investment, just like Coca-Cola."

"A great what?" Capehart asked.

Costello repeated, "Investment—like Coca-Cola. There are fourteen different brands of soft drinks that are equivalent and as good; yet you buy Coca-Cola because they do so much advertising, and they come first. With newspapers I come first. They have an investment in me, in a lot of newsprint, that they want to get their money out of."

Evidently, Costello had public relations on his mind. Letting himself be called a gambler suited his public relations needs. He had made money in bootlegging. Now he had investments—but he was not a retired man. No one on the committee asked him how he spent each hour of a day, and what kinds of people from what walks of life he was most likely to see. Probably, many committee members would not have liked the answers if he had given them frankly.

By 1950, Frank Costello may or may not have had a serious voice in bookmaking matters. But he had a great deal to say about New York politics and perhaps about national politics as well. He spent much of a typical working day holding court at the Waldorf-Astoria Hotel, as any political power broker might, and the people he talked to included politicians of all ranks.

In the 1950s, political sophisticates spoke knowingly of "the hidden force" in politics. Costello was the very symbol of that force. He wielded it skillfully, and the people he helped into office with money and influence were grateful for it. Sometimes they were so grateful—as in the case of Magistrate Thomas A. Aurelio in 1943 after Costello helped him get a Supreme Court nomination—that they expressed their gratitude on phones tapped by the New York district attorney.

Costello, let it be noted, practiced a quite modern form of politics. He used the leverage of money and connections. He did not, in the rough-and-tumble nineteenth-century style of John Morrissey, provide the muscle to control the polling booths.

But at the time of Costello's testimony in 1950, a more old-fashioned kind of politics was still being carried on. It involved bookmakers, bribes, and police, in Brooklyn. The people controlling matters in Brooklyn were not the bookmakers, but—the police.

12

HARRY GROSS ENTERPRISES — AND THE LAW

THE GOVERNMENT NEVER PROVED THAT A CRIME SYNDI-
cate had taken over a national system of bookmaking. What
was proved, in the early 1950s, was that local police owned
considerable parts of the bookmaking action outright.

In the mid-1950s the Pennsylvania Bar Endowment sponsored a study of wiretapping. Their advisors included the
distinguished civil libertarian, Justice Learned Hand. As
chief investigator they retained Samuel Dash, a lawyer later
better known as counsel for the Senate Watergate Committee.
Dash and two associates looked into wiretapping in half a
dozen American cities. They found, as all policemen knew
and people hunted by policemen took for granted, that the
bug was mighty and it had prevailed. In particular, Dash and
his associates found wiretaps widely used by local bookmaking rings—and equally by police in the same towns. But this
did not mean that the local police put the bookmakers out of
business or kept them on the run. Rather, both sides had
much the same information, and they had become, in effect,
partners.

For example, in Philadelphia the bar group found that
police received $100 for letting a gambler know that his line

was tapped. But the connection started higher up. Recordings from taps on gamblers' phones revealed that they received warnings of coming raids.

In Chicago, Dash indicated he could find scarcely anyone in authority willing to discuss the weather with him, much less the state of lawbreaking. Nevertheless, he did develop some private sources of his own. As he later reported in his book, *The Eavesdroppers*, he learned, aside from what now seemed to be customary illegal procedures, that: "There is abundant evidence that a number of searches and seizures are made without warrants for the purpose of *making evidence unusable* in court. [Author's italics.] Such raids are naturally carried out by police in collusion with racketeers."

The same practices existed in Boston, though there, at least, the Massachusetts Crime Commission had been on the same trail before the Pennsylvania team came calling. It found specifically "that police officers are on the payroll of the gamblers and provide protection for their activities." Thus, Dash said: "According to one gambler, the gamblers are not worried about police tapping their phones, since they are sure that police are not engaged in this practice. . . . They feel confident that if the police ever did try to tap their phones, they would immediately be warned by a friendly telephone company employee."

Boston bookmakers, around 1952, tried to revive the national racing wire service. They brought in wiretapping experts, not so much to listen to other people's conversations as to devise an installation by which one person would speak over eighteen telephones at once. The Boston gamblers found that they only ran into trouble "when they attempted to set up installations on their own without first buying police and telephone company employee protection."

In New Orleans, Dash said, "wiretapping cannot be evaluated." But he did quote from a Special Citizens' Investigating Committee on crime in New Orleans. In 1954 the committee said that duly licensed "public gathering places" were actually being used as disguises "for maintaining handbooks, poker games . . . and prostitution." These places, the committee added, "exist with the New Orleans police alternately encouraging and harassing them while sharing in their profits."

A moment's reflection is enough to suggest the reason for the widespread collusion. No place could be more vulnerable to arrest than a horse parlor or even a wire room. Some brothels might also have had elaborate quarters, difficult to move. But compared with patrons of prostitutes, horseplayers are models of consistency, punctuality (based not on impulse but post time), and therefore predictability. A bookmaker with a fixed address could only stay in business with the consent of local police. Such consent strongly suggests some sort of partnership.

The system operated along model lines in New York. The Pennsylvania Bar team interviewed a former New York plainclothesman with the following result:

> QUESTION: Were some of the plainclothesmen working closely with some of the bookies?
> ANSWER: Yes, that's very true . . . if I'm a plainclothesman and I'm making $80 a week . . . and I come up on a hot pair—in other words it's not a pair that is being given to me as a friend . . . and I went in on it on my own—well, that could be worth anywhere from $500 to $1000 to me personally.
> QUESTION: You mean to keep them in business?
> ANSWER: No, just leave them in business. Just walk away from it.

The questioner went on: "And the figure, I imagine, would be based on the amount of business they're doing."

> ANSWER: That's right. . . . It's a standard practice. If you grab a bookie's worksheet . . . and he wants his worksheet back, you charge him . . . according to the amount of play he has on his worksheet. If he doesn't come across, as the saying goes, you just pass the word in the neighborhood or just let everybody see him get pinched, and then everybody puts in a winner. He has no way of knowing who plays what and you put him out of business. Then all he can do is pay everybody. So it's cheaper to pay you.

The practice of taking from the bookies was very common, the plainclothesman said: "Any man who is susceptible and needs an extra dollar will do it." And the reasons for doing it were not just greed. He said the average policeman might want "a couple of dollars to see that his children's teeth were fixed and so forth. But public opinion was—I think—the most important thing—the disrespect shown to policemen in the past couple of years."

How far up the line did the practice extend? The plainclothesman answered by saying that keeping a telephone cost a bookmaker $1,500 a month. That total "has to be divided all the way down the line." The plainclothesman enumerated ten others of his own rank who would have to be cut in, and possibly a lieutenant or a sergeant. And finally, he said, "The borough office has to go in. His boss has to go in—it goes right up the line."

> QUESTION: What does the plainclothesman think about taking this kind of money?
>
> ANSWER: Well, sir, I'll tell you. The average policeman doesn't look on bookie or policy money as dirty money. Unfortunately I know it's wrong to take it . . . but what I do say is this—it's a well-practiced policy. If you take prostitution money, it's dirty money, and a patrolman who's been taking from a bookmaker will look down on you for taking prostitute's money. . . . You can offer me $100,000 to let you walk away with an ounce of heroin and I'd lock you up. But plainclothesmen are not worried about gambling anyhow. . . . They gambled for Christ's clothing . . . so how am I to knock it out.

Taken alone, the answers might suggest that the Dash group had laid hands on a peculiarly disgruntled retired cop. In truth, though, the retired plainclothesman could talk with utter frankness because the situation had already been aired before a jury, just a few years before, in the trial of Harry Gross. In 1950, Gross was much the most important bookmaker in Brooklyn. From all the evidence, he had casual contacts with leading Mafia figures, but they were generally not essential in his business. His police contacts, however, ran the length and breadth of the department.

Gross was born in Brooklyn in 1916. His parents were immigrants who struggled, not very successfully, with poverty all their lives. His father at various times ran a small laundry, drove a cab, and worked as a waiter. As a boy, Gross never made a name for himself for strength, toughness, or any sort of athletic ability. But he did leave a faint trail as an energetic hustler from the start. When reporters years later had reason to probe into his school days, they found teachers who thought they remembered the young Gross as a canny businessman.

Any teacher who truly recalled Gross had an excellent memory. He quit school at fourteen and got a job as a soda jerk. He also had a newspaper route but persuaded other boys to deliver for him and so enlarged his routes—and profits. He explored the pleasantries of pool tables and crap games and quickly learned that dice could be loaded. He freely spent money for show, but also developed a reputation for chiseling where he could.

Gross became a bookmaker by now familiar stages. He did odd jobs, carrying bets for a bookmaker's runner. He became a bookmaker's runner himself and while still in his late teens was booking his own bets on the side. Like some of his predecessors, he fancied himself as something of a handicapper. His taste for betting would later get him into serious difficulties.

By the time he was in his early twenties, Gross was bookmaking on his own. He operated a luncheonette in Manhattan and used it as a place for booking bets. He continued to expand and soon had horse parlors in Brooklyn and a connection with a wire room across the Hudson River in New Jersey.

In 1942 a draft board tapped Gross, as it did most men in their twenties that year. He served four months in the army before he managed a medical discharge—presumably because a broken leg he suffered as a schoolboy had been poorly set.

During his brief army career Gross kept his bookmaking establishments going with the help of a partner. After his discharge he more than made up for the slight interruption. By the end of the war he was making so much money that he could invest the surplus in half a dozen New York restaurants and nightclubs. By 1949, still in his early thirties, he was quite simply the leading bookmaker in Brooklyn, with perhaps as many as thirty horse rooms going. He had now attained so much elevation in his calling that many of his customers did not know his name, and he remained a shadowy figure in the background known as Mr. G.

The question may fairly be asked: Did he somehow manage to keep his steady and rather rapid progress a secret from the New York Police Department? The answer, of course, is that he did not and could not have done so. Gross was well known to the police and had been for years. They had promoted his rise.

New York newspapermen Norton Mockridge and Robert H. Prall made a study of Gross's career in their book, *The Big Fix.* They tallied Gross's arrests in the years from 1937 to 1944: nine arrests in the seven years. But Gross did not serve a single day in jail, and his fines came to a total of $75. By the end of World War II he might understandably have thought himself immune from serious punishment.

Sometime around 1941, when his career as a bookmaker was still at an early stage, Gross had a crucial conversation with an unknown Brooklyn policeman. He quickly understood that he needed permission to operate an uninterrupted business. And he understood, too, that the price of his invisible license was a share of his proceeds, to be pieced out among the many policemen who inevitably would keep an eye on him. The piecing out, as Gross had to do it at the beginning of the 1940s, followed very much the pattern described by the retired plainclothesman to the Pennsylvania Bar investigation in the 1950s. The sharing applied to every horse room—to every bet booked and collected by Gross's organization.

But sharing implies a passive relationship. That is, Gross booked the bets and managed the business. The police quietly took their share, as a price for letting him operate peaceably.

By the late 1940s, however, the relationship was no longer passive. It had become something more like an unofficial partnership, active on both sides.

Probably Gross excelled his rival bookmakers in two qualities above all others. He did not grudgingly consent to payoffs to the police, but welcomed them and sought them out eagerly. And he had a keen sense of police character. He cultivated his circle of acquaintance among detectives and asked their advice on where to set up new locations.

In 1945, Gross made his single most important connection, with an able and politically well-connected young plainclothesman, James E. Reardon. According to Mockridge and Prall, Reardon saw to it that other bookies were kicked out of locations that Gross wanted for himself. Reardon and Gross together gave parties for police officials, handed out presents and tickets for Broadway shows, and on occasion paid for the services of prostitutes.

One bookmaker, a man named Pledge, resisted being forced, in effect, to join Gross's combine. He went to a Queens county grand jury to complain about shakedowns. Nothing came of Pledge's complaints except that Reardon was demoted and assigned to a uniformed police patrol. In a matter of months, he retired from the police department and from then on served, in effect, as Gross's chief executive officer. Reardon's brother, Michael, remained on the force.

At this point, in 1949, prosperity seemed unlimited for both Gross and his police associates. And then Gross's ego led him to try to prove that he was a better handicapper than the customers who had made him a successful bookmaker. He began betting heavily himself. According to one story, he set out to beat the horses, betting thousands of dollars on single races. Presumably, according to this story, Frank Erickson booked his bets. Another account (provided by a highly credible source) has it that Gross went broke betting on baseball. He had relied on information given him by a pair of touts so notorious that a clever bookie should have dismissed them on sight. In either case, Gross bet heavily, and lost just as heavily. He redoubled his bets, to recoup, and continued to lose. He went on a final three-day betting spree, and wiped himself out. For the first time in a dozen years as a bookmaker, he could not pay off the winners at the end of a day.

Gross lost his nerve as well as his bankroll. He did the unpardonable: bought a ticket on the first plane for California. After three days in the West, Gross mustered his courage and telephoned Reardon, conceivably to find out who, if anyone, was out looking for him. Reardon was as angry and abusive as he had expected. But it turned out that no one was gunning for Gross. The bettors had been paid off. The bookmaking operations had gone on as usual.

Money had to be raised. Apparently with Reardon acting as a finance committee of one, a sum well into six figures had been borrowed—some of it certainly from New York policemen themselves, some of it, according to plausible rumor, from high-ranking mob sources. The borrowed money paid for Gross's expenses on the West Coast and for his trip back. He returned in good time, took charge of the operation again, entertained more lavishly than ever, and within a few months the profits of the business were enough to pay off the loans. Gross's partners had evidently concluded that it was simpler, and cleaner, to hold his place open for him than to find a successor.

Gross had escaped from his first disaster, in 1949. In 1950 he faced Nemesis again—and this time there was no escaping. On September 15, 1950, a special team organized secretly by Brooklyn District Attorney Miles McDonald arrested Gross for a tenth time. Although Gross knew that he could not expect to get off with a $75 fine this time, he assumed that he could at least walk out of jail by posting $50,000 bail. But Judge Samuel Leibowitz set bail at $250,000. Gross stayed in jail, subjected to constant interrogation.

In coordinated raids that started with Gross's arrest, the District Attorney's teams also took over the bookmaker's headquarters on Long Island, his chief telephone room, and eventually, after some of the arrested bookies started giving information, his bookkeeping offices as well. The sweep was nearly complete.

By the beginning of October, District Attorney McDonald

had gathered enough information about the bookmaker's friends among policemen to justify the arrest of James Reardon too. Reardon first evaded questions. His younger brother Michael went before the grand jury, refused to talk, and was held in contempt of court. On October 11, authorities said they had placed guards around James Reardon twenty-four hours a day. Evidently he had started to talk. Two days later, the elder Reardon, having discussed his partnership with Gross, was placed under a doctor's care for "nervous exhaustion." His testimony went no further. He acknowledged having run Gross's business when the bookie was in California, but he stopped short of naming the other policemen who had raised the money to keep Gross's business afloat. For the time being, Reardon was released. Eventually, as one by-product of the Gross case, he was brought back into court, tried, and sent to jail for perjury.

Actually, Gross, Reardon, and all their associates on both sides of the law had had ample warning of coming trouble for most of the preceding year. Late in 1949, Ed Reid of the Brooklyn *Eagle* had written a series of articles about the prevalence of bookmaking in Brooklyn and charged that the bookmakers were being protected by police.

Before writing the series, Reid discussed his findings with District Attorney McDonald. Allegedly, Reid had been put onto the story by a conversation he had overheard in a saloon—a conversation in which he said he had heard mention of a mysterious Mr. G., the boss of the bookies, who operated with the consent of some of the most highly placed officers on the police force.

McDonald had been elected to office four years earlier. He said that during those years he had been accumulating evidence about gamblers too. After his talk with Reid, McDonald discovered that Mr. G. was in fact Harry Gross. Secretly he ordered a grand jury inquiry. To carry it out, he virtually set up a secret police force of his own.

Fearing that if they asked the police department for help they would simply alert Harry Gross's friends, McDonald and his closest assistants asked Police Commissioner William P. O'Brien for a detachment of twenty-nine young men taken directly from the Police Academy. McDonald claimed that he needed young probationers to study gambling on college campuses. But soon enough the regulars of the police force learned of the rookie investigators. In the months that followed, several times young cops found themselves trailing older cops. In at least one confrontation, an assistant district attorney feared a gun battle—with police on both sides.

By late summer of 1950, McDonald and his rookies had gathered enough evidence to persuade the grand jury to bring in indictments. The raids of September 15 followed, and shut down the Harry Gross bookmaking operation. Ten days later Commissioner O'Brien, who had assigned the rookies to McDonald, announced his retirement from the department. He was quickly followed into retirement by a stream of other police officers, including Inspector John E. Flynn (who had taken part in a bookmaking investigation himself) and Chief of Detectives William T. Whalen.

As for Harry Gross in jail, he continued to make trouble for the district attorney's staff. He talked in torrents, bragging about his feats as a bookmaker, about people he had cheated, and about the payoff money he had given to the police. In his account, the sums he gave mounted by the hundreds of thousands and came to rest finally at a flat million dollars a year. But still he blew hot and cold about identifying the officers who had been paid. Among other things, he may well have thought he was risking being killed. Eventually, he seemed to have made up his mind to testify as the district attorney wished. A trial of police officers was set. Then it had to be delayed because of the suicide of one of the indicted men.

Nearly a year after the first arrests, in September 1951, the trial actually began. By this time Gross's bail had been reduced to $25,000 and he had been allowed a fair amount of freedom while being kept under guard by two of the district attorney's men. On the second day of the trial Gross and his guards drove to Gross's home. During the evening Gross went into another room "to wash his hands," walked out of the house—and disappeared.

Mockridge and Prall suggest that Gross actually walked

away from his guards to go by car to a meeting with several leading mobsters in New Jersey. The writers say that he may have been paid—and they give the sum as $120,000—to withhold testimony about the police officers.

What is certain is that Gross did drive to New Jersey and continued on to Atlantic City. Under the name of Harry Green, he registered at an ocean-front hotel and asked for a room with a view of the sea. The next day he went to the Atlantic City racetrack. He had lost about $400 in bets when the head of the racetrack police force saw him, recognized his face from pictures, and led him off to a New Jersey state police barracks.

The trial resumed. Gross seemed just about ready to name his police accomplices when, in another sudden twist, he refused to say anything more. Judge Leibowitz, in a rage, denounced Gross. The district attorney's people, seeing years of work crumbling, could not hold back tears. The charges against the policemen were necessarily dropped. And a week later Gross was sentenced to twelve years in jail.

In 1952, after one year in jail, Gross changed his mind once more and this time he did identify policemen, in a courtroom, in a series of departmental trials.

Of the first twenty-nine police officers tried in the departmental court, twenty-three were found guilty. The court punished the guilty with dismissal from the force, with loss of pension rights, and with no back pay for the period under suspension. The twenty-three included five captains, a lieutenant, and a sergeant.

By the end of a series of departmental trials, the number dismissed had risen to more than fifty. In a sweeping overhaul, a large number of plainclothesmen were transferred back to uniformed patrol. More than four hundred officers retired or resigned. Several of the men who had spent their working lives with weapons at their sides preferred death to disgrace and committed suicide.

The scale of the police shake-up had no precedent. In remarks of appreciation to the Brooklyn grand jury, McDonald said: "As far as I can tell, the Gross case is the only case in the lifetime of New York in which a whole ring, including runners, bookmakers, telephone clerks, bookkeepers, chauffeurs, and the top man himself were all arrested and convicted. . . . But it has also meant an entirely new plain-clothes division for the Police Department, a new police commissioner, a new chief of detectives—and many resignations among the top brass."

But effects of the case went far beyond Gross and his employees and the policemen they worked with. The case also caused political upheaval, seen most clearly in the career of William O'Dwyer, New York's mayor.

O'Dwyer had served as district attorney for Brooklyn. McDonald succeeded him in the same year O'Dwyer was elected mayor of New York. They bickered continuously for the next five years. McDonald complained that the mayor tried to stop his investigations, particularly in the bookmaking case. As the grand jury probe continued, O'Dwyer denounced it as a "witch hunt." He later had to apologize for the remark.

Two weeks before Gross's arrest, O'Dwyer resigned his office as mayor. New York Democratic leader Edward J. Flynn arranged with the Truman administration to have O'Dwyer appointed ambassador to Mexico. The U.S. Senate approved the nomination, and O'Dwyer at once moved to Mexico, leaving behind a cloud of unanswered questions. Why had he left what many politicians regarded as the third most significant political office in America? And why had he taken a substantial pay cut to do so?

O'Dwyer's friends pointed out that he was a warm-hearted man, up from the ranks, a one-time uniformed cop himself. As a magistrate he had made something of a specialty of family counseling. As a district attorney he showed his keenness to put down crime by prosecuting the notorious ring of killers known as Murder, Inc. During his last year in office, they said, he was in bad health, upset by the death of his wife, and then emotionally off balance as he courted another woman, the young and beautiful Sloan Simpson.

But inevitably, by 1950, his enemies outnumbered his friends. They included most Republicans, as a matter of course, and all Democrats who assumed they might benefit by having a new mayor. They charged that once O'Dwyer became mayor, he grew fidgety every time crime investigation was mentioned seriously. He failed to prosecute Albert Anastasia, they charged, though he had ample grounds to do so. His friend and assistant, James J. Moran, may even have suppressed evidence about Anastasia. Moran compounded the difficulties by going to jail himself, for corrupt practices after he was appointed to office. And the police department that touched bottom in the Gross case was O'Dwyer's department, headed by his commissioner and his inspectors.

In reality, O'Dwyer's problem lay deeper, and the Gross case would inevitably bring the problem up from the depths. On his way to the mayoralty, as well as in office, O'Dwyer had readily accepted, in secret practice, what was unmentionable in public. Like many other ambitious big-city politicians of his time, he reckoned and did business with the most important mob leaders. The money that flowed into loansharking, or marginal garment shops, or olive-oil importation, flowed, if anything, more readily into politics.

Frank Costello smoothly wielded great power among Tammany Democrats in New York. O'Dwyer had reason to think he could not be mayor without Tammany support. The Gross case and the ambassadorship to Mexico made it inevitable that the Kefauver Committee would call O'Dwyer to testify. And once he appeared before the committee, it was certain too that he would have to answer questions about a meeting in 1942 at Frank Costello's own apartment, a meeting attended by a number of other Tammany figures. He could only answer that he wanted information from Costello about an obscure man he was investigating for the Air Force. Even his friends had difficulty believing that.

Mob connections did not disappear from politics with the Gross case and O'Dwyer's downfall. Mob money remained attractive. Mafia leaders continued to regard some officeholders as their own. But the rules of the game changed. The connections had to be concealed more carefully. The concealment made it increasingly difficult for old-fashioned city political machines to function. Basic forces—including the middle-class flight to suburbia—were causing the machines to break down. But the Gross case marked at least a turning point, away from what Lincoln Steffens, at the turn of the century, had called the System.

And, finally, the smashing of Gross's organization had to change the nature of bookmaking. Obviously, bookmaking continued. But now bookies had to practice their trade in other ways. The changes practically wiped out the old, well-established bookmaker who could call himself his town's "betting commissioner." In town after town, with no more fuss than a phone call or a conversation over drinks or a meal, the betting commissioner took down his blackboards and locked his door. Conceivably police departments too moved a step closer to decently paid and efficient civil service operation. For bookmaking, the Gross case guaranteed the breakup of large-scale organizations, to be replaced by smaller, more flexible ones—which in the not very long run would do an even larger volume of business.

13

THE KEFAUVER COMMITTEE: A NUMBERS GAME

IT IS POSSIBLE THAT IN 1950 NO ONE IN THE TOWN OF Madisonville, Tennessee, had ever seen a bookmaker or laid hands on a *Daily Racing Form*. It is even more likely that the racing wire never entered the town (population about 2,500 in the 1970s). Madisonville lies midway between Knoxville and Chattanooga, in the hills of eastern Tennessee. Its importance in this narrative comes from the fact that, in 1903, Estes Kefauver was born there.

From all the evidence it appears that at the beginning of 1950 Kefauver himself was also innocent of any intimate knowledge of gambling, or crime—whether organized or unorganized. He had left home to go to the University of Tennessee and then to law school, at Yale. He practiced law in Chattanooga. He entered politics and won a seat in the House of Representatives in 1938, and the U.S. Senate in 1948. In no part of this successful career had gambling seared his character.

None of this implies that, behind his modest manner, Kefauver was politically naïve. He came from a political family. His father, who owned a hardware store, had had political ambitions of his own. A distant relative had been a governor of Missouri and had figured somewhat in Lincoln

Steffen's probings into corruption. Kefauver won his Senate seat over the opposition of Boss Ed Crump of Memphis. His victory helped break the Crump machine, statewide.

But when it came to organized crime and gambling, Kefauver chose to investigate them because—like the mountain—they were there. The investigations made him a national figure. He headed them for less than two years, yet when they were done he was being talked of as a presidential candidate.

It should be added that he remained a long shot for the nomination. The leaders of his own Democratic Party were at best wary of him. Some even despised him:

"HST thinks Humphrey 'too radical'; dismisses Kennedy as a Catholic; has no use for Kefauver. Mentions [Albert] Gore and [George] Leader."

The "HST," of course, referred to Harry Truman. Arthur M. Schlesinger, Jr., made the notes after a conversation with Adlai Stevenson and used them in his biography of *Robert F. Kennedy.*

Stevenson was about to be nominated for the uncertain privilege of running against Dwight Eisenhower a second time. He was mulling over his options for a possible running mate. In the end, Stevenson threw the choice back to the nominating convention. And the convention, in spite of Truman's unconcealed dislike for Kefauver, picked him as its vice-presidential candidate in the foredoomed campaign.

In person, Kefauver seemed a quiet and agreeable man, more polite to witnesses than most committee chairmen. He listened closely to questions, and ideas, from reporters. Presumably he angered his own peers most when his committee, in its voyage of discovery in the underworld, revealed that illegal money had found its way into politics. Here at least Kefauver's committee drew blood. And this may be taken as a form of equalizing justice. On its original charge from the Senate, the committee produced a mixture of results, some of it dubious.

In 1949, during his freshman year in the Senate, Kefauver talked about crime and gambling with a number of newspaper people, according to William Howard Moore, in his book *The Kefauver Committee and the Politics of Crime: 1950–1952.*

He absorbed the doctrine that gambling financed the underworld. That idea was being pushed by, among others, the
American Municipal Association. Particularly active was Virgil W. Peterson, a former FBI man, who in 1942 became
director of the Chicago Crime Commission.

On January 2, 1950, Kefauver filed his claim to jurisdiction over crime. He introduced Senate Resolution 202,
calling for "... investigation of interstate gambling and
racketeering ..." Another ambitious, first-term senator who
threatened to grab the subject as his own specialty was
Joseph R. McCarthy of Wisconsin. Just a month later McCarthy diverted himself with the discovery of Communists in the
State Department and launched another sort of career.

For several months Kefauver picked his way through the
labyrinth of Senate politics. He had to stand by while the
Senate Commerce Committee (through its McFarland subcommittee) took the first cut at "transmission of certain
gambling information in interstate and foreign commerce."
With the help of the press he had to ease past the reluctance of
the Truman administration to support his investigation. He
had to placate a Senate elder, Pat McCarran of Nevada. He
did so by broadening the resolution to cover a greater variety
of rackets and crimes and by ignoring state gambling laws
(including the laws of Nevada).

Finally, early in May 1950, the Senate approved the resolution, calling as it now did, simply for a "Special Committee to
Investigate Organized Crime in Interstate Commerce." Kefauver became committee chairman, without a contest.

Kefauver himself, his chief counsel Rudolph Halley, and a
dedicated staff at once set to work overtime. They kept up a
fast pace for the life of the committee. The committee's
hearings lasted less than a year and a half. Still they covered
fourteen cities, heard about six hundred witnesses, and produced thousands of pages of testimony and exhibits.

In a time of investigations which were stormy enough and
filled with the stuff of live drama, the Kefauver Committee
pulled more than its share of press notice. And yet, the
committee's work did not result in new legislation. Another
ten years passed before any of its recommendations were

enacted. Kefauver by that time was near the end of his life and had long since moved on to other interests.

Kefauver picked up where Attorney General Howard McGrath left off—looking for the trail of interstate horse-race betting. Gambling in general nearly always headed the committee's agenda. Nevertheless, as it moved along, the committee's encounters forced it to take a broader view of crime.

One force pushing the committee was the Bureau of Narcotics. Bureau Chief Harry Anslinger, unlike his opposite number, J. Edgar Hoover of the FBI, had long been a Mafia theorist. One of Anslinger's people, George White, worked with the committee staff. As a result, in its final report the committee concluded: "There is a sinister criminal organization known as the Mafia operating throughout the country with ties in other nations, in the opinion of the committee. The Mafia is the direct descendant of a criminal organization of the same name originating in the island of Sicily."

Within a few years this conclusion would appear to have been partly overstatement and partly gross oversimplification. Still, the committee's sources were limited. It heard testimony largely from crime commissions and police officials. Some of that testimony took remarkable shortcuts through history. Police Chief M. C. Beasley of Tampa, Florida, for example, answered a request for his concept of the Mafia:

> My concept of the Mafia is that—well, I believe it consists of Italian people who have come from the southern part of Italy, Sicily—I believe they are known as Sicilians—that have immigrated into this country. . . . There were criminal bands, as I have read the history of it, running wild and rampant over Italy and Sicily especially, that came over here and, as a result, we have the Al Capones and other different people that organize into a crime syndicate.

It is easy enough to point out that Chief Beasley vaulted over years of many kinds of thuggery and racketeering in America and over generations of experience of immigrants from all parts of the world. But the committee itself, in somewhat more sophisticated form, did only a little better.

Understandably, the committee did treat drug pushing in

some detail. It probed bootlegging and the later influence of mobsters in legal distribution of liquor. It received testimony on the numbers racket and other forms of gambling besides bookmaking. Somehow it skipped lightly over what would later turn out to have been one of the mobs' major interests —loansharking. One brief passage in the committee's final report touched on the Ford Motor Company and its use of thugs to keep out union organizers. In New York, the report said, "the same situation prevailed in connection with the Phelps-Dodge Co. which invited in hoodlums from the gang of Albert and Anthony Anastasia to help break a strike."

In California the committee made use of earlier material developed by the Philbrick Committee. Those hearings had little to do with organized crime as such and still less with gambling, but they did abundantly document corruption in government—much of it centering around the figure of lobbyist Artie Samish.

As for New York, the hearings there were saved for the end to climax the committee's work. Frank Costello and former Mayor O'Dwyer unwillingly played the leading roles in the dramatics. The committee made the links between the two men abundantly clear. Big-city politicians all over the country watched the performance, certainly with close attention, often with unease. As a side issue of importance, the hearings demonstrated the power of television to grab public attention. At the very least, changes in political styles and techniques inevitably followed.

In summing up its work, the committee paid particular attention to what it called "infiltration into legitimate business." On this point, the committee in its travels often enough encountered unchallengeable evidence. That is, they found witnesses who had Italian names and long jail records. These witnesses probably were members of what later would be called Cosa Nostra families. They also clearly had legitimate business interests.

The Kefauver Committee suggested that "rehabilitation of offenders should be encouraged in every possible way." But then the committee immediately cast doubt on how much a gangster could reform: "A gangster or racketeer in a legitimate business does not suddenly become respectable. The methods which he used to achieve success in racketeering and gambling enterprises are not easily sloughed off."

The committee had little doubt "that the public suffers from gangster penetration into legitimate business," and alleged that, consequently, "higher prices must be paid for articles and services"—and this as the "result of the monopoly which is often secured."

Evidently the presence of mob figures in legitimate businesses caused the committee acute difficulty. It produced no evidence of monopoly at all. And it demonstrated its quandary best when it listed alphabetically all the industries in which it had found one or another racketeer. The list included as a matter of course: "amusement industry," "ballrooms, bowling alleys, etc.," "basketball," "boxing," "liquor industry," and "racing and race tracks." But it also included "advertising," "banking," "construction," "electrical equipment," "insurance," "newspapers," "shipping," and "steel." It seems unlikely that, even with the most earnest efforts, the Mafia could have achieved a monopoly of ballrooms and bowling alleys. But banking? Insurance? Steel?

The further the committee searched, the more the difficulties compounded. Thus, even charity caused confusion. According to the final report: "The committee found that hoodlums, behind the front of their respectable enterprises, contribute enormous sums to hundreds of worthy causes. While the committee in no way wishes to reflect on the worthiness of such causes, it has found that hoodlum contributions do tend to fool uninformed people and thus contribute to the relaxation of public vigilance."

At bottom, it may be that the committee suffered most from belief in its own statements. It may truly have believed in the huge sums it claimed organized crime absorbed. And this requires some reexamination of gambling, because early and late the committee still maintained that gambling was the heaviest producer of mob income.

In its conclusions the Kefauver Committee said: "Gambling profits are the principal support of big-time racketeering and gangsterism. These profits provide the financial resources whereby ordinary criminals are converted into big-time racketeers, political bosses, pseudo businessmen, and alleged philanthropists."

The statement is sweeping. Unfortunately, the committee never could back it up with numbers. Moore reported that when the investigation began, Kefauver apparently believed that the gamblers' "take" fell somewhere in the range of $15 billion to $30 billion. Presumably by "take" was meant gross income. In 1950 the gross national product was $286 billion. Hence the upper end of the very wide range would put income from illegal gambling at more than 10 percent of the entire GNP—a dizzying concept.

Around 1980, in California, the press featured estimates that placed the value of the marijuana crop first in the state's agriculture. Two questions could be raised about such an estimate: Who said so? And based on what information? In the end, a county agricultural agent who knew the crop, and the people who produced it, and the ways of estimating production, supplied the needed correction. The assumed value of the state's pot crop, substantial to be sure, receded to a more modest position, somewhere in the neighborhood of almonds or artichokes.

Somewhat the same situation prevailed in regard to income from illegal gambling. Illegality invites wild estimates. The estimator feels no fear of correction, and his guess is based on the kind of policy he promotes.

The committee demonstrated its freewheeling ways with numbers in its first foray into Miami, Florida, where it seized records in the offices of the S & G bookmaking syndicate. According to the committee, the S & G records showed a total income of about $26.5 million in 1948, a net of about $467,000. The net seemed far too low to the investigators. They therefore fixed it, by estimate, at something between $4 million and $8 million. Actually, the syndicate's own numbers seem more reasonable. The total take-out on the volume bet could not have exceeded 15 percent (since track odds were paid)—or about $4 million. But that sum had to be split several ways. Sheet writers and runners got their share. Lesser bookmakers, who were given locations by the S & G syndicate, had to be cut in. The syndicate also had to pay protection money. In fact, in the course of its own Miami hearings, the committee demonstrated how large the payoffs must have been. It seems impossible for the syndicate to have retained more than a quarter or a fifth of the take-out as profits—something in the range of $500,000 to $1 million. And not all of that could have made its way back to a presumed national crime center (though indeed a connection with Frank Erickson and Frank Costello was shown). Seemingly, the bookmakers prepared reasonable numbers with a view to avoiding prosecution by the Bureau of Internal Revenue. The committee took those numbers and then inflated them, four to eight times.

In other cities, too, the committee focused on horse-race betting. It did take testimony on the numbers racket and betting on fights and sporting events. But the committee was probably right in assuming that horse-race betting, both legal and illegal, remained the dominant form of gambling at that time. And the emphasis on horse-race betting led the committee into yet another difficulty. The official argument ran: Gambling finances the national crime syndicate. Horse-race betting is the most important form of gambling. Therefore, go after crime by going after betting on horses.

But by 1950 it was obvious, that anyone could bet on horses, perfectly legally, throughout much of the country. Even leaving out Nevada and church basements with their lottery games, racing was *the* legal form of gambling in the United States. Betting at the track might help balance a state's budget, but it could hardly finance the Mafia.

The committee solved this problem with another pair of numbers. It assumed that for every dollar bet at the track, four dollars were bet off-track, with bookies. This assumption lay behind the allegation of gambling wealth pouring into the Syndicate. (It may also have deflected attention from other illegal, and sometimes violent, ways of making money.) The

4-to-1 ratio, off-track compared with on-track, has proved to be one of the hardiest and most long-lived of the numbers games—and one of the wildest.

To unravel the numbers, it is necessary to devote some thought to the nature of horse-race betting. It should be noted first, in passing, that some critics thought the Kefauver Committee should have listened to academic people as well as to law enforcement officials. Conceivably some scholars might have helped. However, the committee might also have profited from conversation with experienced horseplayers— though in fairness it should be said that many horseplayers, for their own reasons, accepted the 4-to-1 myth.

As noted earlier in this work, at the beginning of the 1920s racing was stifled in much of the country. A relatively small number of horses ran in a relatively small number of races. It was perfectly possible for a bettor, in San Francisco, say, or Chicago, with no racetrack nearby, to follow the horses competing in New York. Knowing something about the New York horses, he might wish to bet on one of them. The out-of-town bettor backed his opinion with a bookmaker, or not at all. Under those circumstances it was perfectly possible that more money was bet away from the track than at it. How much more would be impossible to say. The ratio could have been 1½ to 1—or 4 to 1—or even 5 to 1.

By the time of the Kefauver hearings of 1950 the situation had reversed—in my opinion. Comparing 1920 with 1950: The number of racing days had increased threefold, the number of races and the number of horses racing had increased four- and fivefold, and the amount bet at racetracks had increased proportionately. It was no longer necessary, or practical, for a Californian to follow New York racing. It goes without saying that the volume of illegal betting is hard to measure—which is one reason the 4-to-1 myth has proved so durable. But a factual analysis of the nature of horse-race betting strongly suggests that betting with bookies decreased, as betting through the pari-mutuels increased, to the point where the illegal part of the action came to no more than a third of the total.

1. Betting on horses is a game of judgment. Even losing players rely on judgment, though unsuccessfully. Some people do have random or whimsical ways of picking horses—using name, or color, or numerology, or signs of the zodiac. They are largely occasional visitors on an outing.

2. In spite of legend to the contrary, some horseplayers do win. They are a very small percentage of all players. Statistical demonstration that winners exist would be out of place here. But even if many players merely believed in the existence of winners, a majority would continue to bet. Without that hope, horse-race betting would be totally irrational. In the days of on-track bookmaking the take-out (or vigorish, the bookies' edge), was never less than 10 percent. With modern pari-mutuels the take-off often amounts to 17 percent and sometimes more. In the random games like craps and roulette, the take-out (the house edge, in this case) varies a little with rules changes, but it is less than a third of the take-out at the track. Only the slot machines are greedier —and they cater to a large, unthinking, and transient public. If playing horses were like playing slot machines, few could remain long in the game. A single visit to the track should be sufficient to convince a newcomer that some players have been going for years and continue to go.

3. The exercise of judgment, the crucial difference at the track, depends on information. Given a choice, the player will make his bets at the track. He can learn more there. He can see the actual running of each race. He will bet with a bookie if he has an opinion about a horse and cannot get to the track. He may also bet with a book, marginally, because he can do so on credit. But he cannot continue on the cuff if he loses.

4. The horseplayer finds the bulk of the information he needs in the *Daily Racing Form*. The player is hooked to the *Racing Form*, not by habit, but as if to a lifeline. Moe Annenberg built his monopoly on solid ground. It remained intact forty years after his death.

Over vast stretches of the country no one sees a *Racing Form;* none can be found. It may be taken for granted that in such places no one bets on horses. The McFarland and Kefauver committees heard talk of scratch sheets and tout services. The scratch sheets were largely a convenience for bookmakers. Tout services did, and do, exist, and people buy them. And if they depend on them entirely for their opinions, they do not stay long in the game.

The circulation of the *Daily Racing Form* then, provides one solid starting point for estimating the number of horseplayers, on and off the track. The Kefauver Committee apparently did not consider it. It was used, however, in an extended article on gambling in *Life* for June 19, 1950. The article assumed that there were about three players for every two copies of the *Form*. It then pyramided a succession of assumptions on this base and came up with a figure that would have satisfied the congressional investigators—a total of $6 billion in profits for illegal gambling ($2½ billion for racing alone) per year.

The number of horseplayers per copy of the *Daily Racing Form* seems to me, if anything, *too low*. I could easily believe that the number of players is twice as great as the number of papers. But all the other numbers are stretched beyond sight of reality. The circulation of the *Form* is given as a million. That is nothing less than a fourfold exaggeration. The average daily circulation of all editions of the *Form* combined has scarcely ever approached a quarter of a million.

The *Life* article assumed that the average player's bets total $7,000 in a year. That average twenty-five years later was only about $5,000. *Life*'s number for 1950 was probably a twofold inflation (on top of the fourfold inflation of *Racing Form* circulation). And finally, the amount of profit extracted by bookmakers was set impossibly high (at 25 percent).

With all corrections applied to the *Life* figures, it appears that the total amount bet by all horseplayers in 1950, on and off the track, was actually about $1.6 billion. But, of the total, just about $1 billion was bet at tracks, through the pari-mutuel machines. The remainder, about $600 million, seems a reasonable guess for the bookmakers' actual handle, nationally. The vigorish taken by the bookies from the total on racing bets cannot have been much more than $100 million—instead of the $2½ billion assumed by *Life* and, in effect, by the Kefauver Committee.

By Kefauver's time, bookies may already have been handling more action on sporting events than on racing. Whatever the grand total handled by bookmakers may have been, it appears from the Gross case and other evidence as well that more of the bookies' profit went to policemen than to the Mafia. Certainly racketeers also profited from some casinos and from the numbers racket. Overall, though, the Kefauver Committee did well not to come to grips with reasonable numbers on the Mafia's illegal gambling profit. The numbers would have cast a shadow over the statement that gambling was "the principal support of big-time racketeering."

The Kefauver Committee did make one sensible adjustment to reality, as it encountered it. By the time the committee had toured the country, it had for the most part quietly shelved that ancient bugbear of law enforcement, layoff betting.

The McFarland Committee had made much of the presumed national network of layoff betting. It used the device to skewer Frank Erickson and start his downfall. And layoffs did exist—but not quite on the grand scale first conceived, and not always in interstate trade.

The Kefauver Committee in summarizing its work noted the presence of layoff betting and then proceeded at once to what it considered a more fertile area: come-back betting. As noted earlier, a come-back bet is one placed with a bookmaker, which the bookmaker chooses to send back to the track by a messenger, to be bet through the pari-mutuels. The bookmaker avoids a possibility of loss (and of gain as well), and may further aim at depressing the odds on a given horse.

In its Washington hearings, the committee heard factual and interesting details on how come-back betting operated. Three witnesses described how they themselves made come-back bets for bookmaking organizations. Representatives of the Thoroughbred Racing Association were given a chance to speak against the practice.

In passing, it might be noted that some tracks, far from disapproving of come-back bets, are believed to have solicited the business. Such bets do increase the pari-mutuel handle and therefore the track's share of the take-out. At least two accounts of the early history of Santa Anita allege that in the first days (around 1934), when the future of the track seemed dubious, an infusion of come-back money from the East kept the track alive. At any rate, bookies undoubtedly made come-back bets then, and a generation later they still did. But the Kefauver Committee slighted one question: Was the practice illegal?

Clearly, in most places a law was broken when someone booked the bet in the first place. But did the bookie break the law again when he made the bet, or caused the bet to be made, at a racetrack mutuel window? In due course, federal law barred interstate transmission of gambling information. But most come-back bets are carried out within the track's own state. In this case the person carrying the come-back bet may well describe himself as simply a messenger.

In New Orleans and in Chicago, during the 1970s, downtown offices accepted bets for delivery to nearby racetracks. In both cities authorities suggested that "accepting" a bet in this sense might well mean booking it. The messenger service might simply decide to pocket some bets, if it thought a particular horse had no chance of winning. The issue remains alive.

The committee's final report also dwelt at length on the racing wire. Without question, the wire transmitted racing information between states for gambling purposes. The committee said, "The wire service is as essential to a bookmaker as the stock ticker is to a stockbroker." Therefore, "the organization which controls the wire service can, in effect control bookmaking operations." The report then traced some of the bloody and complex maneuvers in the wire service business. After the murder of James A. Ragen, it said, the racing wire came under control of the "gangsters who constitute the Capone crime syndicate."

The historian deals mainly with the past, sometimes the immediate past. Perhaps it is unfair to expect him to project the future. Fair or not, it must be said that the Kefauver Committee failed to see what was about to happen to the wire service. At the moment that the committee completed its work, the racing wire was dwindling. But its decline by no means ended bookmaking. On this point, and others, the committee might well have listened more closely to one of its own witnesses, the St. Louis betting commissioner, James Carroll.

The racing wire added greatly to the prosperity of the horse parlor. But after the Gross case, the place where horseplayers gathered to hear results and make bets was near extinction. The racing wire declined with it.

Actually, on this point the committee again overlooked information close at hand. In the 1930s, as a by-product of the prosecution of Moe Annenberg, the American Telephone and Telegraph came under fire for handling the racing wire. Annenberg's service, it was said, was the phone company's fifth-largest customer. Annenberg walked away from the business. So did A.T.& T.—but not before it revealed to the Federal Communications Commission that its racing wire revenue came to about $550,000 a year. Western Union stepped in to take the phone company's place. And it defended its right to do so before the McFarland Committee.

In its published hearings the McFarland Committee incorporated a staff report of the Federal Communications Commission, prepared late in World War II. The FCC report dealt at length with Western Union's transmission of racing news. It quoted a letter from a telegraph company vice-president encouraging his people "to insure expeditious handling" of the racing wire business, and adding that it might involve revenue of about $30,000 a month—compared with about $46,000 a month received by A.T.& T. in the late 1930s. Making allowance for increased costs during wartime, it appears that in the few years after the phone company stepped aside, wire service traffic had already been cut nearly in half.

Overall, the Kefauver Committee viewed bookmaking in the way that French generals, presumably guarded by the Maginot line, looked at trench warfare in 1940. They believed in a state of art that was already more than twenty years old. Actually, the Kefauver hearings took place during a time of change for bookmakers in America. New forms of bookmaking were already appearing—brought about by legal parimutuel betting, by unforeseen effects of World War II, and perhaps most of all by the boom in television.

14

A NEW STYLE IN BOOKMAKING

FOR 150 YEARS PEOPLE THOUGHT OF BOOKMAKERS MAINLY in connection with horse racing. True, bookmakers did handle other kinds of bets. British sportsmen wagered heavily on prizefights, cockmains, and human footraces as well. In the United States, too, betting spread over all sports. Arnold Rothstein made large bets on fights and on team games. He obviously bet on baseball and not just on a fixed World Series.

But always in the background, unstated, sensed if unknown, was the commandment given by a veteran nineteenth-century English bookmaker to one of his apprentices: "Never, my son, bet on anything that talks."

The tried, the sensible, the reliable business for bookies lay at the racetrack. And so, what happened in American gambling after World War II was something of a revolution. Congressional investigators early in the 1950s set off in hot pursuit of the racing wire, layoff betting and come-back betting, and the vanishing horse parlor. Meanwhile, the American bettor and the bookmaker who handled his action had already turned more and more to sporting events.

To be fair, the Kefauver Committee did hear a small amount of testimony about bets on baseball. By the 1960s, when the McClellan Committee had taken the place of the

McFarland and Kefauver committees, sports betting, with football now leading the way, occupied perhaps a quarter of the committee's attention. In the real world, outside the committee rooms, sports betting had already taken the lead over all forms of illegal gambling.

One obvious reason for the change was the state-by-state legalization of horse racing. Though congressional committees and the Department of Justice refused to believe it, many horseplayers enjoyed themselves more, and found they had a better chance of holding their own, at the track, betting through the mutuel machines.

Even more important was the increase in gambling as a whole, from the late 1940s on. Horse-race attendance and betting also continued to increase. But the volume of betting on baseball, basketball, and football swelled far more rapidly.

The postwar period can be described in many ways. Victory released years of tension. A country that for more than ten prewar years had never recovered from economic depression was finally enjoying prosperity. Families had been reshuffled, whole populations had moved about the country. With each year, old rules seemed to fit less well. And, for at least fifteen years after the war, speculators had their longest continuous period of success in the country's history. If millions could take up a small position in the stock market, other millions could do their speculating in sports betting.

The horseplayer had his special body of knowledge, which he hoped might bring him profit and occasionally did. The knowledge was not easy to acquire; the number of horseplayers grew only slowly. But a majority of men, and increasing numbers of women, read the sports pages. For better or worse, they regarded themselves as experts in professional sport. They had, in short, opinions. Whether these opinions were valid or not, they were bettable.

In the face of the trend, Congress chose, for the first time, to concern itself with gambling. In 1948 it had passed a law aimed against offshore gambling ships. During the time of the Kefauver Committee it passed another gambling control measure—the Johnson Act of 1951. This law limited inter-state transportation of "gambling devices." Congress was still flexing its interstate regulatory powers, and it had heard testimony that Frank Costello had moved his slot machine enterprises from New York to New Orleans. Most of the Kefauver Committee recommendations lay dormant.

Meanwhile a much younger and equally ambitious politician, Robert F. Kennedy, joined the pursuit of gamblers' illegal money. John Kennedy's next younger brother had served an apprenticeship, hunting Communists, as a member of Senator Joe McCarthy's staff. In 1957, having earlier become counsel to Senator John McClellan's committee on investigations, Robert Kennedy launched his assault on the Teamsters' Union. At the end of it, James Hoffa had been sent to jail and driven from the presidency of the Teamsters' Union, and eventually he was killed. Robert Kennedy became attorney general in his brother's cabinet in 1961. And the McClellan Committee continued in the crime-hunting business.

Like the Kefauver Committee, the investigators of the early 1960s clung to the theory that illegal gambling profits—bookmakers' profits in particular—financed the underworld. But the numbers used, like the inflation beginning to wrack the country, were wilder than ever.

In August 1961, Senator McClellan and his colleagues heard the testimony of three high-ranking experts from New York. They were Myles Lane, a federal prosecutor; Jacob Grumet, a long-time official in New York City; and Judge Goodman A. Sarachan of Rochester, New York, who now headed the New York State Commission of Investigation.

Sarachan informed the committee that the take-out at a racetrack amounted to 30 percent—a number so remarkable that if true it would have ended organized racing within a month. The actual figure, for most of the country at that time, was about 15 percent, but no one at the hearing saw fit to set the record straight. Sarachan also reassured the committee that gambling money did operate other and yet more sinister rackets. Of a man named Genovese, he said that "he, along with others, got their principal revenues to operate the narcotics and white slavery and other rackets out of the gambling proceeds."

And finally the group from New York repeated the Kefauver Committee doctrine that horse betting with bookies far exceeded betting at the track. But now the ratio was no longer 4 to 1: it had grown to 16 to 1. Senator McClellan himself repeated this amazing message, apparently to reassure himself that he had it right, as the hearings continued the next day.

"As I understood yesterday," McClellan said, "it was stated that for every dollar bet on the races at the track, about $16 is bet off the track, it averages that."

Against this kind of background, and with proposals now being sent to Congress by Attorney General Robert Kennedy, 1961 saw passage of three anti-gambling laws.

The key to the Kennedy package was a law to prohibit interstate transportation of wagering information. It was aimed particularly at the old target of congressional investigators, the racing wire. Kennedy testified in support of his bill that: "It is quite evident that modern organized, commercial gambling operations are so completely intertwined with the Nation's communications systems that denial of their use to the gambling fraternity would be a mortal blow to their operations."

Congress enacted this measure, and with it two others. One penalized interstate travel done in order to carry on illegal gambling and other crimes. The other barred, again in interstate commerce, transportation of illegal wagering paraphernalia. This last aimed at slips, papers, and various materials needed for the numbers racket and other illegal lotteries.

The "mortal blow" promised by the Attorney General proved less than fatal. Gambling, and especially sports betting, continued to grow.

In 1962, Congress broadened the gambling devices law of 1951. In 1964 it enacted a measure against bribery in sporting events.

By 1970 a new administration, under Richard Nixon, had taken office. In that year it got through Congress an Organized

Crime Control Act, a law that inevitably contained gambling sections. And now new ground was broken. The key section of the 1970 law banned illegal gambling businesses that met two conditions: (1) they violated the law of the state in which they were carried out, and (2) they involved five or more persons. The gambling business must also have operated at least thirty days in succession or have had a gross revenue over $2,000 in any single day. The key point is that this time "interstate commerce" was not mentioned. Congress simply assumed that any gambling business over a certain size had to reach beyond one state.

The government also moved against gambling through tax laws. A tax law of 1951, strongly influenced by the Kefauver hearings, placed a 10 percent excise tax on all betting conducted for profit. The law that year also required professional gamblers to pay what amounted to a $50 head tax. Those who favored the tax law predicted that it would a) cripple illegal gambling and b) produce revenue of perhaps $400 million a year. The law could hardly have had both effects. (How could a demolished industry yield such revenue?) And, in fact, it produced neither. It did not cripple illegal gambling, and it produced less than $10 million a year over the next decade. In 1974 the tax law was overhauled once more and the gambling excise tax dropped to 2 percent. Congress accepted the reality that the excise tax served mainly to handicap legal gambling—as in Nevada—in its competition with the outlawed product.

The Internal Revenue Service, incidentally, thought from the start that the excise tax was unenforceable. An IRS spokesman pointed out in 1951 that failure to collect the tax might breed contempt for other taxes. In 1952, Commissioner Mortimer M. Caplin said the tax service would need more than 4,300 new agents to handle the excise tax burden. Congress did not grant money for the vast staff increase.

Two inventions set the pattern for modern sports betting and bookmaking. The first and more obvious was television. For thirty years, from the early 1950s on, live telecasts of sports events steadily gained popularity. The franchise for a professional football or baseball team became a passageway to wealth. Star players, with some help from the courts, also bargained their way to startling wages. Some of them, for the short span of their careers, earned as much as corporation presidents. Sports betting was simply the unrecorded part of the flood of money set loose by TV broadcasts.

Among other things, television, in its own oblivious way, provided a background of mocking laughter for the old and tired refrain from congressional committee hearings: "Cut off the wire service and you stop bookmaking." On Saturdays, Sundays, and Monday evenings during football season, every saloon in the country had its own wire service hanging on the wall. It was free, too, courtesy of advertisers, and it came complete with instant replay and in color.

In millions of homes, rooms, or apartments the television set took on some of the functions of the horse parlor of the past. The bettor watched the game to see the outcome of his bet. What he saw gave him a new set of opinions. During the week ahead he would back those opinions with further wagers.

The second invention involved not a machine but simply an idea—the bookmaker's point spread. For two hundred years bettors had wrestled with the problem of setting the stakes in an event in which one party (a horse, a fighter, or a team) seemed clearly superior. In mid-nineteenth-century England, Admiral Rous took one step by assigning different weights, or handicaps, to the horses in a race.

But only rarely did the weights bring the field together. As Pittsburgh Phil observed, a really good horse running against a poor one could most often pick up an extra twenty pounds, take the track, and win going away. And so it became the function of bookmakers to make a race bettable by offering different odds against each runner in a field. If an unlikely horse, held at long odds, actually won, he rewarded his backers with a rare but handsome return.

Overall, the bookmaker's list of odds, or prices, against each horse in a field represented in part his judgment of the horse's chances. In part, the list also represented his judgment of the betting public's opinion about each horse. What he wanted above all was to attract different amounts of betting, at the different odds, so that no matter which horse won, the payout would be about the same, and he would be guaranteed a profit.

In a prizefight, or a contest between two teams, one side or the other was likely to be favored, sometimes heavily. Again, the bookie split the bettor's action by offering odds. For example, if a team was heavily favored, the bettor might have to stake $6 to win $1. The bettor who backed the underdog, if he was lucky enough to win, might get back $5 for the $1 he wagered. And here again the bookmaker tried to adjust the odds to the strength of the bettors' opinions—in this case producing about five times as much betting on the favorite as on the underdog, and protecting his own commission no matter which side won.

The bookmaking trade went along more or less happily for at least a century and a half, using the odds to split the action profitably. And then someone came up with the point spread.

Newton and Leibnitz invented calculus at about the same time, unknown to each other, in different countries. It is possible that ingenious American bookies in different cities independently hit upon the idea of the point spread. Gerald Strine and Neil D. Isaacs, who seem to have gone into the matter as deeply as can be done, in their book *Covering the Spread* suggest that the point spread may have originated in Minneapolis in the late 1920s or early '30s. Certainly giving or taking points was a rarity before World War II, though it was commonplace afterwards. In football and basketball betting, use of the points quickly became standard practice.

In betting with the point spread, no odds are offered. Everyone bets at even money. In placing a bet with a bookmaker, the bettor stakes $11 to win $10: the difference is the bookie's commission.

The favored team must win by a set number of points. Or, taken the other way round, the underdog may lose in the actual game, but its backer wins his bet if the margin of defeat is less than the number of points offered.

To take an example from the early days of the point spread: In 1950, the Cleveland Browns met the Los Angeles Rams in a playoff game for the National Football League championship. Suppose that the public favored the Browns. To get a bet down on the Browns you had to give three points. If you were willing to back the underdog Rams, you were given three points.

The teams settled the issue on the field. The Browns won, 30–28. But backers of the Browns lost their bets—because in effect they had to give away three points, one more than the actual margin between the teams. Backers of the losing Rams won their bets. For purposes of wagering, with the gift of three points, they had finished a point ahead. If the point spread had been two—two points given or taken—the game for betting purposes would have been a tie and all wagers would have been off. In some cases, an extra half point is added to the points given or taken. Then there can be no ties.

Clearly, the purpose of the points is to split the bettor's action roughly equally between the two teams. But offering odds serves the same purpose.

The advantage of the point spread—and it is a powerful one for bookmakers—is that it stimulates more action. It does so by encouraging a bettor to act on his opinion.

Suppose, for example, that a league champion is playing a mediocre team. The champions, naturally, are strongly favored. Offering odds of, say, 5 to 1 may split the action properly. But the total volume of bets will be low. Many people will not want to bet at all. Backers of the champions may think they are offering a great deal of money to win a little. Backers of the underdogs may think the odds reasonable but in fact they simply do not expect to win, and so they too pass the game without a bet. With the points, on the other hand, enough of a margin can be offered—ten or eleven or more points—so that in the end every bettor can persuade himself that he has reason to favor one side or the other. The total amount bet thus increases vastly—and the bookmaker's commission increases in proportion.

Strine and Isaacs point out that the spread is good for the advertising business too. In a game between poorly matched rivals, the issue may be settled long before the end of the game. Normally, viewers watching on television would turn away. But the points separating the teams may not be settled until the final minutes. And so the bettor remains fixed to his TV screen, waiting to learn from that free, universal, all-purpose sports wire, whether he will pay or collect.

Baseball before World War II was the leading professional sport and the chief betting medium among sports. The odds split the baseball action effectively enough. For the most part they still do today. Among other things, margins of victory or defeat in baseball tend to be narrow. But the point spread suits football and basketball admirably. With a powerful assist from television, betting on football with the points by the 1970s had become the largest part of the bookmakers' handle.

Basketball is something of a special case. Very tall athletic wizards play it with such speed and skill that the game, as seen on television, is something of a jumble. Basketball's television audience—a fair gauge of the volume of betting—is less than half the size of football's. And something else must be added: a basketball team has only five starters. The condition, or intention, of just a few players can strongly affect the score of the game.

Early in 1951 two former basketball players for Manhattan College in New York were arrested and charged with bribery and conspiracy to fix basketball games. They confessed to having paid members of their old team to shave points in Manhattan's games. Since the point spread was not yet widely known, *The New York Times* explained, "Gamblers do all their betting on points in any given game, rather than on the over-all result. Players in their hire agree to 'go under' a fixed score margin, or 'go over'."

Presumably the players might have refused to lose a game on purpose, but they saw little harm in winning by a narrow margin. If the spread was eight points, they might miss just enough shots to win by only five or six points and thus win bets for backers of the weaker team. In practice, it was not always possible for players to control a game so exactly. Sometimes they played so badly that they lost outright, against mediocre teams.

The case against the Manhattan College players turned out

to be only an entering wedge. It will be remembered that in 1951, Estes Kefauver was preparing to bring his committee to New York, and on a nearby front the Harry Gross bookmaking trial was underway. New York District Attorney Frank S. Hogan now widened the basketball investigation. The next team to go was the College of the City of New York. C.C.N.Y. players also confessed to taking money for tailoring the results of their games. And soon after, it turned out that another leading college team, at Long Island University, was also involved in point shaving. A *New York Times* sports columnist, Arthur Daley, proclaimed: ". . . the gambling craze has swept the country with the avariciousness of a prairie fire. . . . The flames are out of control. Nothing can extinguish them now. And the faggot that fed the blaze is the satanic gimmick of the point spread. It made gambling irresistible to those hitherto uninterested in a wager."

What to do about it? Daley said: "The personal preference here would be boiling in oil for all fixers. That would deter them."

Actually, fixing scandals in college sports had already come to the surface in at least three cases between 1945 and 1951. But now the problem clearly had spread. For a moment it looked as if only the tough and sophisticated players in the country's greatest metropolis were doing business with fixers. But then it was discovered that basketball players from the University of Kentucky, in pastoral Lexington, and Bradley, in Peoria, Illinois, had also shaved points. Bradley and Kentucky, like the New York schools, C.C.N.Y. and L.I.U., consistently had teams of championship caliber. Clearly the problem was national. At least a half dozen other schools were named, and the number of players who slept uneasily can never be known. The players with ruined careers (and sometimes jail sentences) included some of the finest athletes of their time.

A New York judge, Saul Streit, heard the testimony against the Bradley players and issued a lengthy report on the case and its background. He flayed the players, to be sure, but he looked beyond at the broader picture of college sports. He pointed to the blandishments—bribes in reality—offered by colleges to young high school athletes. He denounced the fake standards behind athletic scholarships. He listed the benefits, amounting to pay, offered to varsity athletes. In short, he exposed the sham of amateurism in collegiate sports.

The governing body of amateur sports, the Amateur Athletic Union, also managed to overlook bent standards. At the same time that the collegiate basketball scandals were multiplying, the manager of an AAU team admitted that he had used a professional player in a tournament in Connecticut. The championship AAU basketball teams of the time were in fact subsidized by major corporations, in the interest of public relations. The supposedly amateur players earned wages for doing supposed company jobs.

Charles Rosen, himself a former collegiate and professional basketball player, in his *Scandals of '51*, pointed to a number of quiet ways in which coaches and athletic departments saw to it that their players made extra money. The New York college basketball players, for example, made money in an informal summer camp league.

Actually, commercialism in amateur sports had been common knowledge for many years. A generation before, in magazine articles, John Tunis had given a graphic picture of how the amateur tennis champions were financed (and the tennis pros of the time only taught or gave exhibitions). The young tennis stars had to be suitable, socially and ethnically, to circulate among members of sponsoring clubs. They then picked up money in a dozen demeaning ways and became hustlers in the process.

Amateur boxing not only served as a school for the professional prize ring, but itself offered prize money. The phrase, "to give someone the works," may have come from the amateur fights. Amateur tournaments offered watches as prizes. Often the watch movements were removed and the watch cases stuffed with money. If given an intact watch, the fighter felt betrayed: he had been given the works.

Naturally the basketball fixes did genuinely betray a number of people. A fair number of the players' classmates felt betrayed, even shaken. For whatever reasons of their own a number of sportswriters also expressed outrage. And a special wave of anger swept the ranks of old grads who sat in gymnasiums and stadiums, seeking a glimpse of the youth of their imaginations. Their fury over the point shaving was greater even than their rage at a football game when a nineteen-year-old, standing alone on his goal line, dropped a punt as eighty thousand spectators watched. Close behind the alumni came the guardians of athletic virtue, the officials of athletic organizations, who wore uniform blazers to matches and games and presided in dignity over their athletic betters.

But more was at stake than dreams of glory or the massaging of ego. Collegiate games attracted tens of thousands. Full arenas produced large sums of money, sums worth scrambling for—by athletic departments and tournament organizers as well as gamblers. Money makes its own rules, and those rules do not match the rules of amateur sport.

Colleges depended on winning coaches to maintain budgets and keep up the flow of donations from satisfied alumni. No coaches were implicated in the point-shaving scandals. But it is scarcely an accident that several among them led their fellows in petty tyranny, dedication to winning at all costs, and flagrant violation of recruiting rules. Judge Streit, in his lengthy report on the basketball scandals, singled out the University of Kentucky as "the acme of commercialism and over-emphasis." He said the Kentucky coach, Adolph Rupp, had admitted (1) knowing Lexington bookmaker Ed Curd, and (2) having called Curd to find out the point spread in a Kentucky game.

After the scandals of 1951 the schools could go in either of two opposite directions. Some chose to go back to amateurism—to take their chances with their alumni, to accept the possibility of lesser gate receipts, and to play teams in their own class. The other way out was the exact opposite—to move even closer to professionalism, and to police the games better. This semiprofessional route proved possible, too, with some help from the expanding professional leagues in football and basketball—and from the bookmakers as well.

Nothing in the dogma of the Kefauver and McClellan

committees could have prepared anyone for the true role of the bookmakers and established gamblers in the basketball scandals. As Rosen documents abundantly, the fixers were small-fry gamblers and freebooters, trying to take advantage of other gamblers and in particular of the books. The man behind the New York fixes was one Salvatore Sollazzo, a businessman who made money from illegal sales of gold but spent more than he made and was seriously in debt. First press accounts credited the unknown gamblers behind the scandal with making hundreds of thousands of dollars. In truth, according to Rosen's detailed study, Sollazzo made little enough from his bribes and was nearly broke again when he went off to jail.

When point shaving was at its height, the bookmakers were the intended victims. They defended themselves in the most effective way possible: they simply refused to book bets on suspect games. And they were aware of the shady games before anyone else. It was their action that led to police investigation.

A leading bookmaker in the Midwest was Charlie McNeil. According to Rosen, McNeil observed that the fixers had gotten to a referee "in a major college conference." McNeil went to the conference's commissioner—who indignantly refused to listen to evidence about an "honorable" man, coming from a disreputable source. McNeil went to another official and this time offered to predict which games the referee would be working—and the outcomes of those games. His predictions were right—though assignments of referees were supposedly secret. McNeil had simply kept a shrewd eye on the flow of betting money and the sources from which it was coming. Without doing anything else about the matter, the conference allowed the referee's contract to lapse, and he was hired by another conference.

As professional sports continued to expand, into the 1960s and '70s, the schools were saved from the cost of their own commercialism. More and more openly they began functioning as the farm system for the pro leagues. The college athlete now had rich contracts waiting for him—if he was good enough at his trade to be a target for bribes. He had to be peculiarly foolish to risk a career for the sake of dumping a few college games.

During the 1960s some questions were raised about betting (not fixing) among professional football players. Paul Hornung and Alex Karras were suspended for allegedly betting on their own teams. Did any teams ever do business to win bets—on one side or the other? An occasional rumor spread quickly. The professional football and basketball leagues set up their own security systems, staffed by investigators and former policemen. The early warning system for all of them remained—the flow of bets around the country and the point-spread line. If a team was dropped from the line— meaning bets on that team's games would not be booked— the team was immediately placed under the closest observation.

On September 7, 1961, Leo Hirshfield of Minneapolis told the McClellan Committee that he had arranged with the head of the National Basketball Association to act as a watchdog for professional basketball. Hirshfield ran a sports information service, for bookmakers among others. He said:

> Now, Mr. Podoloff can tell you that we set up a system whereby I have a private number so that in the event I ever find out that there is any undue activity in any professional basketball game, I can call that number, and they will be able to reach him wherever he is . . . and he will immediately get in touch with . . . the officials and the players and the coaches, and everybody will be called into a huddle and they will be told that this game is being played under a spotlight . . . and that they better watch themselves.

This information so startled Senator McClellan that he asked several clarifying questions on his own. But it did not fit into the committee's overall view, and the committee counsel did not pursue it.

Thus, basketball survived its scandals, and for the most part football evaded them. The professional leagues expanded, and with them—though condemned by them— bookmaking flourished. The point spread, once called the instrument of the devil, proved to be a remarkably simple and flexible device for regulating an industry.

Symbolically, the old-time horse parlor gave way to the phone booth. In a mechanical sense, a phone line, and preferably an untappable line, was as necessary to modern bookmaking as the point spread. If organized crime was to take over bookmaking nationally, as in the gospel of the congressional committees, it would first have to deploy an army, many divisions strong, around the pay phones of the country. The bookmaker remained the very model of a small, independent businessman, the thew and sinew of free enterprise.

But if bookmaking has no ruling syndicate or board of directors, it does in fact have a center. Its affairs are regulated and held in balance by the more or less official line, the list of point spreads offered on coming games. Without contract or written understanding, or flow chart of any kind, the line originates for the most part in one place, Las Vegas. And the Las Vegas line itself is mainly the work of one man of rare judgment and ability, Bob Martin.

15

PRACTITIONERS OF THE ART

USUALLY IN ANY DIFFICULT ART OR CRAFT SEVERAL PER-
formers cluster at the top. In most years, any one of three or
four quarterbacks might fairly be called the best. Or, in
recent years, how could one choose among such pianists as
Horowitz, Rubinstein, Serkin, or Richter?

Much more rarely one figure stands above the rest. At some
point around 1960, people who listened to Jascha Heifetz
realized suddenly that they might never hear such violin
playing again. Or take chess: For years American chess
masters doggedly resisted Robert J. Fischer and criticized his
character. Then, when he had beaten all of them often
enough, they capitulated altogether and called him the best
in the world. On a different scale, for at least twenty years
after World War II, every photo-journalist in the country who
wished to be taken seriously had his camera shutters worked
on by one man in midtown Manhattan.

In the subtle and complex business of football linemaking,
one person is also accepted as the leader in his craft. Bob
Martin is the linemaker for the Union Plaza Sport and Horse
Book in Las Vegas, Nevada. No learned critics invent vocabu-
laries to describe his point spreads in leading newspapers and
magazines. You cannot refer to standard tables for his evalua-

tions of professional football games. But, for all that, he is accepted as the key man in his trade. The work he does at the beginning of every week during football season—work done independently and without obligation to anyone—shapes the flow of football betting over most of the United States.

I suppose a parallel might have been found in the work of Tex Grenet as pricemaker at the New York and Florida racetracks fifty years ago. But the differences between them are important. Grenet sold his numbers to any bookmaker. Martin works for one legal book, the Union Plaza. The results of his work spread around the country by a kind of instant osmosis, without his lifting a hand to help it. And Grenet's influence was meager compared to Martin's. After all, on autumn weekends tens of millions are watching football on television more or less in unison.

Martin was born in Brooklyn just after the end of World War I. He might thus have spanned the two major kinds of pricemaking and betting—in horse racing and team sports. Actually, in his early sixties, active, alert, and observant, he is completely attuned to modern sports betting. He never was interested in handicapping or betting on horse races. He recognizes the names of some of the outstanding horseplayers and respects their abilities, but he knows of them simply because he is an expert on the national betting markets. Thus, on hearing the name of an unusually able racing handicapper (an amateur, better known in another field), Martin was able to identify him—accurately—by a poker game he frequently played in.

Martin as a schoolboy went to Brooklyn Dodgers baseball games as often as he could and was betting on games before he was well into his teens. He attended New York University, studied journalism—and continued to learn about betting. He had his true apprenticeship when he came home from service in World War II. His campus then was a small area on the West Side of midtown Manhattan, bounded roughly by Madison Square Garden, Stillman's Gym, and the out-of-town newsstand at Times Square.

In common with others in the handful of elite who have made a great success by backing opinions, Martin obviously has much intelligence, but more important are his originality and capacity to work at an idea. He early observed that the fight cards in New York, aside from the feature bouts, were made up of young fighters coming to the big city from other parts of the country. He started buying several dozen out-of-town newspapers, to follow the fights in the other cities. When the youngsters arrived at a New York arena, Martin already had an advance line on them. He came to be reckoned so astute a judge of fighters that managers and promoters sought his advice.

In those days Martin bet on his own account and also booked bets. During a stay in Washington he was arrested. With Edward Bennett Williams (a distinguished defense attorney and owner of professional sports teams) as his counsel, he won his case in the U.S. Supreme Court. The police had been watching him so eagerly that they had driven a spikelike instrument through the outer wall of his home. The spike lodged in a heating duct and turned the entire house into a microphone. The later proceedings revealed that the police had been able to listen in on a conversation between Martin and a fight promoter—on the sidewalk, in front of the house.

Martin journeyed west to Las Vegas in the 1960s, just as the Nevada boom was getting under way and sports betting was surging upward. He still shows marks of an eastern background. A sophisticated man, he dresses comfortably but leaves high-heeled boots and cowboy hats to tourists (and showmen). In Las Vegas his talents and the national trends came together and meshed. He cannot be called the most important sports bettor (though he might still be tempted into a bet on occasion). Rather, he is the indispensable man for other sports bettors of high and low estate, wherever they may be.

By the early 1980s, Martin was concentrating mainly on football. According to a detailed *New York Times* survey of sports betting in January 1975, the baseball line originated somewhere in the East. The basketball line, with its murky background, remains something of a mystery. In any case, that sport is the least heavily bet of the three major team games.

According to Martin, "A line originates wherever someone is capable enough and confident enough to put up some numbers." And this is just what he himself does for the heavy action on football at the Union Plaza.

Except for the single Monday night game, a week's games have been played by Sunday evening. Martin immediately gets to work on the line for the coming week. By Monday he has a point spread on every game, ready for trial. A handful of professionals, knowledgeable bettors in Las Vegas, bet into the Union Plaza's line. From their reactions, Martin may sometimes, though not often, make some adjustments in the spread.

From Las Vegas, the line goes out across the country. It moves on its own, through no visible or official mechanism. It flows naturally and quietly—and fast, like water cutting its own channels. The sports pages of newspapers frequently carry a Las Vegas line or something based on it. Bookmakers everywhere cite the line to each other and to their customers, generally on the telephone, with one party or the other frequently in a phone booth. Late in the week, but still before the last flurry of wagering on Saturday and Sunday morning, heavy bets have started to go down. Signs of the action have flowed back to Las Vegas, sometimes resulting in more shifts in the points—again, more often than not, minor.

Football bets in the final round of action in Las Vegas itself may be very large. Smaller books may place a limit as low as $2,000 on single wagers. Books like the Union Plaza, Churchill Downs, and the Stardust may raise the limit as high as $10,000 or even $20,000 for individuals. A bet as high as $50,000 has been reported. At the higher limits, the books like to know whom they are dealing with. In such cases they are inclined (in the local phrase) to "play faces."

The regional variations in the line are generally small. This too may be a triumph of television: the bettors are looking simultaneously at the same major source of information, the games themselves. But here Bob Martin notes some important exceptions. When Oakland played Philadelphia in the January 1981 Super Bowl, the difference in spread varied scarcely half a point between the two coasts. On the other hand, a game pitting Denver against Houston might be much more strongly influenced by local feelings and might produce a difference of more than a point in the spread. It was this kind of local feeling that a betting commissioner like Jimmy Carroll of St. Louis went shopping, by phone, to find and exploit in the 1950s.

As for what goes into the making of a line, here Martin follows in the tradition of Admiral Rous and the leading handicappers from the nineteenth century on. A line would necessarily start with comparison of teams, with specific strengths and weaknesses paired, with the complicated evaluation of intertwined form and momentum, physical condition and injuries, and motivation. But selecting what may be a better team is really just a step on the way to deciding which team is likely to be favored. That in turn is another step toward the ultimate goal: finding the handicap—or point spread, in the case of football—that will split the action or bring out an equal volume of bets on either side.

In other words, doing the major part of his work in just a few hours after the last game is played on Sunday, Martin has to conjure out of his own head and feelings a sense of how millions of bettors will react to the following week's games. Politicians go through weeks of laborious poll-taking before launching campaigns. Martin has to launch a campaign weekly by dead reckoning. Linemaking anticipates what a poll would show and thus contains something very like a political quality. Martin, like Carroll and Tom Kyne and other betting commissioners before him, has followed election campaigns with more than passing interest.

In short, the linemaker is not at all the detached handicapper looking only at numbers and abstract factors. Basically, Martin is concerned with people. Understanding them may be the most important part of his talent, and this shows in his personality. He is accessible. He is widely known in the world of bettors. At lunchtime in Las Vegas, a slow procession stops by his table to exchange greetings and jokes or compliments.

He is cool, pleasant, and sometimes downright funny. And all this time, even while engaged in conversation, Martin is doing his job. In a word, he is keeping an eye not so much on the action as on the actors.

One crucial factor in the linemaker's weekly equations is knowing what the important bettors are doing. Martin points out that the opinion of a $1,000 bettor may be more significant than the action of a $10,000 or $20,000 bettor. In football betting particularly, the size of the bets can soar toward six numbers, and still the linemaker must ask himself: Who bet such amounts, and why?

In the imaginary Old West of the grade-B movie, the Kid rides into town, with his six-gun oiled and ready, to make his reputation. That Kid probably never existed, but his counterpart in modern sports betting assuredly does.

In the late 1970s one such young man came to Las Vegas with a bankroll and for one sensational season ran it up to huge proportions. Then he hit bad going and disappeared from sight. He was known only as Sneakers. Why Sneakers? Martin explained, "That's what he wore—tennis shoes." Then in the spring of 1981, at the end of the basketball playoffs, Sneakers reappeared. He had healed his wounds, acquired another betting roll, and now made his way along Las Vegas Boulevard, going from one sports book to another, sending a trail of rumors before him. As it happened, he backed the right team, the Boston Celtics. Was he on his way to another sensational year? Martin shrugged. His standards for successful players are stringent. They must bet substantially and win consistently, year after year, and have no other source of income. In Martin's opinion, only a small handful of players meet the requirements.

The measurement of Martin's own success is simpler. People he has never seen continue to use his numbers. They use them because week after week they split the action neatly enough to assure the bookie his vigorish in all but the hardest of times.

Betting on sports clearly became an important growth industry by the 1970s. In January 1975 *The New York Times* estimated that illegal sports bets totaled about $50 billion. (With the notable exception of about twenty legal books in Nevada, such betting is almost entirely illegal.) Numbers of that sort defy checking. Conceivably the $50 billion figure is too low. Much more probably, it overstates—as such numbers generally do. For example, Paul Screvane, making some estimates for the New York Off Track Betting system, calculated that if OTB could handle sports bets, it might add about $1 billion to its gross. Some simple (and not necessarily reliable) extrapolations from the OTB numbers suggest a national total for sports betting in the range of $20 billion to $30 billion. In either case, the number is large.

A firm number, for purposes of comparison, is the volume of legal betting on horses—which comes to about $7 billion. Football leads in sports betting, and with the help of television it attracts far more players than horse racing. On the other hand, its action is concentrated into about twenty weekends, from September to January, whereas racing goes on daily in one part of the country or another all year round.

However calculated, the sums involved in sports betting are high enough to guarantee that two groups have a strong interest in keeping the business going smoothly and without scandal. They are: (1) the bookies, and (2) the teams in the National Football League.

The NFL team owners, as a matter of writ, or official doctrine, ignore the bookmakers—or decry them (though some owners have been bookmakers themselves). Meanwhile, the league's security officers keep at their job of preventing fixes. And to do this they use the bookmakers as an early warning system. To profit from his bribes, a fixer would have to bet heavily on what he hoped was the sure winner. The bigger books are constantly on the alert for very large bets from strangers—or for $20,000 bets from $500 bettors. They have as much interest in the matter as the NFL itself. The bookies profit from a random result. If games were fixed, they would face the threat of ruin from betting coups. The customers in the business, the bettors themselves, buy information and pry for inside information—about injuries, or the chance that an athlete has been reached. The books keep an eye on such information too. But what they really want to know is: Who is betting, and how much?

With all this, the bookmaker has to run a relatively efficient operation. He also gets by on a rather low margin of profit. A vast and rounded number—like a supposed $50 billion volume of sports betting in 1975—can mislead. For example, in 1975 the American people also spent about $50 billion for foodstuffs. But any comparison would be specious. Money spent on food is done with and gone, except as it returns in the form of other commodities. Betting money is sometimes lost, but sometimes it comes back with interest. The total, whether it be $50 billion or $30 billion, or less or more, represents turnover, the sum of all betting transactions. Since sports betting does not use a pari-mutuel system, it is impossible to say exactly how much of the total stays in the hands of the bookies as vigorish. The number might vary somewhat from year to year—depending, for example, on the proportion of favorites that win, or on the efficiency of Bob Martin's line. But in the long run the bookmaker's margin cannot be far from a little less than 5 percent. The player bets $11 to win $10. Suppose he has a random result, betting randomly on either side of the spread. For every two bets, he wins one. The two bets cost $22. The winning bet pays him $21—his own stake plus a profit of $10. The bookmaker's profit is a single dollar on a base of $22—a margin of just a little more than 4½ percent. (In practice, the bettor usually lays his wager, on credit, on the phone. He and the book settle at agreed intervals. But he does not pay for the credit and the calculations come to the same result.)

Two conclusions follow from the bookmaker's low margin of profit:

1. Leading bookmakers may know, or know of, each other, but bookmaking remains a competitive business. In days before the point spread, even-money or pick-'em bets were laid at 6 to 5, yielding a bookie's profit, or vigorish, of more than 8 percent. From time to time, the bettors hear talk of a return to 6 to 5 in football. Yet the 11-to-10 odds remain, evidently as a result of competition.

2. The gross vigorish, even on an estimated $50 billion handle in sports betting, can come to no more than $2.3 billion. From what is known about bookmaking operations, at least a third must be allowed for costs, leaving a net of about $1.5 billion. This is scarcely a quarter of the profits that gambling allegedly contributed to organized crime, to finance other rackets, according to official doctrine in the days of the Kefauver and McClellan committees. And by every sign, the volume of illegal betting has increased greatly since the days of the committees. Considering that the bookmakers had to take their own livings (rather handsome ones, in some cases), and pay wages and commissions as well, out of the vig, the leftovers for organized crime must have been modest.

One other basic number about bookmaking still needs deflation. In some of the earlier estimates presented to Kefauver, the number of bookmakers was set at about fifteen thousand. As the hearings continued, that number, like so many others, grew with the zeal of the investigators. In 1961, a New York State crime commissioner told the McClellan Committee that in 1958 there was one bookmaker for every 2,500 in the population. The number was based on a limited area in New York state, and it included everyone who worked for a bookmaker in any capacity.

In 1974 the 1-to-2,500 ratio made its way into scholarly literature—pure and undiluted. Professor Michael E. Canes of the University of Rochester used the ratio in a paper delivered at a conference on gambling in Las Vegas. After granting that the number of bookmakers "is not known with accuracy," he said that "simple extrapolation of the 1958–59 figures [from central New York state] suggests there are something like 85,000 people in the United States today deriving income from bookmaking activities."

Now, the number of people a prosperous bookmaker might support could be large indeed. It could include runners, other employees, aged parents, cousins, and assorted deadbeats. That number is not only "not known with accuracy"—it is not known at all, nor could it be.

Numbers do cling stubbornly to life once they have been turned loose with an official stamp on them. But another problem here is one of definition. Who really is a bookmaker?

Suppose a friend calls me. He knows I am going to the racetrack. He asks me to make a bet for him, on Up Like Thunder, in the seventh race at Santa Anita. I decide Up Like Thunder is a stiff. I do not buy a ticket for my friend. If the horse happens to win, I owe my friend the amount his ticket would have paid. If my handicapping was right, and the horse loses, he owes me the amount of the bet I did not make. For a few minutes I was acting in the role of a bookie—but I was not one in any serious sense.

At a step up the ladder stands an elderly man called Hank whom I sometimes see at another track. He has owned horses; his son trains horses. Hank knows many trainers, and some of them, wanting to keep bets on their own horses a secret (to protect the odds), give him money to bet for them. A friend of mine referred to Hank as a bookie. Why? Because Hank has faith in his own opinion, and sometimes thinks the trainers' horses are a poor lot, and therefore pockets the money and hopes for the best. But realistically he cannot be called a bookie either. It seems to me a genuine bookmaker must spend all or most of his time at the job, must derive his livelihood from it, and must have at least some of his own money at risk. Thus defined, the bookie is a much rarer species than the 1-to-2,500 ratio suggests.

The New York Times survey of January 1975, citing police information, estimated that all of New York City had about two hundred full-fledged or major bookmaking offices. None of these was even remotely near the scale of the Erickson or Carroll offices of twenty-five years earlier. A typical office in the *Times* survey had four or five phones, three or four clerks, and handled from $3,000 to $50,000 a day. Higher up in the betting hierarchy, the layoff offices, handling perhaps $400,000 a week each, totaled perhaps thirty.

Reuter and Rubinstein's estimate for *The Public Interest* in 1978 is even lower. They suggest that "the very largest operations, of which there are perhaps five in New York, handle about $500,000 per week in bets." In general, Reuter and Rubinstein seem wary of inflated bookmaking numbers. As they remarked about an overall estimate of illegal betting, ". . . we suspect that the real failing of the estimate was that no one really cared precisely how it was developed, but only that it produce a large number."

It would appear that full-time, at-risk bookmakers probably can be numbered in the hundreds rather than the thousands in a major center like New York and in the thousands nationally. It seems unlikely that the grandest of totals could exceed ten thousand.

All this bears on the overall picture of bookmaking. What bookmaking looks like, at ground level, from the customer's point of view, of course, is a matter of nearly infinite variety. Where generalization seems impossible, one must revert to interviews, one at a time. This I have attempted to do. And, as it turns out, the working bookmakers—who face their customers, and possibly the law, directly—in spite of their human variety, do have much in common.

GUS: THE PAST REVISITED

In 1980, I found a ninety-year-old survivor of bookmaking in San Francisco in the 1930s and '40s. He was called Gus. He lived alone in a dusty apartment, a second-floor walk-up at the intersection of two alleys in the center of a working-class block—now largely Latino.

Gus waited for me in the doorway, then led me through an apartment too large for him. What furniture remained looked as if it had come from a nearby Goodwill. He may well have bought it new, but it would make its way in due course to Goodwill or St. Vincent de Paul. Gus was very thin, very frail. When he started in motion, it was not clear where he was headed, or where he would arrive. He said that in the last year his memory had faded. He seemed guileless, obliging. He was born in 1890 in Nevada and was brought to San Francisco as a child of six months. He no longer remembered the names of the schools he attended. He became a journeyman electrician, and he remembered clearly that he earned $5 a day— "Not much compared to now, hey?"

He had outlived two wives and had no children, only distant relatives. He made his own breakfast, he said, waving a spidery hand toward the kitchen where the burners of an electric stove looked rusty. Other meals? He went out, he said vaguely. On the back of one chair I saw a metal cane. A stool was placed squarely in front of a TV set; another stool rested beside the telephone. I saw no books, no papers, no decorations. Over his street clothes Gus wore a bathrobe. He muttered, "It's cold in here." We sat on a dusty sofa smelling faintly of cigar smoke, and Gus tried to remember when he had first learned something about gambling.

"My father was unlucky," Gus said, as if that were a fitting introduction to matters of chance. Unlucky three times: as a saloon keeper, as a brewmaster, and as a miner. Gus himself first went to work for a bookmaker (his name sounded like Bill Slotman) in the 1920s. By the 1930s he had a card room of his own, with a book in the back room, on a main street in San Francisco's Mission District. The bets he handled were almost entirely on horses. At first he paid prices based on his own line. By the 1940s he was paying track odds. No, he wasn't a good enough handicapper to make a line. He bought a line from Charlie Glynn (a handicapper remembered by old San Francisco horseplayers). Later he also bought a line from a man he called Apples. He admired Apples very much and averaged his line with Glynn's.

The people he remembered best were sheriffs and police captains. He ticked off their names on his fingers and recalled the restaurants to which he took them. He never went to jail.

By 1940, Gus had three clerks, "a man to figure tickets," and a janitor. He was firm on the amount of his handle: about $5,000 on a Saturday, maybe $3,000 or at most $4,000 on a weekday. Did he lay off bets? He shook his head slowly. Once he said, once, he stood to lose $30,000 on a horse. That time he laid off as much as he could, mainly with Bones Remer. But still he stood to lose $13,000. The horse won. "And then they took its number down," Gus said. I asked if Bones Remer knew much about handicapping. Gus looked at me coolly and said, "He didn't know a horse from a mule."

And then in 1946, Gus quit. He had nearly $100,000. His

second wife had some money too. He did not work seriously again, though sometimes he went to the races. The money, and his life, slowly ran out. He looked back on his active days as a bookmaker and the people he had known then and remarked, "I liked it. You know, it's a service business."

Every other bookmaker I spoke to used almost exactly those words.

LARRY MORSE: PAST INDEFINITE

Larry Morse met me at his office in a small town some fifty miles from San Francisco. (Morse is not the name he gave me, nor is the one he gave me his own name.) The office was tiny, containing two bare desks and little else. It gave absolutely no clue to the business conducted there. Morse's name appeared nowhere. He mumbled something about selling a wall-finishing material. Then he jumped up and proposed lunch at his club, the Odd Fellows. He insisted on taking me. I protested but agreed when it seemed clear that he would continue to insist. We went there in his car—a very large, very old, well-maintained Cadillac.

At the club he was greeted cordially by his brothers. He said to me, as we sat down, "They don't know I was a bookmaker. That's why I changed my name. You know I was one, don't you?" I said I thought that was why my friend, his nephew, had sent me to him.

Larry Morse when I saw him had just turned sixty-six. He said he had been receiving Social Security for a year. I wondered how he had accumulated quarters. He said nothing to clarify the matter. "The checks just started coming," he told me. "I was surprised. Listen. We better go to my apartment. It's a big place. I don't want to whisper."

The apartment was in a building only a few years old and rapidly running down. It looked, in fact, like an oversized motel. His living room was like a motel room. At the far end hung a large painting, possibly done by hand, with very heavy globs of oil paint. He waved a hand toward it: "That's an original," he said. "I had to pay something for that." The only other marks of an individual in the room were pieces of a jigsaw puzzle spread over an otherwise empty table, a jar full of Tootsie Rolls, and one copy each of *Playboy* and *Penthouse*.

Morse answered every question quickly, almost without thought and with every appearance of frankness, but he seldom explained anything. He grew up in Baltimore and came to Southern California as a youth, already a hustler. "I never worked for wages a day in my life," he said. He had hung around poolrooms when he was in school, and he claimed he was booking bets for dimes and quarters in his teens.

When I asked him how he got into bookmaking in Southern California, he replied quickly, "I didn't have any mob connections." Later he made passing reference to Mickey Cohen and, in a reflective way, said his greatest regret was not having accepted an offer from Bugsy Siegel. He said Siegel offered him a job in Las Vegas, as a pit boss. Conceivably he might have been good at the job: he was quick, affable, tough, and believed implicitly that the boob out there exists only to be fleeced.

Morse said he had five betting places more or less of his own. And yes, he said, he did have a handicapper. I had asked what kind of betting line he used, in connection with horses, to determine if his book was much out of balance. He was vague about who the handicapper was. I concluded that he most likely had bought a service—and was reluctant to say so. Actually, the problem of an unbalanced horse book bothered him very little. First of all, by the 1950s most of his action was in sports (baseball in particular), which in his own jargon he referred to as "events." And secondly, he always and unhesitatingly assumed that the bettor was wrong. He just wanted bets, he said: "Just stick it in the box."

Some of his best days, Morse said, were at Santa Anita. He enjoyed naming the Hollywood people for whom he ran bets. Why couldn't they bet for themselves? "They didn't want to attract attention," he said. He did not mention credit—the major reason for betting through a book at the track. In the end, he said, the Santa Anita management asked him to leave.

Much of Morse's business, naturally enough, was done on the phone, and he talked of elaborate codes used in calls to Las Vegas, or Shreveport, Louisiana, or Cincinnati. But his first call of the day, he said, was from a downtown connection: he would be told he had "a Sam Temple line," and that meant he was in the clear to book bets that day. Yes, he said, he was arrested several times but was let off with misdemeanors. And finally, one day in the 1960s, he said, he had a last call from his downtown source. He was told, "If you're busted again, no amount of help can fix it. It'll be a felony." And so, he said, he quit. And he smiled, and spread his hands out, and talked about the women he expected to see later in the afternoon.

I asked someone well informed in the ways of bookmaking about this part of Larry Morse's story. The man wrinkled his nose and said, "It doesn't sound right to me."

I talked again with the nephew who had sent me to Morse. The nephew said, "He didn't get warned off. He owed people a lot of money. He went broke booking bets on the Yankees in their good years. He always thought he could beat them." The nephew looked thoughtful, then said, "But I think he's booking bets today."

MR. A.: A TEACHER

Mr. A. lives with his wife and son in a midwestern city that has both a professional football team and a racetrack. His daughter, evidently very bright, won a scholarship to an Ivy League College. When she arrived there, she had to fill out a questionnaire, about which she wrote him: "I had 260 choices for your occupation, but I still had to use 'other' . . ."

The son is studying pre-law. Meanwhile he helps with collections for his father. Mr. A. quickly points out, "They can't bust him for that."

Asked how he would like his son for a partner, he replied, "I'd love it—and my wife wouldn't allow it." He went on solemnly, "But she's very supportive of myself. We've had twenty-six years of a great marriage. Maybe marriage and partnerships are unnatural—unnatural they should last. But my marriage has and so did one partnership."

Mr. A. went west from an eastern seaboard city when he was in his teens, finished high school where he now lives, did army time, went to a state college on the G.I. Bill, and became a schoolteacher.

"I did it just one year. I really didn't take to it at all."

What Mr. A. did take to was cardplaying. As a boy he played a game known in his neighborhood as banker-broker. It was a form of card matching, in the faro family. The boys believed chances were even, but pushes (ties) went to the banker. "I was the banker," Mr. A. said. "My vigorish was seven-point-seven percent."

In the army Mr. A. became an expert at hearts. He thinks he might even have been of world championship caliber at that game. At the Cavendish Club in New York after he came home from the army, he played it so successfully that he ran up a profit of more than $10,000. In one afternoon he won $1,400 at $1 a heart—and at that point the game was broken up. Mr. A. regards himself as a little below the very best in the major card games—like bridge, gin, pinochle, and klabiosh. But he thinks he would be a reasonable bet to win against anyone at a combination of ten games of cards. Poker he puts in a category by itself (it seems not to be one of his games), as a psychologic contest.

At bridge, he routinely became a life master, after learning the game in college, and has helped train international team members. After his year as a teacher and an attempt to sell insurance, he organized a bridge club. In one form or another he has been a professional gambler ever since.

A local ordinance barred gambling in clubs like Mr. A.'s. Police arrested him, padlocked the club, drove him out of business, and fined him. A bookmaker friend, whom he had met playing cards, invited Mr. A. to join him. He did, and has been moving up the ladder in the bookmaking profession ever since.

In his town, Mr. A. said, only a handful of bookmakers specialize in horse bets, and their clientele is dwindling. Most books handle only sports. A third group books both sports and horse bets; he is one of those. He does not regard himself as an expert handicapper in either field. He simply regards both with equal interest as a matter of sound business—and convenience for his customers. "After all," he said, "this is a service business."

When Mr. A. first set off on his own, he had a partner who

bankrolled him to the extent of $10,000. "I never needed to draw on it," he said. "I wonder sometimes if he really had the money."

As matters now stand, Mr. A. has about sixty sports bettors and about thirty horse bettors, with some overlap between the groups. He says he could make a living on the horse betting alone. He pays wages to three or four people whom he calls "the front." They receive phone calls and record bets. He has one and sometimes two others whom he calls "the back." Front and back connect by phone. The back has two phones; the number of one phone is known only to Mr. A., and that line is always open, the back relaying information on it to Mr. A.

"The only one who has much chance to stiff me," Mr. A. said, "is the back." To prevent this, he is careful in his selection of personnel and pays what are regarded as good wages for the area. The front makes from $250 to $300 a week, while the back gets from $400 to $500. Mr. A. pays bonuses for good work done in a good week.

In spite of his precautions, he was once hit for $17,000 by collusion between a back and an entertainment industry boss (whom he described as "a front for Mafia types"). The affair reached a point where threats were delivered against Mr. A.'s family. He became more and more angry as he told the story, recalling a visit he had had from a man with a gun in his belt. But then he added, "You see, we don't really have any muscle in this town."

Mr. A. said he knows police officials, including the head of what he called "administrative vice." He implied that he could expect no trouble as long as everything went smoothly, with no threats of muscle and with winners paid off promptly. He therefore schools his fronts in politeness. Some of the best have been women, both white and black, he said. I remarked that he seemed to be an equal opportunity employer. His own last arrest—for which he was fined and given probation—came early in his career when he was working as a front for the man who gave him his start.

Mr. A. will take no horse bet over $500—and a bet that large is rare. He pays track odds with limits—up to 30 to 1 on a $5 bet, only 15 to 1 on greater amounts. He handles place, show, exacta, and daily double bets, all with a variety of limits.

On professional football, Mr. A. will take bets of from $20 to $500. He is less interested in college football (he fears regional experts on the college game), still less interested in baseball, and downright dubious about basketball. Some of the other books he knows seem not to care what bets they take, and from whom. Mr. A. keeps a wary eye on who is betting and on the balance of his book. As for layoffs, he says he very seldom needs them but when he does he calls a friend he identifies as "Lou." He says of Lou only that he is an older and bigger bookmaker than he. Lou may not have a large number of customers, but Mr. A. thinks his vigorish comes to more than $1 million a year. Lou's scale of operations is so big that he changes his spread only half a point for every $100,000 of action supporting one team over another. Mr. A. assented to my thought that such a large operation suggested a number of people in the background.

At one point Mr. A. remarked that some of his neighbors think he is retired. I said that he did not look a proper age for retirement. What do his children tell people he does?

Mr. A. smiled. "I go by a bridge club at least some time every day," he said. "You see, I still am a bridge instructor."

G.F.: A MAN WITH A BAD COLD

G. F. and his wife live in a town in the Southwest. I met them when they were on vacation in my neighborhood. Such a meeting of course depends on an intermediary. That person was someone closely related to G.F. I have no way of knowing what G.F. was told about me, but whatever it was, it did not serve to put him at ease. Nor could I improve his outlook. He and his wife had stopped off in Las Vegas, where he had lost heavily at the crap tables. Somewhere along the way, he had caught a heavy cold. When I met him, he looked like an unhappy businessman at the end of an unrewarding vacation. His wife, too, hovered over us uneasily and unhappily, and only reluctantly went for a walk.

G.F. was indeed a businessman and still worked at his

original job—selling in a branch of the insurance industry. His business partner did not know that he also booked bets—mainly on football. G.F. was offered a chance to book bets by people he met at their country club.

In his area, he said, he observed three types of bookmakers. One type he called "independent." At the end of an involved explanation, it appeared that these people simply worked for themselves. The second type he called "connected." And the third was "both." He obviously was what he thought of as connected.

Actually, G.F. was what in some places would have been called a bookie's runner. That is, he was an agent for someone else—in his case what he called the Office. He implied that the Office in turn answered to people somewhere along the line who might meet the description of organized crime. "You might call it the Jewish Mafia," he said. I asked if they had an Italian opposition. He said, "No. Irish."

G.F. has no need of a bankroll. He takes, for himself, somewhat less than 50 percent of the winnings. The Office absorbs the losses. But G.F. has to make up the losses, from winnings, when he has those. At such times he is on "make up." He has no overhead except for the rental of a small apartment and a phone used for nothing else.

In spite of his connection, G.F. insists that no muscle is used for collections. And, he said, "I've been stiffed for serious money." Pressure is applied, though. G.F. said he might talk to a bettor's wife or even his boss.

In his area, G.F. thought, the person most likely to be busted is the independent. "He might be squealed on by a connected person," he explained.

By far the largest part of G.F.'s action is football. He books bets on other sports when people want him to. As for horse bets, he does not seek them out at all. He will book such a bet only to accommodate a regular customer. "It's a service business," he said. "You've got to be there when he wants you."

Though he does not seek horse bets, he regards them as the most profitable. He calls the horseplayers "the most degenerate." He is uneasy about horse betting for quite another reason: it gives him a sense of greater exposure, because he has to sit at the phone from noon until evening. (Mr. A. had spoken with some sympathy of the front who has to sit waiting for the possible "knock on the door.") With football bets, G.F. only has to sit at the phone for an hour, starting at 6:30 P.M. during the week, and on weekends from noon to 4:00 P.M.

No matter what the sport, G.F. does not think about layoffs or a balanced book. He said, "Most people think the book wins on vig. Actually, most times the book is in a position on a game." G.F. has an almost mystical faith in the proposition that the bettor is always wrong. He hinted heavily that the Office has *information*—that it knows what is going to happen. He does not think it is chance when a losing team catches up somewhat, late in the game, and beats the spread while losing the game.

Are any of his customers winning players? G.F. said he had fifty people betting football with him; and no, not one winner. Could he win over a whole season himself? Yes, he could: he would bet the opinion of the man who runs his Office.

His own favorite game? With friends at the country club, he said, it is poker. But he added, "I'm not very good at it." He is a large man, somewhat overweight. He said he really is not an expert on any sports and never played any of them well. He smiled ingratiatingly and said, "I'm not really very good at anything."

Quite suddenly, toward the end of our conversation, G.F. said: "You ought to know this: I've quit bookmaking. I only got into it because I used to gamble too much. I figured if I had to gamble I might as well be on the winning side. I've kicked the habit, and so I've quit."

A little less than a year after I met G.F., he was arrested. Apparently a friendly local plainclothesman, talking football with people in a saloon, said he needed a bookmaker. Someone gave him G.F.'s name and phone number. G.F. was fined and given probation.

DON

A friend introduced me to Don at a Southern California racetrack. They had played basketball against each other for major Catholic schools in the Midwest. My friend said Don was a legitimate star. These days Don looks more like a tight end than a former basketball player. Don himself pointed out that he was not tall enough (at three or four inches over six feet) or quite talented enough to play with the pros. He grinned and said, "Last year I coached a girl's team." He lives in an apartment near the beach and still plays on a nearby playground when he can.

For fifteen years after graduation from college, Don held selling jobs and played the horses. "I spent fifteen years being wrong," Don said. A friend, already an established bookmaker, took him on. Now Don is on his own. He has several employees working for him, on telephones—one in a nearby smaller town.

Football bets make up by far the largest part of his action, but he still spends most of his afternoons at racetracks. He likes being there, and he still has about twenty-five customers who bet horses (twice that number, betting larger sums, for football). It occurred to me that he might also want a record of having made winning horse bets—for income tax purposes. He is a cheerful man, and calm about the obvious risks of taking on new customers. But he knows some history, and mention of the Internal Revenue Service makes him uncomfortable.

Don moves up and down the grandstand stairways fast. He has fast reflexes and makes fast decisions. And so he makes limits for bets—and then varies them if he likes a situation. At the races, he likes to limit win bets to $200. But he adds that he has booked bets as large as $800. "If it's a steady customer," he said, "I want to keep him happy." He hates to book any bets on the first race, and he is lukewarm about daily-double bets.

Don said his limit on football bets is $500. But again he stretches the limit. He has taken bets as high as $2,000. "I can lay off as much as $10,000 if I have to," he said.

At first Don laid off bets frequently. He does it hardly at all now, he said. He, too, has faith in the power of the book to beat the bettor. When he does lay off, he goes to the man who set him up in business.

His football line comes from that man too, and he gets it from Las Vegas. Late in the week Don talks again with his former boss, to learn about late shifts in the flow of football betting money.

Other sports bets? "I'll take a baseball bet if a guy really wants." The fights? He shook his head. Basketball? He grinned and said, "I don't touch the stuff. How do you like the six horse in the next race? That one could really hurt me."

LIZZIE'S FRIEND: THE VOICE ON THE PHONE

One bookmaker, the youngest of the lot, I think of as Lizzie's Friend, or The Voice on the Phone. I have no name to attach to him, because I never knew his name and therefore have nothing to alter.

He called me one day and announced himself for what he was, a friend of Lizzie's. That made it necessary for me, first, to recall who Lizzie was. He waited patiently while I wasted words trying to prod my recollection. Lizzie was a friend, of a friend, who . . . and then, what Wolfgang Koehler called Gestalt!—the pattern snapped into focus. Someone had offered him up to me, as a live bookmaker on the hoof. Through a series of phone calls, beginning half a year before, Lizzie's Friend presented himself, from a pay phone, in a booth perhaps fifty miles away from my home.

He was an agreeable fellow. He said, "You're a friend of Lizzie's and she's a great girl. We'll set up a meet, okay?" We talked several more times on the phone, and never did quite set up the meet, and after a while it did not seem necessary.

I had long since learned the one thing about Lizzie's Friend that made him unique among the bookmakers I knew: he was a second-generation bookie. His father was a bookmaker. In his late teens, Lizzie's Friend ran bets to racetracks ninety or a hundred miles away from his home town. Come-back money? "What else?" Lizzie's Friend said.

Now Lizzie's Friend has the business himself. And yes, football is his meat and potatoes. And yes, he still has some of the horse bettors. And sometimes he sends come-back money down to the tracks. "I don't know what he knows, do I? But I don't want to turn down the bet. Gotta keep the client happy, right?"

None of the bookmakers I spoke to even remotely resembled any of the others. I have no way of knowing whom Lizzie's Friend resembles. Yet all shared points in common. The similarities were so striking that I doubt if multiplying the sample ten, or fifty, times over would change the results:

1. All regard themselves as businessmen, and they spoke, uniformly, of being in a service industry. They also take for granted that they are in a competitive business and must pay off promptly.
2. As an article of faith, all assume the bettor is wrong. As a result, they lay off bets far less often than government doctrine states. When they do lay off bets, they do so in their own town, and with someone with whom they have an established relationship.
3. Without exception they deny having recourse to violence.
4. All seem to be, to some degree, gamblers themselves. Again without exception, though, none regards himself as genuinely expert in the fields in which he books bets.
5. All obviously recognize the risk of accepting new customers—and much prefer good introductions. All but one faces the risk with fair equanimity. The one clearly the most anxious is the one who fairly soon afterward was arrested.

16

BACK TO BRITAIN

BRITAIN LED THE REST OF THE WORLD BY MORE THAN A century in Thoroughbred horse breeding. It led by at least half a century in development of bookmaking. And, though the lead narrows, it still shows the way in the blending of public and private interest in the control of betting.

As with monuments or ancient manuscripts, old forms of betting have been preserved. Somehow they manage to coexist with newer forms. Presumably this feat owes much to three hundred years of experience with the kind of political contrivance which makes social pressures bearable.

In practice, the British bettor has his choice of four systems of wagering, all interrelated, in a pattern of wonderful complexity. Three of the systems are legal.

At a racecourse, a visitor sees at once the very symbol of British gambling—the on-course bookmaker. The visitor cannot help it. If he even glances at the horses running, he looks over an array of bookies' pitches, set up in the open, between grandstands and the grassy racing strip. Should he look resolutely away, as if fearing bewitchment, he will still hear the bookmakers, though he may not understand them, as they shout the changing odds.

If the visitor is restless, or weary, and wanders to the rear of the stands, he will see a quieter, usually more neglected, betting apparatus. This is the Tote, operated by the Horse Race Totalisator Board. Though they invented almost everything connected with racing, the British have been willing to borrow on occasion. Thus, after a suitable number of years, their jockeys adapted an American riding style. They even borrowed some American training practices. And, finally, after a delay of some fifty years, they began to use Pierre Oller's totalizator, that product of French reason applied to betting. Official figures indicate that he Tote system has begun to come into its own. From appearances, it remains a neglected younger child at the racecourse. Because they arrived late on the scene, the Tote buildings are consigned to the rear: find them if you can. Otherwise, except for some minor differences in the bets permitted, they operate as American pari-mutuels do.

It is also perfectly possible that the bettor will never see a Thoroughbred (or a greyhound) run. Still he will almost certainly see the third, and largest, system of betting in operation, as he walks through London or any sizeable town. Strategically placed, it would appear every few blocks, are betting offices. These frequently bear the sign: TURF ACCOUNTANTS. At the time of the *Final Report* of the Royal Commission on Gambling in 1978, betting offices in Great Britain totaled 13,254. As the sheer weight of numbers suggests, the betting offices account for roughly 95 percent of all betting on horses, and for much other betting as well.

And finally, the fourth system of betting is the illegal one. After passage of the gambling law of 1853 the only forms of legal horse-race betting were (1) on-course, or (2) by credit, for the most part at relatively exclusive clubs. The rest of betting, and of course it was vast, was illegal. The present betting offices only became legal in 1962. For a few years after that, illegal bookmaking did not disappear, but it remained inactive. Then, with attempts to extract tax revenue from betting, the illegal bookies returned—in force, according to some opinion. The illegal bookie, of course, did not pay taxes. He could therefore cut into the betting market by offering somewhat better odds.

According to the Royal Commission's report: "The evidence about illegal betting is impossible to quantify because it is almost entirely anecdotal. We have heard from time to time of punters [bettors] who said they knew where to place a tax-free bet—it is, after all, only necessary for each punter to know and use one such place for the whole system to collapse. There are stories from betting office proprietors who send agents to take bets in factories, and then find that one day, like the dove from the Ark, they fail to return because they are prospering on their own."

The report also implies (again with commendable restraint and without grabbing wildly for numbers in the fashion of a Kefauver Committee report) that it is possible some betting office proprietors do part of their turf accounting—with trusted clients—in their heads. That is, if the bettor wagers £100, the proprietor might record only a £10 bet. The other £90 would be tax-free. It would pay off, if at all, at a higher, illegal rate.

It should be noted that large-scale casino gambling has also had a rebirth in Britain. As of 1976, 121 clubs had been licensed throughout the country and it was thought that about 300,000 Britons gambled in them. The high-stakes play was thought to take place largely among foreign visitors in a few London clubs.

Clearly, in the last decades of the nineteenth century the legal and illegal systems of betting existed side by side, with full knowledge of the police and most of the rest of the country. According to Wray Vamplew, in his *Social and Economic History of Horse Racing:* "One law for the rich, another for the poor is undoubtedly the theme of Britain's gambling legislation throughout most of the nineteenth and twentieth centuries."

The Royal Commission on Gambling, chaired by Lord Rothschild, summarized the effects of discriminatory law (before passage of the Betting and Gaming Act of 1960): "Bookmakers satisfied the wish of the ordinary British punter to stake a few shillings on a horse either by operating illegal betting offices or by employing runners to receive illegal cash bets in the street. Instead of suppressing betting among poorer people, the law produced resentment and attempts to corrupt the police, contempt for authority and a bookmaking trade operating outside the law, prey to protection rackets and gang violence."

At the racecourses, and on the breeding farms and downs of Newmarket, racing remained very much the affair of the landed upper classes. The list of stewards of the Jockey Club continued to bristle with titles of nobility and military ranks. The focus of betting in London shifted slightly after 1860, to such clubs as the Victoria. The bulk of punters who flocked to the races on holiday, most often by train, by now were working-class. As late as the 1970s the occupational group with the highest proportion of bettors remained skilled manual workers (57 percent, according to the Royal Commission on Gambling, closely followed by the semiskilled and ordinary labor).

The Victorian middle classes despised and feared gambling. In 1897, through the Anti-Gambling League, they nearly succeeded in driving the bookmakers off the racecourses too. The league found a judge who declared the on-course betting enclosures to be in violation of the law of 1853. The bookmakers, and the gentry whom they served, won their case on appeal. In 1899 the House of Lords reaffirmed the right to on-course betting. The wave of gambling reform in Britain, unlike the parallel movement in the United States, receded.

By 1900, though the law of gambling would be modified only slightly for the next sixty years, a series of small but effective changes began to even the chances between the favored few and the many who wanted to join the bettor's game. *Sporting Life* and other journals gradually improved the racing information that the average player could study before betting. (It will be recalled that in 1894, in the United States, the *Daily Racing Form* first appeared. From an American viewpoint, nothing as detailed and precise as the *Form*'s charts and past performances has yet been offered in Britain. Conceivably this lack favors the full-time, year-round student of form, who can invent his own system of recordkeeping.)

Also helpful to the 10-shilling bettor was the gradual standar-
dization of bookmakers' practices. Of greatest importance
was the adoption of a system of Starting Prices. This enabled
the bettor to demand a uniform—rather than a whimsical
—payoff should he be fortunate enough to win his bet from
the bookie. Starting Prices represented a consensus of prices
shown on bookmakers' boards at the racecourse at the moment the horses went off. By agreement near the turn of the
century two newspapermen (presumably more objective than
either bettors or bookmakers—backers or layers) determined
what the consensus was. Representatives of two sporting
papers still do that job.

World War I made the problems of racecourse gambling
seem trivial. Postwar tensions made the same problems more
acute. A historical sketch prepared by the Bookmakers' Protection Association notes: "The on-course racing scene prior
to the 1914–18 war was outwardly a peaceful one. Bookmakers were the sole medium for betting and although they paid
a certain tribute to a Midlands organisation for a form of
'protection' this was all very much under the surface and
incidents on the racecourse were extremely rare."

After the war, rival gangs fought for control of the lucrative
protection racket. The bookies found that a little protection
went a long way and too much of it resulted in overturned
stands, stolen cash, and severe beatings. The bookmakers,
with some help from punters, organized. It was, as the BPA
history put it, "a question of fighting fire with fire in the early
stages, and 'strongarm' men were recruited to defend the
members of the new Association. . . ."

At the start, the bookies had to do their own policing. The
sports editor of the London *Evening News*, J. M. Dick, remarked at a BPA banquet late in 1921: "It is a strange thing to
find the governing authorities of the sport saying 'We have no
authority to curb these people'. . . . You have had the privilege of stepping in where every other authority has failed."
The Jockey Club did send a letter of endorsement to the same
banquet. At the racecourse, newly organized flying squads of
the Metropolitan Police came rushing to the bookies' aid
when thugs set upon them. By 1926, according to the BPA

history, "there were no more incidents of gang warfare on the racecourses."

What also started in the 1920s—and never went away—was the idea that racecourse gambling should help pay for racing and could also be made to yield tax revenues for the state.

Winston Churchill, then chancellor of the exchequer, made the first tax proposal, in 1926. It failed to produce significant revenue. Its author, if not an economist, was something of a realist; he proclaimed the levy "a fiasco."

But the notion that betting should give back some sort of income to the racing industry, and perhaps to the state, had caught hold. It led to establishment of the Tote. The reasoning was: If bookmakers' profits proved too slippery to grab, why not try a pari-mutuel system, under government sponsorship? In such a system, the money lay in a visible pool, which could be tapped from the top. Advocates of the Tote could point to experience in New Zealand, to say nothing of the United States and, of course, France.

The parliamentary struggle on the question went on for two years. It produced, against the bill, the unlikely alliance of bookmakers and antigambling forces. The government was supported by the racing industry itself. In 1928, Parliament approved the act setting up the Tote system, under a statutory body appointed by the home secretary.

Having created a pari-mutuel alternative to bookmaker betting, Parliament sat back and let the new organization fend for itself. In a short history of the Tote, F. G. Reekie observed: "It would appear that in giving birth to the Tote the 1928 Parliament had a twinge of non-conformist conscience. It was willing to enter the betting business, but unwilling to risk any taxpayer's money in it. . . ."

The Tote had to finance itself. It began operations literally without a roof, under a tent. And hoodlums cut its telephone wires on its first day. It had the added disadvantage of beginning in the trough of a depression. With all that, it progressed steadily, if slowly. It trebled its action in the course of the 1930s, appearing particularly to the smaller bettors at the races.

Also in the 1930s came an upsurge of betting in the football pools. On the surface, since the players try to pick a number of winners, this would seem to parallel American sports betting. In actuality, the bettor gambles on chances involving more than a billion combinations, so that what he is joining is more like a lottery than a handicapper's game of opinion. The tickets are cheap, the payoffs enormous. But the popularity of the pools must have acted in effect as a political endorsement of gambling. By the 1970s, according to several independent surveys, more than a third of the adult British population was taking part in the pools every week.

In Britain, as in the United States, gambling boomed in the years following World War II. According to Richard Kaye, of Ladbrokes, "There was plenty of money about. The civilians were still earning well, while those still in uniform were coming home eager and willing to spend their gratuities. . . .

"The young bloods who had served during the war, and many not quite so young, were aching to have a tilt at the bookmakers . . ."

Included among the newcomers to racing were "the Black Market brigade eager to make their ill-gotten gains appear legitimate, paying their losses in bundles of pound notes and receiving their winnings in the form of respectable checques."

Out of the postwar flurry emerged the modern shape of British gambling, culminating in legal, cash betting off-course and in tax levies on wagers.

The postwar years also saw head-to-head competition between the bookmaking concerns that came to dominate betting. By the 1970s four firms had drawn away from the field. These were: Ladbrokes, the William Hill organization, Joe Corals, and Mecca. Of the more than thirteen thousand licensed betting offices in Great Britain in 1978, about three thousand were owned by the Big Four.

Among the four, Ladbrokes could claim priority. In *The Ladbrokes Story*, Richard Kaye traces its origins to the late nineteenth century. The actual founder, who picked the name for the firm, was Arthur Bendir. He ran the organization through most of the years from 1902 until his retirement in

1952. The original members of the firm had been commissioners for backers of horses (that is, large-scale bettors). They graduated into layers (bookmakers, in the American sense). Bendir devised what was then a novel system of using agents who collected a 40 percent fee on the profits from new business.

According to Kaye: "Among those who enjoyed the benefit of the commission terms that he offered were junior members of the aristocracy, particularly from the Brigade of Guards, who discreetly introduced their friends and relatives, thereby no doubt helping to pay for their mess bills and general entertainment."

Ladbrokes also engaged the "first lady bookmaker to appear on a racecourse," according to Kaye. She was Helen Vernet, ". . . born Helen Cunningham, of a noble Scottish family, in 1877. Her father died when she was thirteen and left her eight thousand pounds, which as soon as she was old enough she squandered on gambling."

Her health broke down and her doctor advised her to seek the open air. She found open air, and a career, at the racecourse. But, rather than making bets, she began taking them. She booked bets for her friends in the Members Enclosure. Professional bookmakers, understandably, protested. Ladbrokes persuaded her to represent them making book "on the rails."

The rails, it should be noted, act as a physical barrier between the Members Enclosure and the Tattersalls ring. "Tattersalls" in this sense has only a dim historical connection with the horse sellers and represents the several dozen on-course bookmakers' pitches fronting the main grandstand at the racecourse. Along the rails, bordering this area, some of the largest bookmakers take up their positions. They handle members' bets—some of them very large. They also serve as the racecourse terminus for "the blower." The blower is a system of remarkable efficiency which, within minutes, can convert the whole of Britain into a single market for a particular race. Far more is bet with the licensed offices than at the track. But in the offices payoff odds generally are at Starting Prices, locally determined by bets at the track. The blower, then, handles what an American would recognize both as layoff and come-back money. If bookmakers around the country are holding a large volume of bets on a horse that seems a possible winner, and the price on the horse threatens to be high, betting instructions over the blower may drive the price down. Or, some of the same money, under other circumstances, may seek a different price by being bet, behind the grandstand, with the Tote.

The on-course bettor, incidentally, receives the odds chalked on his individual bookmaker's board, at the moment of his wager. The dazzling hand signals of the tic tac men (which make the hand gestures of floor men in a stock exchange seem crude) serve to flash shifts in betting money back and forth from the rails to the Tattersalls ring, and as far away as to the Silver ring. This last props up class structure in racing and represents the cheaper seats and generally smaller bets.

William Hill, Ladbrokes's great rival for fifteen years after the end of the war, was born in Birmingham in 1903, one of eleven children of a coach painter. He started early as a bookmaker and made his way up, by way of provincial tracks, greyhound racing, football betting, and finally the rails on the major racecourses. His competitors regarded him as able, energetic, and fearless in backing his own opinions. He did not hesitate to take bets on heavily backed favorites—if he thought the horse could be beaten. The British bookmakers, like their American descendants, rarely enjoyed the quiet and comfort of a balanced, or round, book. The bookmaker demonstrated his skill, and profited greatly, with the right kind of unbalanced book. That is, he aimed at holding the greatest part of his action on horses he correctly gauged as losers, the least on the horses he feared. A member of a rival bookmaking firm said of Hill that he played with numbers like a great pianist at a keyboard. He was also, and necessarily, a keen judge of horses. He owned several himself, as early as the 1930s. He bred, among others, Nimbus, the 1949 Derby winner.

During the 1950s, Hill's firm and Ladbrokes vied for the record of handling—and sometimes paying off—the largest wagers. Both firms could demonstrate payoffs that, translated into dollars, would have run into six figures. They also competed for shares of the football betting action and carried their rivalry into the courts.

On at least one important occasion, though, William Hill made a mistake in business judgment. On the eve of legalization of betting offices, Hill was quoted as saying he thought only a third of the newly licensed offices would be open after a year. A spokesman for his firm said, "We regard the betting shop as legalising the street bookmaker and we are not in that business."

It was as if a Thoroughbred swung wide on the turn for home, allowing fresher horses to slip through on the inside and grab the lead. The racers that thus burst out of the pack were Joe Coral's firm, and somewhat later, Mecca. They did not waste time debating the future of the licensed betting office—or its connection with the illegal street bookmaker of the past. They set about taking leases on as many locations as they could. Within a few years, the Big Two had become the Big Four.

The William Hill organization remained strong. It, like the others of the Big Four, became publicly held. Ultimately, William Hill became part of Sears Holdings, Ltd., under Sir Charles Clore, and retained an estimated 15 percent of the betting market.

Joe Coral, according to Barry Campbell's *Horse Racing in Britain*, was brought to England in 1912 as an immigrant boy from Poland. By 1923 he was what amounted to a bookie's runner. By 1930 he had become a full-fledged bookmaker on his own. By 1960 he had built up a legal credit business but had evidently served his apprenticeship in street bookmaking. His firm, Joe Corals, thrived with the opening of a string of licensed betting offices. When they became a publicly held company in 1964, they were many times oversubscribed. In 1971 they absorbed the Mark Lane chain of betting shops, which had come up by a similar route. The merger produced a network of nearly 650 betting offices.

In the 1970s Joe Corals diversified. Their holdings included hotels, gambling casinos, a marina and yacht club, stadiums in two towns, and a number of restaurants. And the kinds of bets they booked were diversified as well.

At the end of the 1970s the Joe Corals offices gave the impression of a cheerful, aggressive organization prepared to accept your bet on any question of enough interest or substance to offer a fair chance of making a betting line. A knowledgeable American in late 1979, if he had a strong opinion which happened to be correct, stood to profit from a bet with Corals on the 1980 American presidential election. They made Edward Kennedy the favorite, laying 7 to 4 against him. They made Jimmy Carter 3 to 1, and offered what turned out to be a generous 10 to 3 against Ronald Reagan.

Ladbrokes, too, books bets on elections. It lost about £36,000 on the London municipal elections of 1967. Generally it gauged election results well. In the American presidential election of 1968, it made Richard Nixon the odds-on favorite, and so adjusted the odds that (in American terms) it split the action perfectly. It made a profit of £4,800 on Nixon's victory. Had Hubert Humphrey won, the profit would have been slightly under £4,300. Ladbrokes has maintained a tradition of betting on anything not involving suffering or loss of human life. It has offered price lines on beauty queen contestants, on candidates for Oxford Professor of Poetry—and on the number of days a lost golden eagle might stay away from its zoo.

Joe Corals, on its floodtide of expansion, took one further step. It bridged whatever gap may have remained between gambling and business. It set up a separate concern, called Coral Index Ltd., which simply permits a bet on whether security market indexes will go up or down. In the words of Corals Managing Director Christopher J. Hales: "With Coral Index, clients are invited to back their judgment, or their instinct, against the rise or fall of the Financial Times Ordinary Share Index in London, the Dow Jones Industrial Index in New York, and the Hang Seng Index in Hong Kong."

Coral Index sold £1 units, each unit representing the value of a one-point variation in the chosen index. The minimum stake on the London market was five units; on the New York and Hong Kong exchanges, two units. The maximum was a hundred times the minimum. The bookmaker's edge came from a spread between bid and asked prices.

It is difficult to think of any comparable way of speculating in a security market with so little capital needed and so great a chance of immediate gain or loss. A client's position, incidentally, is automatically closed out in thirty days. The bookmakers leave the long-range risks in the hands of more steady-gaited speculators, with heavy capitalization—the insurance companies.

The problem child of betting in the late 1920s, the Tote, also came of age in the 1970s. Increasing taxes, a temporary shutdown of racing because of a hoof-and-mouth epidemic, and spells of foul weather—on top of the Tote's built-in limitations—brought the Tote to the edge of bankruptcy for several years. Then the rules were changed to permit the Tote to compete on more nearly equal terms. The basic machinery still consisted of the pari-mutuels paying off at prices created by bettors themselves in racecourse pools. But now the Tote, working in consortium with a separate group, City Tote, was able to open a chain of more than 250 betting shops. It could offer, besides Tote prices, S.P. and Board prices as well. It could book bets on foreign races and on sports other than horse racing. And it was allowed to open twenty-nine credit offices as well.

For the whole of British bookmaking, the dramatic change of the early 1960s was permission to take bets in cash in licensed betting offices. But credit betting continued, and on a large scale, for all the firms. For a big concern like the William Hill organization, the betting shops deal mainly with cash bets. The central office handles the major credit accounts. Some of the credit customers may bet in the tens of thousands of pounds. Some of them, too, win more often than others. And, equally hazardous for the bookmaker, is the credit bettor, who, having lost, cannot pay.

On balance, of course, credit betting must prove profitable to the bookmakers—since they continue it. And not the least of its virtues is the view of betting practices it gives the central office. The bookmaker quickly comes to know who acts on impulse, who bets only on what might be called "insight"—in American terms, stable information. If a bettor seems to have sound information, his choice may make its way back from the central office to the rails, at the racecourse, with the instruction, "Watch out for this horse."

On the general matter of bookmakers' profits, the *Final Report* of the Royal Commission on Gambling said: "As Jane Austen might have said, it is a truth universally acknowledged that bookmakers make too much money. In fact, one might say that this opinion is held by everyone except bookmakers. In one form or another it found expression in most of the proposals we received for raising money from the proceeds of betting."

The Big Four cooperated fully in the examination of their own records. The report said it thought the accounts supplied them by the bookmakers were "no less trustworthy than those of firms of similar size in any other line of business."

For the period 1974 through 1976, the commission found that the gross profits of the Big Four averaged a little over 11 percent per year. Profits of the Tote during the same period averaged 10½ percent. Profits of a sample of 570 smaller betting offices were somewhat lower—a little over 10 percent.

What the bookmaker makes, the bettor loses—which accounts, of course, for the Royal Commission's "truth universally acknowledged." It is worth noting, though, that the Big Four's margin in the 1970s was very similar to what it is thought Oller and the French government abstracted from the first pari-mutuel pools in the 1870s. In the American sense, it is evidently an amount of vigorish the player can live with. It is substantially less than the amount of take-out from the mutuel pools at American tracks today. And, through the years, the British bookmakers' profits have still permitted at least a few successful bettors. Conversations in each of the leading firms confirmed this.

What has made a crucial difference in Britain is the betting levy. It is not at all clear how many consistent winners have survived a tax superimposed on the expected bookmaker's profit. And here of course is the point at which the illegal, and tax-free, bookmaker enters his wedge.

Overall, the public and private betting apparatus of Great Britain offers a remarkable exercise in adaptation through variety. It also demonstrates tolerance in the midst of strife. According to Geoffrey Hamlyn (in "Bookmakers and Backers," *The British Racehorse*, June 1978), before passage of the betting laws of the early 1960s, "there was a noisy clamor for a Tote Monopoly, and it was known that the Jockey Club Stewards of the day favoured the proposal."

It is hard to grasp the notion of any sort of monopoly being imposed on a betting structure so quirky, or downright baroque. I can imagine the bookmakers offering long odds against it. But whatever happens to gambling in the future, it would seem certain that the on-course bookies' tic tac men will be the last to go. Their hand signals are as much a timeless symbol as the changing of the guard at Buckingham Palace—and a good deal more skillful.

EPILOGUE:
NEVADA AND THE FUTURE
OF LEGAL GAMBLING

IN 1931, IN THE DEPTHS OF THE GREAT DEPRESSION, NE-vada legalized gambling statewide. At the time it had a population of 91,000, by far the sparsest of any of the forty-eight states, or less than one person to the square mile. What mining and ranching it had could scarcely support even that number.

Ultimately, of course, legalization of gambling transformed the state beyond anyone's imaginings. The full effects nationally, fifty years later, have yet to be measured. At the time, though, legal gambling seemed a modest affair.

In truth, gambling had scarcely ever been outlawed in Nevada's history. People who intended to gamble did gamble. They took for granted a certain amount of reform and moral uplift in their state's politics. To maintain a reasonable balance, they kept their games for the most part in back rooms—usually behind saloons. If a tourist went looking for such a game, he would not necessarily find one, unless he had local connections. Twice in the late 1920s, Bill Kyne of San Francisco organized Thoroughbred horse racing in Reno. He lost money both times and had to conclude that the gamblers of Reno (then Nevada's principal town) had firm notions of their own about what was worth a wager.

In 1913 the clergy and the women's organizations, with an assist from the Progressive movement, did pass a law banning gambling. It lasted just two years. What took its place was a law permitting games of cards in which the deal changed hands—enough of a loophole for most games popular locally. The law of 1931, backed by the governor, Fred Balzar, did not so much install gambling as push it into the open.

Liberalization, rather than mere legalization, of gambling, was one of several moves designed to bring people into Nevada. Otherwise, the state presented a bleak aspect to newcomers. One attraction offered to male travelers was more-or-less open prostitution. From time to time local authorities made gestures toward cleaning up the ancient calling—not by shutting down the brothels but by giving their residents medical inspections.

Probably the best known of Nevada's permissive laws had to do with divorce. By easy stages, over a period of twenty years, the legislature lowered the residence requirement for purposes of divorce. In the end, a stay of only six weeks was enough. This rule did not imply hostility toward matrimony. Nevada made marriages easy, too, particularly for visiting Californians.

Less publicized and of more lasting importance were Nevada's tax laws. By the middle of the 1920s, Nevadans paid scarcely any local or inheritance taxes. As a leftover of the wild days of mining speculation, Nevada also made it easy to incorporate any kind of business locally. California lawmakers repelled this lure to their business community by tightening their controls over corporations doing business within the state. Long after the gambling boom was under way the tax laws continued to have effects of their own. By the 1960s and '70s, shippers with goods destined ultimately for the West Coast warehoused them in Nevada to avoid inventory taxation.

But gambling drove the engine and caused everything else to expand. Three amateurs, who were also outsiders, took the first big step. A carnival operator, Raymond Smith, and his two sons came to Reno in the mid-1930s and opened a gambling club named Harold's after one of the sons. None of the three knew anything about gambling. They were also blessedly ignorant of the secretiveness afflicting the local gamblers. They advertised their club nationally, on highway billboards. And they catered to families, opened a museum as a sideline, and generally spread an atmosphere of wholesomeness. Another outsider, William Harrah, whose experience with gambling had been confined to bingo, took Nevada gambling still closer to mass markets of middle- and lower-middle-class visitors from California. He operated out of Reno, and at the same time opened an establishment on the shore of Lake Tahoe, as close to the California border as he could get. He organized tour buses, and demonstrated that gray-haired women in leisure clothes could tackle his gambling equipment all day (occasionally winning) and then return to ordinary life undebauched—and perhaps even refreshed.

The last giant step in Nevada gambling took place some four hundred miles south of Reno, in the tiny railroad town of Las Vegas. And this time what was said about organized crime (or the Syndicate, or the Mafia) was true. They were there. Las Vegas had its first spurt of growth during the building of the Hoover Dam. During and immediately after World War II, Las Vegas experienced a boom in resort hotels and casinos featuring star entertainers. A man named Benjamin Siegel built one such casino. When Siegel was murdered in 1947, it turned out that he was in fact Bugsy Siegel, that his police record was long, and his connections with high-ranking mobsters unquestionable. Later accounts suggested that he had been holding back money from his partners. It would be naïve to believe that no one in authority in Nevada knew about Bugsy Siegel's connections. His murder made them impossible to overlook. By the middle of the 1950s, Nevada gaming authorities were as self-conscious about criminal records as the horse racing industry. And meanwhile, Las Vegas had moved far ahead of Reno, the older center in the north. The huge and flashy Las Vegas casinos and hotels had found the right mix of gambling and entertainment. They tapped the largest entertainment market in the West, in Southern California, and became national tourist attractions as well.

By the 1950s gambling in both Reno and Las Vegas was firmly established. Its revenue, combined with tourist trade and the service industries it spawned, were the main supports of the state. And still people wondered if the pace could continue, if interest in gambling might wane. In fact, the boom was only getting under way. Through the 1960s and '70s, Nevada became the fastest growing state in the United States. By the 1980s, Las Vegas, a city with essentially no past, a dot on railroad maps just two generations before, approached a population of 400,000.

And Nevada as a whole, with no plan or expectation of doing so, had taken its place as a social experiment on a grand scale. For a century or more, reformers had talked of gambling as addictive, as a destroyer of character, as a danger above all to the young. In Nevada people gambled everywhere. Gambling was inescapable, as much a part of the fabric of life as the automobile and telephone in the rest of the country. For that matter, Nevada's entertainment was gaudy, and whorehouses were handy in towns which exercised local option to have them. What, then, had happened to the quality of life in a gambling state?

In June 1974 a number of scholars met in Las Vegas to hold a conference on the theme, "Gambling and Society." Some presented technical papers in probability mathematics. Some discussed purely business aspects of the gambling industry. Some repeated familiar arguments about gambling as addictive and soul destroying. And some people at the meeting took new positions. Thus Felicia Campbell, from the University of Nevada at Las Vegas, pointed out that the psychologists who set forth the classic positions (gamblers want to lose, they want to punish themselves), really knew very little about gambling. Campbell commented that in Las Vegas, where they were meeting, "gambling is simply a fact of existence." The crime rate in the town, she said, "is about average for America, and one may walk alone at night without fear."

In prisons, Campbell said, permission to gamble is downright humane. A former inmate told Campbell that "being allowed to gamble was all that saved his sanity during his years of incarceration."

Campbell also conducted interviews with elderly gamblers in smaller downtown Las Vegas casinos. For them, she found, gambling restored activity to barren lives. An elderly woman from Kansas, living on a small pension, told Campbell she refused her daughter's invitation to live with her: "I didn't want to be no built-in babysitter. I raised my kids. I kept my house. Now I want something different."

The older people whom Campbell interviewed play steadily. As a matter of course, overall, they must lose. None loses enough to suffer harm. The occasional big wins are what they remember. They seem worth the price.

Among younger players, Campbell found some for whom gambling supplies the only dream, or slim chance to advance, in otherwise dull and unpleasant lives. A cleaning woman regarded gambling as a straightforward transaction: when she wins, she is buying herself time off—time in which she can rest, relax, and feel in command of her life.

All of Campbell's observations, incidentally, have long been familiar to people at racetracks. The approach may be called anecdotal, and it is. But anecdotes—based on careful reporting—are more valuable than moral assumptions. In any case, a larger question remains unanswered: What is the effect of gambling on everyone else, on the nongamblers, young and old?

Perhaps Las Vegas is in a class of its own. Nothing seen there proves anything about other places. Reno, though, has a history and a wide range of business.

It is common to begin comparisons among countries by looking at health records. But it is hard to match health numbers for single towns. They have different mixes of age and ethnic groups. They have different climates, face different occupational hazards. Still, it should be said that county health officials in Reno believe they do cope with more than their share of health problems. But these problems relate mainly to an oversized group of transients and drifters. Reno, sited at an entrance to the West Coast, has known such problems since long before legal gambling.

Reno in 1975 had an estimated population of 78,000. Among towns of similar size, Reno's crime statistics were neither very good nor very bad. Reno in 1975 had fewer serious crimes (per 100,000 population) than Muncie, Indiana, or Kalamazoo, Michigan, or Lawton, Oklahoma. It had almost exactly the same rate as Santa Clara, California. It had higher rates than Dearborn Heights, Michigan, or Clifton, New Jersey. The mix of violent crimes and crimes against property was about the same as in the towns of similar size. Between 1970 and 1974 crime rates were going up in Reno —but so were rates in the other towns. And the rates of increase were similar. Overall, the law-abiding in the gambling town of Reno had neither much more nor much less to worry about than their neighbors in towns of that size in other parts of the country.

And finally, what of the young who grow up in a place where gambling is commonplace? From whatever can be learned through school records, it appears that the casinos have no effect—certainly no bad effect—on the young. According to a senior administrator in the Reno schools, the system there is markedly conservative. Reno parents want it that way. It seems almost as if they wish to prove that gaming presents no problem.

Comprehensive achievement scores have been climbing in Reno, and are high compared with other places. Parents looking for innovative programs in math and reading might be disappointed. But almost any parents would be pleased about the seven National Merit Scholarships awarded in one Reno high school in one year. True, that high school drew on a favored population; but for the district as a whole, twelve Merit Scholarships were awarded—high by any standard. To be sure, some problems are looming ahead for the schools. As Reno's industries grow, demand for unskilled workers increases. Children of those workers are having language problems—problems related to all kinds of social pressure and disadvantage, but hardly to gambling.

The casinos in Reno are largely concentrated within the compass of a few blocks. It is possible to walk away from them in five or ten minutes. And then the visitor sees only an ordinary town of medium size, grown prosperous and bustling, with many tax advantages and a thriving tourist traffic. This is also how the residents see their own town.

Clearly gambling has profoundly affected Reno and Nevada as a whole. But perhaps the effects have been just as important for the rest of the country. Some states are looking, enviously, at the wealth created in a place once known best for wasteland. And the most startling change may be in thinking about gambling. Increasingly, gambling in itself seems to be accepted as neither very good nor very bad, but merely as a common part of the human condition. In fact, comparison of Nevada with other states suggests that the worst things about gambling have been associated with its suppression.

Let reformers everywhere take comfort. Nevada's history will not repeat itself in most of the rest of the country. Few other places could thus seek to overwhelm themselves with visitors. But let Nevada's neighbors also prepare for more debate on gambling. The last twenty years have demonstrated, at the least, that public policy on the matter has been remarkably dim.

It could be argued that any public policy, if effective at all, must offend someone. But it is cheap-jack cynicism to say further that all policy is therefore bad. Some policies have certainly done good. As a simple case, it seems provable that we ought to have clean drinking water—though people with privies on riverbanks, or some managers of chemical plants, might not always agree.

With gaming policy the problem is not simply disagreement but ineffectiveness. The congressional committees of the 1950s and '60s used fake statistics to support unworkable programs. In spite of ringing declarations by Kefauver, McClellan, and Bobby Kennedy, it appears that little if any money was diverted from the underworld as a result of their efforts. In fact, both casino and sports gambling increased greatly in the face of congressional disapproval. And if the moral fiber of the country has rotted, other causes must be sought.

Perhaps one difficulty comes from trying to stuff too much into a single package of gambling policy. It seems to me gambling presents three rather different questions of public interest, concerning (1) casinos, (2) pari-mutuel betting, and (3) sports betting.

CASINOS

No doubt bringing a new casino into a town, any town, would present problems. So would building a new steelmill, or semiconductor plant, or staging a sports car rally. Would presence of the casino (or mill, or plant, or rally) violate existing law? What about zoning? Does the town have enough hotel rooms and restaurant seats? Can parking be handled? Who gains? Who loses? And in the end, who has more political leverage—the gainers or losers? All these seem local matters. Each state house has already acted on them, one way or another, though some positions may change. Surely the federal government need not be concerned further.

Left on its own, a casino will succeed or fail simply as a business venture. Aside from any food and entertainment that the casino may sell, it profits from the house edge in a series of games of chance (not opinion). How much it profits works out from the interplay of costs of operation, rules of the game (including how slot machines are set), and how the visitor or player reacts to his losses. None of these three points seems to require new policy, beyond existing law.

As for costs of operation, they offer a standard textbook case in business administration.

The rules of the game are strongly affected by competition. Billboard ads in the northern part of California in 1981 announced that some Reno and Lake Tahoe casinos had "re-set"their slots. They offered customers larger, and more frequent, payoffs. Customers might have concluded that previous payoffs had been stingy. In other casino games, too, management can pare its edge slightly—and as publicly as possible—to woo patrons from the competition.

How the individual bears his gain or loss is the capstone of the whole arrangement—and, again, far beyond the reach of law or righteousness. On the surface, casino play seems irrational. The house margin is fairly low. It is probably somewhat over 5 percent overall—varying greatly with the mix of games offered and the kinds of players. On a given day, with a small house edge, the player may nearly as easily be a winner as a loser. The house rewards the player with diversion, or excitement, for accepting the margin against him. In the long run, though, even a small house edge grinds away inexorably. But, as has been seen, a form of logic supports some players even in the long run. They absorb small losses, without serious damage. Occasionally they score, they win big—beyond the piddling amounts they can save against everyday pressures. And they have done it, excitingly, by beating a machine—instead of hoarding a few dollars at a time, depriving themselves daily. The mathematics of this process are described somewhat by the Friedman-Savage curve. They are illustrated more graphically in Felicia Campbell's interviews with elderly and working-class gamblers in casinos.

The casino game of blackjack presents something of a special case. The player who masters basic strategy can reduce the house edge against him to scarcely half a percentage point. This is the practical equivalent of playing the house even-up—a great waste of time and expense for a casino that provides floor space, cards and tables, and pays the dealers' wages. Worse (for the casino), is the player who can master card counting and varies his bets at strategic moments. By dogged, grueling work, he can actually show a small percentage of profit. Some casinos presumably bar counters from their tables, if they detect them. And here the casinos may have created a policy problem for themselves. Conceivably, the right of a player to use skill against a casino—or conversely, the right of a casino to force him to rely solely on chance—may have to be tested in the courts. In its first stages at least, controversy over card counting in blackjack may already have had two effects: (1) an increase in sales of books on how to win at blackjack, and (2) an increase in the number of players (many of them unskilled) crowding the blackjack tables.

PARI-MUTUELS

Pari-mutuels, with government supervision, take bets on jai alai games, on dog races, on quarterhorses and buggy races, and on such specialized breeds of horses as Appaloosas and Arabians. In spite of all this competition, backing opinions on Thoroughbred horse races remains overwhelmingly, as it has been from the start, the principal business of the pari-mutuel system.

But things do change. Congressional committees used to assume, as a problem, a vast amount of betting, outside the pari-mutuel system, with illegal books. Even funneling that money back to the tax collectors at the racetrack did not make the investigators happy—not if the funneling was done by bookmakers in the form of come-back money. Did they wish off-track betting eliminated altogether? From one committee hearing to the next, nothing seemed to happen. And then it turned out that the players had done it on their own, by moving over to sports betting.

Now the problem turns out to be a wrong shoe on another foot. Some tracks themselves are looking for increased off-track action. Since the mid-1970s Thoroughbred horse racing has teetered on the edge of serious decline. The handle (or total money bet through the machines) continued to move up a little. But it does not move as fast as inflation. Attendance, the crux of the matter, has fallen a bit nationally, seriously in some places. Experienced racetrackers harbor a suspicion that their ranks are thinning faster than they can be replaced with eager new faces at the paddock rails and the mutuel windows. This newer problem mainly concerns the racing industry—including horse owners, track managements, and such specialists as riders and trainers. But state and local governments also have a stake in the taxes they pluck from the mutuel pools.

One way out is to bring the racetrack to the players, lawfully. The name of this approach is OTB, for Off Track Betting, and it has been tried in New York City. Polls there as early as 1963 showed 3-to-1 public support for OTB. The New York OTB, as a chain of official betting shops, is now firmly established. It left a number of racing people unhappy. Industry representatives first resisted OTB. Then they capitulated in a deal that gave them a meager cut from the OTB pool while hurting track attendance.

But some racing people still see OTB, sensibly handled, as the hope for the future. Louis E. Wolfson owns the Harbor View Farm in Florida. Among other fine horses, he had Affirmed, twice named Horse of the Year. In a 1980 pamphlet Wolfson wrote: "Also essential to the survival of our industry in the 1980's for long-range financial stability, is a nationwide off-track betting operation, providing for a fair and equitable distribution of revenue for the various governments, the horsemen, and the tracks. Live simulcasting will bring the races to the people; and, in due time, the people will flock to the race tracks, just as they did in Japan . . ."

In a modern building in New Haven, Connecticut, connected by microwave television with the New York racetracks, an experiment in OTB has succeeded. Aqueduct and Belmont races are shown on a movie-sized screen, in a clean and attractive cross between a theater and an oversized betting parlor. The theater, called Teletrack, is close to a freeway, with adequate parking. It has 2,200 seats and forty betting windows. Teletrack also handles harness racing at night. Bets made there are combined in a single statewide pool with betting done at smaller, conventional OTB offices throughout Connecticut. State officials, the New York tracks, horsemen, and bettors all seem pleased with the experiment.

At western tracks, OTB is moving more slowly. Because attendance has not yet fallen, some track owners remain as concerned as ever with sale of hot dogs and admission tickets. But even there, younger, more aggressive track managers want to develop the OTB concept. Clifford C. Goodrich, when he was general manager of Golden Gate Fields in 1980, suggested that the two major tracks in northern California might benefit from sharing closed-circuit television for off-track betting. This network could gradually be enlarged to take in towns from 100 to 150 miles outside the San Francisco Bay Area. Goodrich suggested, plausibly, that such a network would build interest in racing. It might then substantially increase the betting handle, with larger shares for everyone: for state and local governments, for the horsemen's purse money, and for the tracks. But Goodrich found no takers and later moved to another track.

In 1981 the OTB concept did go west, for a few major stakes races. Longacres, in Washington, and Centennial in Colorado, for example, showed the Kentucky Derby on television screens and took bets on the Derby through their own mutuel machines. They made their own pools and paid off at their own odds, by arrangement with Churchill Downs in Kentucky.

Out of the OTB discussion emerges another idea—which suggests that regressive taxation might be reversed. If the pari-mutuel take-out is reduced (if the percentages for taxes, purse money, and overhead are pared slightly), winning bettors will be paid off at higher odds. Some small but significant number of players will be more successful.

Will the great chance of success bring out more bettors? Will they so increase the amount of action that everyone profits, even with reduced percentages in the take-out? At the beginning of the 1980s only the New York tracks and a few radical thinkers elsewhere had begun to examine the idea that less might equal more.

SPORTS BETTING

The bulk of sports betting, outside Nevada, also remains outside the law. No one has recently called for a crusade to abolish sports betting. Neither has anyone proposed a reasonable and legal way to handle the many millions wagered on a football game. A New York OTB official proposed that football betting, with the spread, could be handled through the mutuels. If the spread fails to split the action in a mutuel pool exactly down the middle (Bob Martin's finest product could hardly achieve such a miracle), then winning bettors get more if one team wins, less if the other wins. Very sharp players might look for overlays: teams that have a better chance of winning than the money suggests. In general, though, the New York OTB proposal stirred up no waves of enthusiasm.

Is it possible to imagine football betting turned over, by law, to a nationwide network of betting parlors? Conceivably. But the problem would come back to the matter of taxation. As pointed out earlier, the bookie's 4½ percent vigorish represents very efficient management. It is hard to believe that official betting shops could do better, if as well. Granting of licenses would also, almost certainly, go along with a tax bite on the handle. Presumably the greater convenience of licensed betting shops might make some small tax tolerable. But how small is tolerable? If state and local taxes came to as much as 3 or 4 percent, the bite on the players' winnings would be painful. And the result would be inevitable. The illegal channels for sports betting are already established. Bettors would return en masse to bookmakers who offered a higher rate of return.

Veterans of law enforcement (for example, Captain Frederick W. Egen, in his 1952 book, *Plainclothesman*) have pointed out that ignoring a problem is one way of handling it. It may be that football betting, as it stood in the early 1980s, was such a case. Certainly no existing law has made the slightest dent in the volume of sports betting. If any other is to be tried, let it at least reckon with the stubbornness of the human spirit.

At bottom, beneath any question of control of gambling, lies the greater question: Do we seek lives without risk? If such a life were possible, the question certainly would be worth examining. One could vote aye or nay, according to philosophy or disposition. But the least consideration should make it obvious that the riskless life does not exist. Each life, in fact, is a tissue of implausibilities. Every event in it can only be predicted as a matter of probability. An event (sunrise? a falling leaf?) may approach the same certainty as the absence of life. But it will never, so long as life continues, achieve it.

If such is the case, then the search through the labyrinth of law and regulation for a way to stop risk-taking runs counter to the currents of life. It stultifies. It creates rules that work properly only in the minds of the rulemakers. Worse, it creates laws that bring down the idea of law.

Of course law is needed: to mediate reconcilable difference, to prevent some from doing harm to others, to protect people in the exercise of those functions that give meaning to a life. But none of this applies to laws against gambling. Society already approves a risky plunge into the wheat pit or the stock exchange. Is that because much power accrues to successful gambling on the great exchanges? What can be the virtue in antigambling laws which oppose those games that offer relief from the drabness of some lives? Those who break such laws are in no sense heroes; but the net effect of their punishment is hypocrisy on a grand scale.

Let the law pick targets worthy of its might.

Allow the policeman to turn quietly away from two people with wagers before them on the table. Leave the gamblers alone to find out whose opinion is better, or simply whose luck, for the moment, seems most charged with magic.

A SELECTIVE BIBLIOGRAPHY
(including all works mentioned or quoted from in the text)

THE LITERATURE CONCERNING GAMBLING IS LARGE AND of mixed value and reliability. Sources depended on in this study include:

I. GOVERNMENT HEARINGS, U.S. AND GREAT BRITAIN:

Hearings and Reports, Special Senate Committee to Investigate Organized Crime in Interstate Commerce (Kefauver Committee), 82nd Congress, 1st Session, 1951.

Hearings, Subcommittee on Interstate Gambling of Senate Commerce Committee (McFarland Committee), 81st Congress, 2nd Session, 1950.

Hearings, Permanent Subcommittee on Investigations of Senate Committee on Government Operations (McClellan Committee), 87th Congress, 1st Session, 1961.

Hearings of Committee "to Inquire into the Laws Respecting Gaming," House of Commons and House of Lords, 1844.

II. GOVERNMENT SPONSORED REPORTS AND PUBLICATIONS:

Blakey, G. Robert (supervisor of study for Law Enforcement Assistance Administration, U.S. Department of Justice). *The Development of the Law of Gambling: 1779–1976*, Washington, DC: U.S. Government Printing Office, 1977.

Cornish, D. B. *Gambling: A Review of the Literature and Its Implica-*

tions for Policy and Research. (British) Home Office Research Study No. 42, London: Her Majesty's Stationery Office, 1978.

Fowler, Floyd J. Jr.; Mangione, Thomas W.; and Pratter, Frederick E. (for the U.S. Justice Department). *Gambling Law Enforcement in Major American Cities,* Washington, DC: 1978.

Royal Commission on Gambling. *Final Report.* (2 vols.), London: Her Majesty's Stationery Office (Cmnd. 7200), 1978.

U.S. Commission on Review of the National Policy toward Gambling. *Final Report.* 1976.

III. GAMBLING (GENERAL) AND LAW ENFORCEMENT

Caillois, Roger. *Man, Play and Games.* Translated by Meyer Barash. New York: Schocken Books, 1979.

Cardan, G. (Cardano). *The Book of My Life.* Translated by Jean Stoner, New York: Dover, 1962.

Chaftez, Henry. *Play the Devil.* New York: Clarkson N. Potter, 1960.

Cressey, Donald R. *Criminal Organization: Its Elementary Forms.* New York: Harper and Row, 1972.

Cressey, Donald R. *Theft of the Nation.* New York: Harper and Row, 1969.

David, F.N. *Games, Gods and Gambling.* New York: Hafner, 1962.

Eadington, William R., ed. *Gambling and Society: Interdisciplinary Studies on the Subject of Gambling.* Springfield, IL: Charles C. Thomas, 1976.

Egen, Frederick W. *Plainclothesman: A Handbook of Vice and Gambling Investigation.* New York: Greenberg, 1952.

Figgis, E. Lenox. *Gamblers Handbook.* Northbrook, IL: Domus Books, 1976.

Herman, Robert D. *Gamblers and Gambling: Motives, Institutions and Controls.* Lexington, MA: Lexington Books, 1976.

King, Rufus. *Gambling and Organized Crime.* Washington, DC: Public Affairs Press, 1969.

Longstreet, Stephen. *Win or Lose.* Indianapolis: Bobbs-Merrill, 1977.

Newman, Otto. *Gambling: Hazard and Reward.* London: The Athlone Press, 1972.

Skolnick, Jerome H. *House of Cards: Legalization and Control of Casino Gambling.* Boston: Little, Brown, 1978.

Turner, Wallace. *Gambler's Money: The New Force in American Life.* Boston: Houghton Mifflin, 1965.

Weinstein, David, and Deitch, Lillian. *The Impact of Legalized Gambling.* New York: Praeger, 1974.

Wykes, Alan. *The Complete Illustrated Guide to Gambling.* New York: Doubleday, 1964.

IV. OTHER WORKS CITED OR CONSULTED

Alexander, David. *A Sound of Horses.* Indianapolis: Bobbs-Merrill, 1966.

Anderson, Annelise Graebner. *The Business of Organized Crime.* Stanford, CA: Hoover Institute Press, 1979.

Ashton, John. *The Dawn of the XIXth Century in England.* London: T. Fisher Unwin, 1906.

Ashton, John. *The History of Gambling in England.* Reprint. Montclair, NJ: Patterson Smith, 1969.

Asinof, Eliot. *Eight Men Out.* New York: Holt, Rinehart and Winston, 1963.

Baruch, Bernard M. *Baruch.* 2 vols. New York: Holt, Rinehart and Winston, 1960.

Batchelor, Denzil. *The Turf of Old.* London: H. F. and G. Witherby, 1951.

Betts, Toney. *Across the Board.* New York: Crown, 1956.

Bird, T. H. *Admiral Rous and the English Turf: 1795–1877.* London: Putnam, 1939.

Blyth, Henry. *Hell and Hazard.* Chicago: Henry Regnery, 1970.

Bourke, Algernon. *History of White's (With the Betting Book from 1743 to 1878).* London: 1892.

Bowmar, Dan M. *Giants of the Turf.* Lexington, KY: The Blood Horse, 1960.

Brashler, William. *The Don: The Life and Death of Sam Giancana.* New York: Ballantine Books, 1977.

Buck, Fred S. *Horse Race Betting.* New York: Arco, 1962.

Campbell, Barry. *Horse Racing in Britain.* London: Michael Joseph, 1977.

Carswell, John. *The South Sea Bubble.* Stanford, CA: Stanford University Press, 1960.

Chandler, David Leon. *Brothers in Blood: The Rise of the Criminal Brotherhoods.* New York: E.P. Dutton, 1975.

Cohen, John. *Chance, Skill and Luck.* New York: Penguin Books, 1960.

Comstock, Anthony. "Pool Rooms and Pool Selling," *North American Review,* November 1893.

Cook, Fred. *A Two Dollar Bet Means Murder.* New York: Dial, 1961.

Dash, Samuel (with Richard F. Schwartz and Robert E. Knowlton). *The Eavesdroppers.* New York: Da Capo Press, 1971.

Davis, Patricia T. *End of the Line: Alexander J. Cassatt and the Pennsylvania Railroad.* New York: Neale Watson Academic Publications, 1978.

Deane, Phyllis and Cole, W.A. *British Economic Growth, 1688–1959:*

Trends and Structure. Cambridge: Cambridge University Press, 1969.

DeArment, Robert K. *Bat Masterson: The Man and the Legend.* Norman, OK: University of Oklahoma Press, 1979.

Demaret, Kent. *Baptists and Bangtails.* Houston: Cordovan Press, 1973.

Demaris, Ovid. *The Director: An Oral Biography of J. Edgar Hoover.* New York: Harper's Magazine Press, 1975.

Dickens, Charles. *The Pickwick Papers.* New York: New American Library, 1964.

Disraeli, Benjamin. *Lord George Bentinck: A Political Biography.* New York: E.P. Dutton, 1905.

Dizikes, John. *Sportsmen and Gamesmen.* Boston: Houghton Mifflin, 1981.

Egan, Pierce. *Boxiana; Or, Sketches of Ancient and Modern Pugilism.* Selection edited by John Ford. London: The Folio Society, 1976.

Firth, Raymond and Yamey, B.S., eds. *Capital, Saving and Credit in Peasant Societies.* Chicago: Aldine Co., 1964.

Flynn, John T. "Smart Money," *Collier's Weekly,* January 13, 20, 27; February 3, 1940.

Fowler, Gene. *The Life and Times of Jimmy Walker: Beau James.* New York: Viking Press, 1949.

Friedman, Charles. "Portrait of a New York Bookie," *Gambling in America,* edited by Herbert L. Marx, Jr. New York: H. W. Wilson, 1952.

Gambino, Richard. *Blood of my Blood.* New York: Doubleday, 1974.

Gosch, Martin A., and Hammer, Richard. *The Last Testament of Lucky Luciano.* Boston: Little, Brown, 1974.

Havemann, Ernest. "Gambling in the U.S.," *Life,* June 19, 1950.

Hay, Douglas, *et al. Albion's Fatal Tree.* New York: Pantheon, 1975.

Hildreth, Samuel C., and Crowell, James R. *The Spell of the Turf.* Philadelphia: J.B. Lippincott, 1926.

Hill, Christopher. *Reformation to Industrial Revolution: A Social and Economic History of Britain, 1530–1780.* London: Weidenfeld and Nicolson, 1967.

Hobsbawm, E. J. *Industry and Empire.* (Pelican Economic History of Britain, Vol. 3, 1750 to present day.) New York: Penguin Books, 1968.

Hofstadter, Richard. *The Age of Reform: From Bryan to F.D.R.* New York: Vintage Books, 1955.

Hoofprints of the Century. Excerpts from the *Thoroughbred Record, Livestock Record, and Kentucky Livestock Record,* 1875 to 1974. Compiled by William Robertson and Dan Farley. Lexington, KY.

Hore, J.P. *The History of Newmarket and The Annals of the Turf.* London: A.H. Bailey, 1886.

Hulse, James W. *The Nevada Adventure: A History,* 4th ed. Reno: University of Nevada Press, 1978.

Ianni, Francis A.J. *A Family Business.* New York: Russell Sage Foundation, 1972.

Ickes, Harold L. *The Secret Diary of Harold L. Ickes.* Vols. II and III, New York: Simon and Schuster, 1954.

Irey, Elmer L. *The Tax Dodgers.* New York: Garden City Publishing Co., 1948.

James, Marquis. *The Life of Andrew Jackson.* Indianapolis: Bobbs-Merrill, 1938.

Kahn, E.J. *The World of Swope.* New York: Simon and Schuster, 1965.

Katcher, Leo. *The Big Bankroll: The Life and Times of Arnold Rothstein.* New York: Harper and Brothers, 1958.

Katz, Leonard. *Uncle Frank: The Biography of Frank Costello.* New York: Drake, 1973.

Kaye, Richard (with Roy Peskett). *The Ladbrokes Story.* London: Pelham Books, 1969.

Keynes, John Maynard. *The General Theory of Employment, Interest and Money.* New York: Harcourt, Brace and World, Harbinger Book ed., 1964.

Laxalt, Paul. *Nevada: A Bicentennial History.* New York: W. W. Norton, 1977.

Liebling, A.J. *The New Yorker,* July 27, and September 18, 1937.

Maas, Peter. *The Valachi Papers.* New York: G.P. Putnam's Sons, 1968.

Marx, Karl. *Capital.* New York: Modern Library, 1932.

May, Sir Thomas Erskine. *The Constitutional History of England (Since the Accession of George the Third).* New York: A.C. Armstrong and Son, 1880.

McGill, James C., and McCarthy, Clem. "Pittsburgh Phil," *Saturday Evening Post,* August 3, 10, and 17, 1940.

Merchant, Larry. *The National Football Lottery.* New York: Holt, Rinehart and Winston, 1973.

Mockridge, Norton, and Prall, Robert H. *The Big Fix.* New York: Henry Holt and Co., 1954.

Moore, Bob. *Those Wonderful Days: Tales of Racing's Golden Era.* New York: Amerpub Co., 1976.

Moore, William Howard. *The Kefauver Committee and the Politics of Crime: 1950–1952.* Columbia, MI: University of Missouri Press, 1974.

Olmsted, Charlotte. *Heads I Win, Tails You Lose.* New York: Macmillan, 1962.

Orchard, Vincent. *Tattersalls.* London: Hutchinson, 1953.

Phipps, Herb. *Bill Kyne of Bay Meadows.* New York: A.S. Barnes, 1978.

Pusey, Merlo J. *Charles Evans Hughes.* New York: Macmillan, 1951.

Rascoe, Burton. *Before I Forget.* New York: Doubleday, Doran and Co., 1937.

Reuter, Peter, and Rubinstein, Jonathan B. "Fact, Fancy, and Organized Crime," *The Public Interest,* No. 53, Fall 1978.

Robertson, William H. P. *The History of Thoroughbred Racing in America.* New York: Bonanza Books, 1964.

Rosen, Charles. *Scandals of '51: How the Gamblers Almost Killed College Basketball.* New York: Holt, Rinehart and Winston, 1978.

Rous, Henry John. *On the Laws and Practice of Horse Racing.* 1866.

Scheiber, Harry N., Vatter, Harold G., and Faulkner, H.U. *American Economic History.* New York: Harper and Row, 1976.

Schlesinger, Arthur M., Jr. *Robert Kennedy and His Times.* New York: Ballantine Books, 1973.

Smith, Adam. *An Inquiry into the Nature and Causes of the Wealth of Nations.* New York: Modern Library, 1937.

Steigleman, Walter. *Horseracing.* New York: Prentice-Hall, 1947.

Stern, J. David. *Memoirs of a Maverick Publisher.* New York: Simon and Schuster, 1962.

Strine, Gerald, and Isaacs, Neil D. *Covering the Spread: How to Bet Pro Football.* New York: Random House, 1978.

Sumner, William Graham. *Andrew Jackson.* Boston: American Statesmen Series, 1899.

Talese, Gay. *Honor Thy Father.* Greenwich, CN: Fawcett Publications, 1972.

Thackrey, Ted, Jr. *Gambling Secrets of Nick the Greek.* Chicago: Rand McNally and Co., 1968.

Thompson, Flora. *Lark Rise to Candleford.* New York: Penguin Books, 1973.

Thormanby (pseud.). *Kings of the Turf: Memoirs and Anecdotes of Distinguished Owners, Backers, Trainers, and Jockeys.* London: Hutchinson, 1898.

Tobias, J.J., ed. *Nineteenth Century Crime in England.* New York: Barnes and Noble, 1972.

Vamplew, Wray. *The Turf: A Social and Economic History of Horse Racing.* London: Allen Lane, 1976.

Van Cise, Philip S. *Fighting the Underworld.* Boston: Houghton Mifflin, 1936.

Veblen, Thorstein. *The Theory of the Leisure Class.* New York: Mentor ed., 1953.

Waller, George. *Saratoga: Saga of an Impious Era.* New York: Prentice-Hall, 1966.

Weise, Arthur James. *Troy's One Hundred Years: 1789–1889.* Troy, NY: W.H. Young, 1891.

Webb, Sidney and Beatrice. *English Prisons Under Local Government.* New York: Longmans, Green & Co., 1922.

Werner, M.R. *Tammany Hall.* New York: Doubleday, Doran & Co., 1928.

Willett, Peter. *The Thoroughbred.* New York: G. P. Putnam's Sons, 1970.

Winn, Matt J. (as told to Frank G. Menke). *Down the Stretch: The Story of Colonel Matt J. Winn.* New York: Smith and Durrell, 1945.

INDEX

Adonis, Joe, 133, 135
Agnew, George B., 88–89
Agnew-Hart Bill, 88, 90, 91
Alderson, Baron, 22
Alexander, David, 96
Alo, Vincent (Blue Eyes), 135
Amateur Athletic Union, 191
American Conference for the Prevention of Infant Mortality, 85
American Indians, 34, 142
American Municipal Association, 168
American Telephone and Telegraph Co., 114, 115, 124, 179
Anastasia, Albert, 135, 145, 150, 164, 170
Anastasia, Anthony, 170
Anderson, Annelise Graebner, 147, 148
Anderson, Patton, 57
Annenberg, Max, 109, 110–11
Annenberg, Moses L., 106–20, 134, 175, 179
Annenberg, Tobias, 109
Annenberg, Walter H., 107, 115, 119–20
Anslinger, Harry, 143, 169

Anson, Colonel, 19
Anti-Gambling League, 222
Apalachin meeting of Syndicate, 144–45
Aqueduct, 100, 243
Aristotle, 40
Armor, Mary Harris, 85n.
Ascot Stakes, 45
Ashton, John, 52
Athens, 39, 40
Auctioneering of horses, 12, 13, 48
Auction pools, 70–71, 72, 73, 74, 79–80, 88
  wire services and, 75, 80
Aurelio, Thomas A., 151

Balzar, Fred, 234
Bankruptcy Act of 1861 (Britain), 25
Bannon, Joe, 112–13
Barbara, Joseph, 144–45
Baruch, Bernard, 42, 81–82, 86–87
Baseball, betting on, 91, 181, 182, 189, 198
Basketball, betting on, 182, 189–93, 198–99
Bay Meadows racetrack, 97

Beasley, M. C., 169
Becker, Charles A., 93
Before I Forget (Rascoe), 110–11
Bell's Life, 48
Belmont, August, 74, 76–77, 87
Belmont Park, 8, 87, 95, 99, 100, 243
Bendir, Arthur, 225–26
Bennett, Harry, 142
Bennett, James Gordon, 74
Bentinck, Lord George, 10, 15–22, 29, 30, 31, 50, 51
Betting and Gaming Act of 1960, 221
Betting commissioner, 128–30, 136–37, 165, 200
Betting offices:
  in Britain, 220, 221, 225–28, 230, 231
  OTB, 202, 243–45
Betts, Toney, 98, 132, 133
Bible, 36
Big Fix, The (Mockridge and Prall), 157
Bingo, 123
Bird, T. H., 20, 29, 30, 51
Blackjack, 241–42
Bonanno, Joseph, 145
Bookmakers' Protection Association, 223–24
Bookmaking (on horse races):
  betting commissioner, 128–30, 136–37, 165, 200
  in Britain, *see* Britain
  come-back betting, 177–78, 242
  John Gully and, 28–31, 51
  horse parlor, 101–102, 108, 154, 179
  interviews with bookmakers, 207–18
  layoff betting, 94, 123–36 *passim*, 149, 177, 218
  levels of operation, 101–102
  Mafia and, 148–50, 177, 204
  moves outside the law, 90–105
  in nineteenth-century United States, 54, 63–64, 66, 71, 72–82
  number of bookmakers, 204–206

origins of, 12, 14–15, 22, 51, 64
vs. pari-mutuel system, 80–81, 100, 126, 174
point spread, *see* Point spread
police and, 151–65, 173, 177
pricemaker, 102–103, 104, 127, 128–30, 186–87
reforms and investigations, 86, 87, 88–90, 123–24, 127–37, 172–82, 239–40
similarities among bookmakers, 218
vigorish (take-off), 100, 101, 102, 172–73, 175, 177, 183, 201
wire room, 101, 154
wire services, *see* Wire services
see also Auction pools; Pari-mutuel system; Sports events, betting on
Boston, Massachusetts, 153
Bourke, Algernon, 8–9
Bowmar, Dan, III, 87
Boxiana (Egan), 27
Boxing, 191, 198
Bradley, E. R., 97, 132
Bradley College, 190
Brecht, Bertolt, 96
Brisbane, Arthur, 112
Britain, 5–12, 35, 219–32
  bookmaking in mid-nineteenth century, 51–54
  casino gambling in, 221
  debtors' prison in, 23–26
  gambling clubs in, 8–10, 44–45, 49–50, 53–54, 221, 222
  horse racing betting in, 7–8, 10–31, 45, 47–54, 219–28, 230–32
    four current wagering systems, 219–21
  legal status of gambling in, 36–37, 44, 50, 53, 54
  Parliament, 6, 16–17, 21, 25, 30, 53, 222, 224
    investigations into gambling, 44–50, 52
  private enclosure of land in, 10, 12

Britain (*cont'd*)
  South Sea Bubble, 5–7
  sports events betting in, 181, 225, 228, 230
British Racehorse, The (Hamlyn), 232
Brooklyn *Eagle*, 160
Brooklyn Jockey Club, 69
Brothers in Blood: The Rise of the Criminal Brotherhoods (Chandler), 128
Brown, Russell, 103
Brunnel, Frank, 77, 112
Buck, Fred S., 73, 101
Bureau of American Ethnology, 34
Burke, Ed, 78
Byron, Lord, 26

California, 88, 90, 97, 121, 122, 170, 234, 235, 240, 244
Campbell, Barry, 228
Campbell, Felicia, 236–37, 241
Canfield, Richard, 87
Canes, Michael E., 204
Canning, George, 16
Capehart, Senator, 140, 150
Capital, Savings and Credit in Peasant Societies, 38
Caplin, Mortimer M., 185
Capone, Al, 110, 119
Cardan, G., 4
Cardenio, 28
Card games, 67–68, 69, 123, 234, 241–42
Carnegie, Andrew, 33, 86, 87
Carolla, Sam, 128
Carroll, James J., 128–31, 179
Carswell, John, 5–7, 8
Carter, Jimmy, 229
Casinos, 149, 177, 221, 235–39, 240–42
Cassatt, Alexander J., 74–75, 108
Cassel, Sir Ernest, 42–43
Cavanagh, John, 92, 96, 99
Cella, Louis A., 80, 96
Centennial, 244
Cesarewitch, 45
Chambers' Edinburgh Journal, 52–53

Chandler, David Leon, 128
Charles II, King of England, 7–8
Chicago, 109–11, 121–22, 149, 153, 178
Chicago Crime Commission, 168
Chicago Crime Survey, 109
Chicago *Examiner*, 110
Chicago *Tribune*, 110, 111
Children's gambling games, 34–35
Churchill, Jennie, 60–61
Churchill, Winston, 61, 224
Churchill Downs, 72–73, 90, 199, 244
Cincinnati *Post*, 80
City Tote, 230
Cleveland, Grover, 76
Clore, Sir Charles, 228
Cohen, John, 34
Cohn, Harry, 132, 133
College of the City of New York, 190
College sports, 189–94
Collier's magazine, 114
Come-back betting, 177–78, 242
Congressional Globe, 61
Comstock, Anthony, 75–76, 79, 85, 88
Connecticut, 243
Constitutional History of England, 25
Continental Press, 121, 130
Coral Index Ltd., 229–30
Corals, Joe, 225, 228–30
Cosa Nostra, *see* Mafia
Costello, Frank, 96, 128, 131–32, 133, 135, 144, 148, 149, 150–51, 164, 173, 183
Covering the Spread (Strine and Isaacs), 187
Cox, James M., 117
Craps, 123, 175
Crockford, William, 29, 45, 47, 50
Crockford's Club, 49–50
Croker, Richard, 69
Cruchen, Thomas, 75
Cruise, Mike, 98
Crump, Boss Ed, 167
Cumberland, Duke of, 13
Cunningham, Helen, 226
Curd, Ed, 192

Daily Racing Form, 77, 107, 112–13, 114, 116, 175, 176, 222

Daley, Arthur, 190

Darrow, Clarence, 116

Das Kapital (Marx), 38

Dash, Samuel, 152, 153, 155

Davis, Patricia T., 74–75

Davis, William, 14, 30

Day, William, 45–46

"Dead Rabbits," 59

Debt (formation):
  compared to gambling, 40–43
  defaulters on, *see* Defaulters on debt
  moral and legal status of, 39–43
  in preindustrial societies, 38–40

Debtors' prison, 23–26

Defaulters on debts, 18–19, 22, 44, 48, 51, 53, 64
  legalizing collection of gambling debts, 48–49, 50

Demaris, Ovid, 143

Democratic Party, 84, 98, 118, 164, 167

Demosthenes, 41, 42

Dewey, Thomas, 129–30

Dice games, 67

Dick, J. M., 223

Dickens, Charles, 23

Dickinson, Charles, 57

Director: An Oral Biography of J. Edgar Hoover, The (Demaris), 143

Director's Liability Act, 88

Disraeli, Benjamin, 15, 16–17, 20, 21

Dr. McX, 136–37

Domestick Intelligence, 7–8

"Don," 215–17

Dostoevsky, Fëdor, 33

Dowling, V. G., 48

Drommel, Professor, 72

Drummond (bookmaker), 14

Dwyer, Mike, 69–70, 72–73

Dwyer, Phil, 69, 72–73

Earp, Wyatt, 68

Eavesdroppers, The (Dash), 153

Economic function of gambling, 37–43

Edward IV, King of England, 36

Edward VII, King of England, 42

Egan, Pierce, 27

Egen, Captain Frederick W., 101, 245

Egypt, ancient, 35

Eisenhower, Dwight, 167

Elections, betting on, 129–30, 229

England, *see* Britain

English Prisons Under Local Government, 23

Erickson, Frank, 131–36, 148, 149, 158, 173, 177

Fallon, William J., 91

Family Business, A (Ianni), 147

Faro, 67–68, 69

Federal Bureau of Investigation, 140, 143, 169

Federal Communications Commission, 114, 179

Firth, Raymond, 38

Fleet Prison, London, 23, 24, 26

Flynn, John T., 114, 115, 127, 161, 163

Football, betting on, 182, 189, 194, 202, 244–45
  in Britain, 225, 228
  Las Vegas line and, 195, 196–97, 198–201

Ford Motor Company, 142, 170

Fowler, Gene, 91, 95

France, 220, 224
  Mississippi scheme in, 5, 7

Gambling:
  beginnings of, 3–12, 34–35
  in Britain, *see* Britain
  debt formation compared to, 40–43
  economic function of, 37–43
  effects of society, 236–39
  enters the English language, 7, 36
  future of, 239–46
  history of, 34–37

Gambling (*cont'd*)
interlude: on the nature of gambling, 32–43
in nineteenth-century United States, 54–82
reforms and investigations, 81, 83–90, 123–24, 127–37, 166–85, 234, 239–40
see also specific forms of gambling, e.g. Horse races, betting on; Sports events, betting on
Gambling ships, 182
Gaming, 4, 36–37, 40
see also Gambling
Gates, John "Bet-a-Million," 82, 87
General News Bureau, 109, 113
Genovese, Vito, 145, 183–84
Gentleman's Magazine, 23–24
George I, King of England, 7
George III, King of England, 10
Georgia, 85*n.*
Gitt, Jess, 32
Goodrich, Clifford C., 244
Goodwin's Official Turf Guide, 78
Goodwood races, 20
Gore, Albert, 167
Gosch, Martin A., 132–33
Grannon, Riley, 79
Gravesend track, 69, 79
Greece, ancient, 34, 40, 41
Gregson, Bob, 28
Grenet, Augustine J. ("Tex"), 103–105, 127, 197
Greville (bookmaker), 14
Gross, Harry, 155–65, 177, 179, 190
Grumet, Jacob, 183
Gully, John, 15, 22–31, 51
compared to John Morrissey, 58, 59, 61

Hakelburg, Ike, 78
Hales, Christopher J., 229
Halley, Rudolph, 168
Hamlyn, Geoffrey, 232
Hammurabi code, 36
Hand, Justice Learned, 152
Harding, Warren G., 90

Harold's, 235
Harrah, William, 235
Hay, Douglas, 26
Hearst, William Randolph, 88, 110, 111, 112
Heenan, John C., 59
Henry IV, King of England, 36
Hildreth, Sam, 94
Hill, Christopher, 11
Hill, Harry, 29
Hill, William, organization of, 225, 227–28, 230
Hirshfield, Leo, 194
History of Gambling in England, The (Ashton), 52
History of Newmarket and the Annals of the Turf, The (Hore), 8
History of White's (With the Betting Book from 1743 to 1878) (Bourke), 8–9
Hitchcock, Thomas, 87
Hobsbawm, E. J., 10, 12
Hobson, John A., 89
Hoffa, James, 183
Hofstadter, Richard, 83
Hogan, Frank S., 135, 190
Holland, 7
Holmes, Oliver Wendell, 60
Honor Thy Father (Talese), 145
Hoofprints of the Century, 80, 81
Hoover, J. Edgar, 143, 169
Hore, J. P., 8
Hornung, Paul, 194
Horse parlor, 101–102, 108, 154, 179
Horse races, betting on, 8, 11, 54–82, 92, 94–137, 182, 233
in Britain, 7–8, 10–31, 45, 47, 54, 219–28, 230–32
George Bentinck and, 18–22, 31, 50
the blower, 226–27
four current wagering systems, 219–21
John Gully and, 28–31, 51
origins of bookmaking and, 12, 14–15
Starting Prices, 223, 226

Horse races (*cont'd*)
  defaulters on debts, *see* Defaulters on debts
  ratio of off-track to on-track, 173–74, 184
  reforms and investigations, 19–20, 81, 86, 87, 88–90, 123–24, 127–37, 172–81, 239–40
  volume of legal, 202
  wire services and, *see* Wire services
  see also Auction pools; Bookmaking; Pari-mutuel system
Horse Race Totalisator Board, 220
Horse Racing in Britain (Campbell), 228
H.O. Scratch Sheet, 132
Howard, John, 23, 24
Hughes, Charles Evans, 87–88, 90
Humphrey, Hubert, 167, 229
Hundley, William, 143
Hunter, John R., 60
Huntington, Collis P., 106
Hyer, Tom, 59

Ianni, Francis A., 146–47, 148
Ickes, Harold L., 118
Iliona (horse), 45
Illinois, 65, 121
Interest, taking of, 40–42
Internal Revenue Service, 106, 140, 173, 185
  Moe Annenberg and, 113, 117, 118, 119–21, 134
Interstate Commerce Commission, 84
Interstate News, 115
Interviews with bookmakers, 206–18
Investigations, *see* Reforms and investigations
Irey, Elmer L., 106, 113, 114, 115, 117, 119
Isaacs, Neil D., 187, 188
Italo-Americans, 139, 141

Jackson, Andrew, 56–57, 63
Jackson, John "Gentleman," 26

Jail, *see* Debtors' prison
James, Marquis, 57
Jerome, Leonard W., 60, 63, 64, 65
Jerome Park, 64, 73, 103
Jersey, Lord, 29
Jockey Club (American), 77, 82
Jockey Club (British), 13–14, 18, 29, 45, 50, 64, 222, 223, 232
Johansson, Ingomar, 135
Johnson, Andrew, 61
Johnson, Dave, 104
Johnson, Nucky, 119
Johnson Act of 1951, 183
Jones, Orlando, 79

Kahn, E. J., 92
Kalish, Max (Kid Rags), 98
Karras, Alex, 194
Katcher, Leo, 91, 94, 133
Kaye, Richard, 225–26
Keene, James R., 81–82, 87
Kefauver, Estes, 135, 136, 164, 166–80, 181, 183, 185, 190, 204, 239
Kefauver Committee and the Politics of Crime, 1950–1952, The (Moore), 167–68
Kelley, James E., 64
Kennedy, Edward, 229
Kennedy, John F., 167, 183, 184
Kennedy, Robert F., 183, 239
Kentucky, 65, 80, 121
Kentucky Derby, 72, 73, 97, 129, 244
Kentucky State Racing Commission, 80
Kerr, Captain, 16
Keynes, John Maynard, 42, 89
Kid Rags, *see* Kalish, Max
Knight, John, 117
Kuhnsman, George, 78
Kyne, Bill, 97, 233

Ladbrokes, 225–28, 229
Ladbrokes Story, The (Kaye), 225, 226
La Guardia, Fiorello, 96
Lane, Mark, betting shops of, 228
Lane, Myles, 183

Lansky, Meyer, 128, 133, 135
Las Vegas, Nevada, 69, 149, 198, 235–37
  see also Nevada
Las Vegas line, 195, 196–97, 198–201, 203
Law, John, 7
Lawrence, Andrew M., 110
Lawrence Realization Stakes, 97
Laws and Practice of the Turf (Rous), 30–31
Layoff betting, 94, 123–37 *passim*, 149, 177, 218
Leader, George, 167
Leibowitz, Judge Samuel, 159, 162
Leonard, Benny, 93
Lichtenstein, Saul, 78, 104
Liebling, A. J., 98, 99, 103, 104
Life, 176, 177
Linemakers, *see* Las Vegas line; Martin, Bob
Livestock Record, 75
Loans, *see* Money lending
Loansharking, 170
"Loggating in the field," 35
London *Evening News*, 223
Longacres, 244
Long Island University, 190
Lord George, *see* Bentinck, Lord George
Lorillard, Pierre, 74
Lotteries, 67
Lottery laws, 123
Louisiana, 88, 121
Louisville, Kentucky, 65, 72
Luciano, Charles (Lucky), 133, 134, 144
Lynch, John L., 113

Maas, Peter, 148
McCarran, Pat, 168
McCarthy, Clem, 70
McCarthy, Joseph R., 168, 183
McClellan Committee, 143, 181–82, 183–84, 194, 204, 239
McDonald, Miles, 159–61, 162–63
McFarland Committee, 123, 127, 128–32, 134, 135, 140, 141, 150, 168, 177, 179
McGrath, J. Howard, 123–24, 125, 126, 140, 141, 169
Mackin, Bill, 79
McManus, George, 95
McNeil, Charlie, 193
Mafia, 128, 138–51, 164, 169, 240
  Apalachin meeting, 144–45
  bookmaking and, 148–50, 177, 204
  the Commissione, 143–44
  crime and business, 145–47, 170, 171
  ethnic smear, 141–42
  Las Vegas casinos and, 235
  violence and, 142–43
Manhattan College, 189–90
Mara, Tim, 98–99, 103
Marbles, 34, 35
Martin, Bob, 195, 196–201, 203, 245
Marx, Karl, 37, 38
Maryland, 65, 121
Massachusetts, 36, 37, 40
Massachusetts Crime Commission, 153
Masterson, Bat, 68
Mather, Increase, 36, 37
May, Sir Thomas Erskine, 25
Mecca (British bookmaking organization), 225, 228
Mellish, Colonel Henry, 27, 28
Metropolitan News Company, 80, 108–109
Metropolitan Turf Association, 77
Miami, Florida, 115, 116, 117, 149, 172–73
Miami *Herald*, 116, 117
Miami *News*, 117
Miami *Tribune*, 115, 117
Midwest Racing News, 121
Miller, T. G., 114
Milwaukee, Wisconsin, 111–12
Mississippi scheme, 5, 7
Mockridge, Norton, 157, 158, 161–62
Money lending, 41–42
  see also Loansharking
Monmouth racecourse, 74–75

Moore, Joe, 95
Moore, William Howard, 167–68
Moran, James J., 164
Morgan, E. D., 87
Morgan, J. P., 76, 86–87
Morrissey, John, 58–64
Mosaic law, 36, 39
Mostyn, Mr., 21
Murray, Hugh, 112–13

Napoleon Bonaparte, 9–10
National Basketball Association, 194
National Consumers League, 84
National Football League, 202
National Labor Committee, 84
National Tuberculosis Association, 84–85
Nationwide News Service, 113, 114–15, 121, 130
Nevada, 168, 185, 202, 233–29
 legalization of gambling in, 233, 234
 see also Las Vegas, Nevada; Reno, Nevada
New Jersey, 65, 74, 108, 122, 133
Newmarket Downs, 7–8, 10, 11, 12, 18, 19, 20, 29, 30
New Orleans, Louisiana, 153–54, 178, 183
New York City, 62, 170
 basketball fixes in, 189–90, 193
 number of bookmakers in, 205, 206
 OTB, 202, 243, 244–45
 police and bookies in, 154–55, 157–67
 poolroom operators, 74, 75, 108
 Tammany Hall, 58–59, 61, 63, 93, 96, 98, 164
New York *Daily Mirror*, 98
New Yorker, The, 98
New York *Herald*, 78, 79
New York *Morning Telegraph*, 95, 113
New York Off Track Betting System, 202, 243, 244–45
New York Society for the Suppression of Vice, 75

New York State, 64, 65, 80, 87–88, 93, 104, 183, 184
 Jockey Club's control in, 77
 legal status of bookmaking in, 73, 77–78, 90, 99
 number of bookmakers in, 204, 206
 pari-mutuel betting in, 73, 90, 104, 121
 reform movement in, 88–90
New York State Commission of Investigation, 183
New York State Legislature, 76, 77
New York *Sun*, 62
The New York Times, 94, 190, 198, 201–202, 205
New York *Tribune*, 62
New York *World*, 92, 93
New Zealand, 224
Nixon, Richard, 107, 184, 229
North American Review, 76, 79
Numbers game, 67, 149, 173, 177

Obaldeston, Squire, 19
O'Banion, Dion, 110
O'Brien, Thomas, 98–99
O'Brien, William P., 160, 161
O'Connell, Harry, 132
O'Connor, Johnny, 95
O'Dwyer, William, 163–64, 170
Off Track Betting, 202, 243–44
Oller, Pierre, 71, 72, 220, 231
Orchard, Vincent, 19
Organized crime, *see* Mafia
Organized Crime Control Act, 184–85
OTB, 202, 243–45
Oxford Universal Dictionary, 35

Palmerston, Viscount, 45–47
Pari-mutuel system, 70, 71–72, 73, 90, 97, 104
 vs. bookmaker, 80–81, 100, 126, 174, 175
 in Britain (Tote), 220, 224, 227, 230, 231
 come-back betting, 177–78, 242

Pari-mutuel system (*cont'd*)
  future of, 242–44
  legalization of, 121, 127–28, 182
  OTB, 202, 243–45
Paris-Mutuals, *see* Pari-mutuel system
Patterson, Floyd, 135
Payne Telegraph Service, 109
Pearce, Henry ("Game Chicken"), 26, 27, 28
Pendleton Act, 84
Pennsylvania Bar investigation, 152–53, 157
Pennsylvania Public Service Commission, 118
Pepys, Samuel, 3–5, 42
Percy-Gray Law, 77–78
Peters, Elmer (The Eel), 132
Peterson, Virgil W., 168
Phelps-Dodge Co., 170
Philadelphia, Pennsylvania, 152–53
Philadelphia *Inquirer*, 115, 117–18
Philadelphia *Record*, 118
Philbrick Committee, 170
Phipps, Herb, 97
Pickwick Papers, The (Dickens), 23
Pioneer News, 130
Pittsburgh Phil, *see* Smith, George
Plainclothesmen (Egen), 245
Point shaving, 189–92, 193
Point spread, 186–89, 192, 194–95
  baseball line, 198
  basketball line, 198
  Las Vegas line, 195, 196–97, 198–201, 203
Poker, 67, 123
Police:
  bookmakers and, 151–65, 173, 177
  sports fixes and, 193
Policy racket, 67
Politics (Aristotle), 40
Poole (fighter), 59
Pool halls, 71, 74, 75–76, 79–80, 88, 108, 109
  see also Auction pools
"Pool Rooms and Pool Selling," 76
Populists, 83–84

Portland, Duke of, 15, 17
Powell, John Wesley, 34, 60
Prall, Robert H., 157, 158, 161–62
Pricemaker, 102–103, 104, 127, 128–30, 186–87
Prison, debtors', *see* Debtors' prison
Primitive accumulation, 38–39, 43
Prohibition, 85, 95, 116, 142, 149
  see also Bootlegging of liquor
"Property, Authority and the Criminal Law," 26
Prostitution, 234, 236
Purple Gang, 135

Racing, horse, *see* Horse races, betting on
Racing associations, 65–66, 75, 99, 177
Racing wires, *see* Wire services
Ragen, James M., 115, 121–22, 178
Rascoe, Burton, 110–11
Reagan, Ronald, 107, 229
Reardon, James E., 158, 159, 160
Reardon, Michael, 158, 160
Reekie, F. G., 224
Reforms and investigations, 19–20, 81, 83–90, 123–24, 127–37, 166–85, 234, 239–40
Reid, Ed, 160
Reno, Nevada, 233, 235–36, 237–39
Republican Party, 88, 89, 118, 163–64
Reuter, Peter, 148–49, 205–206
Richard, Tex, 95
Ridsdale, Robert, 29, 30
"Ringers," 19–20, 69
Robert F. Kennedy (Schlesinger), 167
Robertson, William H. P., 56, 78, 87
Rome, ancient, 4, 35, 40
Roosevelt, Franklin D., 117
Rosen, Charles, 191, 193
Rosenthal, Herman, 93
Rothschild, Baron Henri de, 86
Rothschild, Lord, 221
Rothschilds, 76
Rothstein, Arnold, 91–96, 132, 133, 181

Rothstein, Carolyn Greene, 92, 95
Roulette, 175
Rous, Admiral Henry John, 20, 29–31, 50, 51, 64, 186
    interrogation of, 45–47
Royal Commission on Gambling, *Final Report* of, 220–22, 231
Rubinstein, Jonathan B., 148–49, 205–206
Running Rein (horse), 19–20, 22, 29
Runyon, Damon, 95
Rupp, Adolph, 192
Russell, Charles Henry, 50

Samish, Artie, 170
S & G bookmaking syndicate, 172–73
Sanford, Sykes and Eaves, 64
Santa Anita track, 178
Sarachan, Goodman A., 183–84
Saratoga Springs, New York, 55–56, 57–64, 65, 70, 87, 92
Scandals of '51 (Rosen), 191, 193
Schlesinger, Arthur M., Jr., 167
Schreiber, Barry, 97
Schwab, Charles, 86
Scotland, 12
Screvane, Paul, 202
Scribner, Ben, 56
Seabury Committee, 96
Sears Holdings, Ltd., 228
Security market indexes, betting on, 229–30
Sheepshead Bay track, 73
Sherman Anti-Trust Act, 76, 107
Siegel, Bugsy, 235
Simpson, Sloan, 163
Sinclair, Harry, 92
Slot machines, 149, 175, 183
Smith, Adam, 12, 18, 37–38
Smith, George (Pittsburgh Phil), 70, 77, 79, 186
Smith, Raymond, 234–35
Social and Economic History of Horse Racing (Vamplew), 221
Sollazzo, Salvatore, 193
Solon, code of, 36, 39, 40

South Sea Bubble, 5–7
Sporting Life, 222
Sports events, betting on, 91, 133–34, 158, 173, 175, 181–95, 240
    annual amount spent on, 201–202, 203, 206
    in Britain, 181, 225, 228, 230
    fixes and scandals, 91, 181, 189–95
    future of, 244–45
    interviews with bookmakers, 206–18
    Las Vegas line, 195, 196–97, 198–201, 203
    number of bookmakers, 204–206
    point spread and, *see* Point spread
    similarities among bookmakers, 218
    television and, 188–89, 199, 202
    see also Horse races, betting on
Stardust book, 199
Starting Prices, 223, 226
Steffens, Lincoln, 165, 166–67
Stern, J. David, 117–18
Stevenson, Adlai, 167
Stoneham, Charles, 92
Streit, Saul, 190–91, 192
Strine, Gerald, 187, 188
Sullivan, Tim, 93
Sullivan, Yankee, 59
Sumner, William Graham, 57
Super Bowl, 200
Supreme Court, 84, 90, 96, 151, 198
Swindell, Frederick, 30
Swope, Herbert Bayard, 92, 93
Syndicate, *see* Mafia

Talese, Gay, 145
Tammany Hall, 58–59, 61, 63, 93, 96, 98, 164
Tattersall, Richard, 12–13, 48–49, 52
Tattersalls (Orchard), 19
Tattersalls ring, 13, 226, 227
Tax Dodgers, The (Irey), 113
Taxes, 66, 67
    in Britain, 220–21, 224, 231–32

Taxes (*cont'd*)
  in Nevada, 234
  pari-mutuels and, 242, 243, 244
  tax law, 185
  see also Internal Revenue Service
Teamsters' Union, 183
Teletrack, 243
Television and sports betting, 185–86, 188–89, 199, 202
Tennes, Mont, 109, 110, 113
Tennis, 191
Theory of the Leisure Class, The (T. Veblen), 40–41
Thompson, George, 59
Thompson, Ike, 79
"Thormanby" (racing writer), 15, 16, 18, 20, 21, 27
Thoroughbred Racing Association, 177
Thoroughbred Record, 70, 80, 81, 82, 97, 108–109
Tiresias, 17
Tobey, Charles, 135
Tolar of New Britain, 38
Tombstone, Arizona, 68
Tote, the, 220, 224, 227, 230, 231 232
Travers, William R., 60, 61, 63
Travers Stakes, 94
Trinidad *Daily Advertiser*, 68
Troy, New York, 62–63
Troy's One Hundred Years: 1789–1889 (Weise), 63
Truman, Harry, 129–30, 163, 167, 168
Tunis, John, 191
Tuohy, William J., 122
Turf Commission Agents, 28
TV Guide, 115
Tweed, Boss, 58, 61–62

Ude, Eustache, 49–50
Union Plaza Sport and Horse Book, 196, 197, 199
  see also Las Vegas line
U.S. Bureau of Narcotics, 140, 143, 169

U.S. Congress, 61, 63, 122, 166, 182–83, 184–85
U.S. Department of Justice, 118–19, 123–24, 182
  Mafia and, 140–41, 143, 144, 147–48
U.S. Immigration Commission, 84
U.S. Senate, 167–68
U.S. Senate Commerce Committee, 123, 140, 168
U.S. Senate Special Committee to Investigate Organized Crime, 135, 136, 164, 167–80, 181, 183, 185, 190, 204, 239
U.S. Steel, 86, 87
U.S. Treasury, 76
University of Kentucky, 190, 192
University of Nevada at Las Vegas, 236
University of Rochester, 204
Usury, 40

Valachi, Joseph, 143, 145, 148, 150
Valachi Papers, The (Maas), 148
Vamplew, Wray, 22, 54, 221
Vanderbilt, Cornelius, 59–60, 63
Veblen, Thorstein, 40–41
Victoria club, 222
Vigorish, 100, 101, 102, 172–73, 175, 177, 183
  on sports betting, 201, 203–204
Volstead Act, 85

Waldorf-Astoria Hotel, 150
Walker, Jimmy, 95
Waller, George, 55, 60, 61
Washington, George, 56
Watt, James, 12
Wealth of Nations (Smith), 12, 37
Webb, Beatrice, 23, 24
Webb, Sidney, 23, 24
Weise, Arthur James, 63
Wendt, Lloyd, 110
Western Union, 109, 124, 179
Whalen, William T., 161
White, George, 144, 169
White's (London club), 8–10, 45

White Slave Traffic Act, 84
Whitney, Harry Payne, 94
Whitney, W. C., 87
Who's Who in America, 107
Wilkes' Spirit of the Times, 61
Williams, Edward Bennett, 198
William IV, King of England, 27
Winn, Colonel Matt J., 73, 90
Wire room, 101, 154
Wire services, 79–80, 105, 106–17, 118, 119, 121–22, 124, 130–31, 178–79, 184
  television as, 186, 189
Wiretapping, 148, 152–53
Withers, D. D., 74, 75
Wolfson, Louis, 243
World Series of 1919, 91, 181

Yamey, B. S., 38
York, Duke of, 16